Art and Context in

Late Medieval English Narrative

A distinguished group of medievalists contribute to this volume in honor of Robert Worth Frank, Jr., Professor Emeritus of English literature, The Pennsylvania State University, editor of the *Chaucer Review*, and past president of the New Chaucer Society. The studies reflect his life-long interest in the poetic art that emerged in late medieval English narrative out of multiple historical contexts, and taken together they illuminate ways in which English writers at the end of the Middle Ages employed the resources of their cultural moment to create narratives that still engage us.

The twelve studies divide into three groups. The first group examines *Piers Plowman* and aspects of Langland's narrative art; the second considers important facets of Chaucer's narrative artistry and its relationship to medieval literary and cultural practice; the third group deals with late medieval English narrative and social custom, reflecting recent increased scholarly interest in the dramaturgy of medieval social life, hence of the symbolic structures that shape narratives in the historical and literary record.

ROBERT R. EDWARDS is Professor of English and comparative literature at the Pennsylvania State University.

Art and Context in

Late Medieval English Narrative

ESSAYS IN HONOR OF
ROBERT WORTH FRANK, JR.

EDITED BY

Robert R. Edwards

D. S. BREWER

First published 1994
D. S. Brewer, Cambridge

ISBN 0 85991 407 0

D. S. Brewer is an imprint of Boydell & Brewer Ltd
PO Box 9, Woodbridge, Suffolk IP12 3DF, UK
and of Boydell & Brewer Inc.
PO Box 41026, Rochester, NY 14604-4126, USA

British Library Cataloguing-in-Publication Data
Art and Context in Late Medieval English Narrative: Essays in Honor
of Robert Worth Frank, Jr.
I. Edwards, Robert R.
821.109
ISBN 0-85991-407-0

Library of Congress Cataloging-in-Publication Data
Art and context in late Medieval English narrative : essays in honor of
Robert Worth Frank, Jr. / edited by Robert R. Edwards.
    p. cm.
Includes bibliographical references.
ISBN 0-85991-407-0 (acid-free paper)
1. English literature – Middle English, 1100–1500 – History
and criticism. 2. Narration (Rhetoric). 3. Rhetoric, Medieval.
I. Edwards, Robert, 1947- .
PR251.A73 1994
821'.109–dc20   94-7066

The paper used in this publication meets the minimum requirements
of American National Standard for Information Sciences –
Permanence of Paper for Printed Library Materials, ANSI Z39.48-1984

Printed in Great Britain by
St Edmundsbury Press Ltd, Bury St Edmunds, Suffolk

Contents

Introduction

The essays collected in this volume honor Robert Worth Frank, Jr., as a scholar, editor, colleague, and mentor. In a distinguished career of research, teaching, and editorial work that now extends more than four decades, Bob Frank has made signal contributions to the study of medieval English literature. *"Piers Plowman" and the Scheme of Salvation*, a study preceded by an important series of articles on *Piers* and medieval allegory, taught several generations of scholars how to read the subtle play of aesthetic and historical contexts in Langland's great poem. *Chaucer and "The Legend of Good Women"* was not only the first book-length critical study of Chaucer's anomalous and fascinating poem; its careful study of Chaucer's incorporation and reworking of sources in the last of his dream visions defined the fundamental terms by which subsequent readers have approached the text. Bob has written valuable and insightful articles on still other important topics in Langland and Chaucer. They range from the image of hunger in *Piers* and amplification in *Troilus and Criseyde* to the structure of the *Parliament of Fowls*, comedy in the *Canterbury Tales*, the nature of Chaucerian pathos, and even Chaucer's "ineptness." In addition, he has turned to works and themes that stand on the margins of the traditional Middle English literary canon, an area of increasing interest in literary studies medieval and modern. His essays examine the miracles of the Virgin, devotional and meditational literature, and medieval pilgrimage. For nearly three decades as his scholarship has continued apace, Bob has edited *Chaucer Review* and made the journal an international forum for scholarly and critical exchange, a generous habitation for the work of "sondry folk" who come together out of their interests in the literary culture of the later Middle Ages. Bob has served us, too, with energy and distinction in the institutions of our scholarly and professional lives, most recently as President of the New Chaucer Society. The scholars who have profited from his encouragement, learning, and wisdom comprise a list too long to rehearse.

Beyond celebrating Bob Frank's achievements, this book tangibly reflects his work. The authors of the essays address an issue that has informed his writing and remains a continuing focus of scholarly and critical interest – namely, the poetic art that emerges in late medieval English narrative out of multiple historical contexts. The art of medieval narrative, as Bob has so carefully demonstrated, is at once universal and particular, accessible to modern readers yet situated in literary traditions, social conditions, and systems of belief whose details scholarship brings to bear on our understanding. The aesthetic achievement of Langland, Chaucer, and other medieval

English writers is fully open to us, but it is not open in just any way. The contributors demonstrate how English writers at the end of the Middle Ages employ the resources of their cultural moment to create narratives with a profound and subtle artistry that still engages us. The essays divide into three groups, which represent the focal points of Bob Frank's scholarship.

The first group examines *Piers Plowman*, Langland's great visionary poem. In the opening essay, C. David Benson addresses the elements of *Piers* that pose difficulties for the modern reader – its indivisibility, religious tone, combination of genres, and above all its frustration of narrative. The last of these is most apparent, argues Benson, in the lack of both a plausible fiction and a programmatic allegorical order. The frustration of narrative stems from a story that does not advance steadily, from abrupt narrative dislocations, and from poetic and intellectual density. But against claims that Langland is an incompetent narrative poet or that his story can be understood only at an allegorical level, Benson contends that the difficulty of *Piers* is calculated to engage the reader in narrative and moral complexities without clear resolutions. Though Langland creates the narrative, its meaning is the responsibility of the reader through his "kynde knowyng," his natural understanding, even when (and perhaps especially if) the text is openly prescriptive. In this respect, he argues, Langland's poem follows the conventions of medieval exegesis and reading.

Elizabeth Kirk addresses the complex relations of theology and narrative in "Langland's Narrative Christology." Focusing on Passus 18 of the B-text, which recounts Christ's Passion and Harrowing of Hell in a dense and shifting imagery, Kirk examines how a theology originally derived from scriptural narrative must be reinscribed in narrative as a way of solving doctrinal problems. Unlike contemporary dramatists and writers of lyrics and meditative pieces, Langland shows not the events themselves but the events as witnessed and interpreted by others, and he juxtaposes an array of short narrative segments, distancing his reader and forcing reflection. Langland's narrative strategy thus allows his poem to contain doctrinal contradictions – Christ's passive suffering and active redemption, God's justice and mercy – and to view them in multiple contexts. In this way, writing serves as a mode not just of recording but also of creating and enacting; through scrutiny and self-criticism, language, especially poetic language, becomes a social instrument and heuristic tool.

Anna Baldwin's essay studies another intersection of narrative art and historical context – the discussion of debt that permeates Langland's poem. She shows how those parts of the poem that occur before Christ's atonement take their debt imagery from traditional laws of contract and vicarious promise. Later parts of the poem take their imagery, however, from historical developments in law that emphasize personal responsibility. Thus, the repeated injunction *redde quod debes* ("Render what you owe") marks the thematic transition in *Piers* from an Old Testament metaphor of bondage and sin to a New Testament debt of love that only mankind can discharge. Furthermore, Langland follows late medieval legal developments so that traditional, one-sided obligations become a new reciprocal debt binding individuals to mankind as a whole and to God. With that development comes "the principle of freedom, of full personal responsibility" that Langland extends in the final part of the poem to a view of debt measured not by one's own sin but by others' need.

In her essay on "The Chilling of Charity," M. Teresa Tavormina shows how Langland's revision in the C-text carefully elaborates an important passage on charity from the B-text by introducing a new metaphor and connecting it to another poetic image. These changes produce an eschatological dimension in Langland's complex representation of charity. Langland's metaphor of "chilled charity" grows out of Latin exegetical tradition, and it is associated with the Apocalypse and later with anti-clerical satire. He connects the metaphor to the image of budding grace in the biblical parable of the fig tree, likewise the topic of considerable exegesis, and thus balances satirical ends with the promise of hope. From such background emerges Langland's Tree of the Church, "partially barren and infected with corrupt, hypocritical clergy" yet still promising strength and comfort. Moreover, in moving the relevant passages from the figure of Anima in the B-text and reassigning them to Liberum Arbitrium in the C-text, he takes the opportunity to rework and intensify the relations of his major themes and images. The revisions, says Tavormina, have "a holographic quality," reflecting not just local adjustments but a global poetic process: "He keeps Anima's whole discourse in mind as he works over its parts, transmuting them into Liberum Arbitrium's speech." The effects carry forward to Langland's final articulation of charity, the church, and the individual soul.

The second group of essays examines how important facets of Chaucer's narrative artistry grow out of medieval literary and rhetorical structures. Monica McAlpine's essay deals with the poem that perhaps best represents the fusion of narrative artistry and cultural resources, the Nun's Priest's Tale. McAlpine locates Chaucer's artistry in a dimension different from both allegorical readings of the tale and critical approaches that have emphasized the mock-epic treatment of language and interpretation. Rather than accept the dominant view that the poem offers no meaning except its escape from meaning, she proposes that Chaucer's masterpiece succeeds in turning satire into a vision. If the tale raises questions about interpreting this story of a fox and rooster, it also raises questions about narrative in general. From this, McAlpine argues, we sense that there is something at stake which gives depth and resonance to the satire of interpretation. Analyzing medieval elements such as fable, debate, the motif of the Fall, and narratorial commentary, she demonstrates how the artful vision of fiction exercises a limited but crucial power to provide human guidance. Chaucer uses these elements to open up his story rather than narrow its meaning. The tale's final vision of frantic energy situates human experience and the understanding of human experience on a temporal plane framed but not defined by eternity.

Mary Carruthers's essay studies Chaucer's use of memory systems, especially in the Knight's Tale. Memory connects the activities of reading and writing in a form of mental production that precedes transcription of the poet's "matter." A sequence of images, each located in a place, serves as the compositional model, which was often expressed in an architectural metaphor such as a building. Carruthers points out that the Knight's Tale, like *Sir Gawain and the Green Knight*, contains a group of well-defined places, that its action is always carefully situated. These places serve both the poet and his audience in their joint effort to draw the poem's matter to "memorie" and thus to grasp its imaginative content and cultural meaning. As Carruthers explains, memory structures account for the large design of the poem as well as its apparent digressions, such as the elaborate descriptions of the oratories dedicated to Venus, Mars, and Diana.

Kathryn Lynch employs another architectural figure – the wall or partition – to examine a concern that remains constant from Chaucer's early dream visions to the *Canterbury Tales*. Lynch points out that walls are a powerful yet ambivalent cultural metaphor, representing both the conditions of civilized life and the loss of the Golden Age. Moreover, the enclosed space depicted in Chaucer's stories has its counterpart in enclosed fictions (tales within tales or sequential narrative segments). The Knight's Tale and Manciple's Tale, for instance, stage a drama of regulating violence within their expanding and contracting spaces. The love story of Piramus and Thisbe uses the wall to complicate the themes of tradition and experience, while *Troilus and Criseyde* converts the walls of the besieged city to the social places of public speech, intimate conversation, and duplicitous language. In the legend of Lucrece, Lynch points out, Chaucer rewrites much of *Troilus*, displacing siege warfare from a military sphere to the political and personal domains of the household and the body.

The authority of feminine speech is the topic of Carolyn Collette's essay, which focuses on the tradition of Mariology in order to locate the cultural assumptions that lie behind the Prioress and the Second Nun in the *Canterbury Tales*. Collette points out that these characters claim an authority quite different from the Wife of Bath's invocation of experience or Griselda's abjection in the Clerk's Tale. The figure of the Virgin, she explains, combines an exaltation of the female with the virtue of humility. Against those critics who emphasize the Prioress's child-like qualities, she reads the imagery of her Prologue for its assertions of spiritual power, goodness, and wisdom. Thus the Prioress's identification with the Virgin is a warrant to speak with an authority independent of male sanction. In the Second Nun's Prologue, by contrast, the Virgin is a figure who exercises dominion over the devil through her purity, and her intercession in man's behalf is re-created in the Second Nun's telling of the life of St. Cecilia. Through the Virgin, both narrators assert the right to speak, and the tales they tell register the cultural ambivalences that this right entails.

Mary Hamel's essay on the descriptions of naval warfare in Chaucer and other Middle English writers analyzes another point at which literary and historical discourse converge. The battle scene in the tale of Cleopatra from Chaucer's *Legend of Good Women* shares important characteristics with similar passages elsewhere in the canon. Hamel proposes that for the most part writers compose not on the basis of contemporary sources but according to a rhetorical topos with well-defined elements. The topos applies, moreover, to both poetic and historical texts. Its antecedents are in classical writers such as Lucan and Vegetius, and in the late Middle Ages, English writers add a coloring of contemporary details to the conventional elements. Hamel shows that there is a sense in these writers, too, that the topos of description is closely allied to alliterative poetry and its traditions of heroic poetry.

The third group of essays deals with late medieval English narrative and social practice. In recent years, scholars have become increasingly aware of the dramaturgy of medieval social life, hence of the symbolic structures that shape narratives in the historical and literary record. Paul Strohm relates the story of the apprentice Perkyn's revelry in Chaucer's Cook's Tale to the official discourse applied to civil unrest in the late Middle Ages. He shows that Chaucer evokes the language of social upheaval from a repertory of terms and motifs that describe the ludic spectacle of the Peasants' Revolt in 1381. These connections pose, in turn, a wider set of relations in which the evocation of events points toward an encompassing representational field, a textual system that includes social performance and literary representation. Strohm points out that revelry applies equally to progressive social change or conservative reaction and that the political meaning of the term becomes clear only in narrative. Chaucer's narrative, like those of contemporary chroniclers, is a device of containment, rebuke, and correction that contends for the dominant social understanding of events by trying to enforce closure on them.

An earlier uprising, the baronial revolt against Henry III under Simon de Montfort, is the topic of Thomas Heffernan's essay. Heffernan, like Strohm, is concerned with the language of the historical record, and his particular interest lies in the case made for de Montfort's canonization. The narratives created around de Montfort show the emergence of a figure in popular imagination who struggles against established authority in the cause of social justice. The rhetoric of the chronicles uses retrospective prophecy to transform the historical individual into a religious figure and innocent victim. After de Montfort's defeat, the chronicles fashion him an English saint, and he is later the subject of religious panegyric. Heffernan explains these developments as efforts to come to terms with the abiding significance of de Montfort's challenge to the conduct of monarchy and to devise a religious rhetoric that would counter the claims of kingly privilege and divine right raised against him. As the barons and commons press de Montfort's case, the royalist opposition portrays him as an ecclesiastical rogue. By analyzing the miracles attributed to de Montfort, Heffernan explores how the cause of popular reform draws on conventional narrative elements to portray a character who otherwise ill suits the topoi of reformist saints.

The final essay, by Peggy Knapp, addresses issues of narrative transformation in both the abstract and the particular. Knapp situates her study between the contemporary claim of Hans-Georg Gadamer that the social and literary understandings of a previous age can be grasped through language and Jurgen

Habermas's critique of Gadamer, which emphasizes that language, particularly as applied to social reality, is an instrument of power. Knapp's focus on the word *thrift* shows how language at once furthers and subverts ideology. In the late Middle Ages and Renaissance, the term comes to signify both propriety and frugality. The two senses repeatedly circle around each other in Chaucer's *Troilus and Criseyde*, supporting and deflating the assertions of love's worth and the characters' motives. In the social pageant of the *Canterbury Tales*, the term enforces social order, while securing the possibility of an internal critique of the social order it represents. In the Renaissance, Knapp argues, *thrift* is part of a changing social narrative in which aristocratic propriety gives way to the political and ethical values of frugality, and Shakespeare's plays register this shift in their linguistic complexity and artistic insight.

As these essays demonstrate, the narrative art of late medieval England is interconnected and strikingly particular. Chaucer, Langland, and the writers of historical documents use the same devices of verbal artistry – richly allusive language, powerful imagery, literary and rhetorical structures. These devices connect their work not only to their contemporaries but to earlier and later writers, and so they offer us a means of understanding the aesthetic meaning and techniques of the texts. But the essays show, too, that verbal artistry has local resonance and acquires meaning within specific contexts. Though Chaucer and Langland participate in broad conventions, their genius is in the details, in transforming convention into new insights and forms of expression. These transformations operate in the domain of social and cultural practice, where theology implies social vision, authority bears on gender relations, ethics and history reveal politics. The art of narrative in late medieval England succeeds equally in literary representation and cultural analysis, and to grasp it fully we need to appreciate both its craft and context. This, too, has been the lesson of Bob Frank's scholarship and criticism, and the essays that follow seek to honor him by showing the power and sophistication of what he has taught us.

Publication of this volume has been generously supported by the Department of English and the College of the Liberal Arts at The Pennsylvania State University. Bob Frank contributed significantly to these institutions throughout his career, and it is fitting that they now help honor him. I wish to thank in particular Robert Secor, Head of the English Department; Susan Welch, Dean of the College; and Raymond Lombra, Associate Dean for Research. I wish to thank as well Dr. Richard Barber for his support of the project and his valuable suggestions. Pat Nickinson worked on this project as a research assistant; her keen eye and tireless checking have been a great service to the authors and the editor.

Robert R. Edwards
University Park, Pennsylvania
October 1993

A Bibliography of Robert Worth Frank, Jr.

"The Conclusion of *Piers Plowman*." *Journal of English and Germanic Philology* 49 (1951): 309–12.

"The Number of Visions in *Piers Plowman*." *MLN* 66 (1951): 309–12.

"The Pardon Scene in *Piers Plowman*." *Speculum* 26 (1951): 317–31.

"Out of Context" (excerpted). *ACLS Newsletter* 3.3 (Summer 1952): 11–14.

"The Art of Reading Medieval Personification Allegory." *ELH* 20 (1953): 237–50.

"Chaucer and the London Bell-Founders." *MLN* 68 (1953): 524–28.

Rev. of D. W. Robertson, Jr. and Bernard F. Huppé, *"Piers Plowman" and Scriptural Tradition*. *MLN* 68 (1953): 194–96.

"Structure and Meaning in the *Parlement of Foules*." *PMLA* 71 (1956): 530–39.

"Piers Plowman" and the Scheme of Salvation: An Interpretation of Dowel, Dobet, and Dobest. Yale Studies in English 136. New Haven: Yale University Press, 1957; reprint, New York: Archon Books, 1969.

The Critical Question, ed. Robert Worth Frank, Jr. and Harrison Meserole. Boston: Allyn & Bacon, 1964.

Rev. of Elizabeth Salter, *"Piers Plowman": An Introduction*. *Speculum* 40 (1965): 750–53.

"The Legend of the *Legend of Good Women*." *Chaucer Review* 1 (1966–67): 110–33.

The Responsible Man: The Insights of the Humanities, ed. Robert Worth Frank, Jr. and Harrison Meserole. New York: Doubleday, 1969.

"*Troilus and Criseyde*: The Art of Amplification." *Medieval Literature and Folklore Studies: Essays in Honor of Francis Lee Utley*, ed. Jerome Mandel and Bruce A. Rosenberg. New Brunswick: Rutgers University Press, 1970. 155–71, 359–61.

Rev. of J. A. W. Bennett, *Chaucer's Book of Fame: An Exposition of "The House of Fame"*. *Modern Philology* 68 (1970): 195–98.

Chaucer and "The Legend of Good Women". Cambridge, Mass.: Harvard University Press, 1972.

"The *Reeve's Tale* and the Comedy of Limitation." *Directions in Literary Criticism: Contemporary Approaches to Literature*, ed. Stanley Weintraub and Philip Young. University Park: Penn State Press, 1973. 53–69.

"The *Legend of Good Women*: Some Implications." *Chaucer at Albany: Middle English Texts and Contexts*, ed. Rossell Hope Robbins. New York: Franklin, 1975. 63–76.

"Miracles of the Virgin, Medieval Anti-Semitism, and the *Prioress's Tale*." The

Wisdom of Poetry: Essays in Early English Literature in Honor of Morton W. Bloomfield, ed. Larry D. Benson and Siegfried Wenzel. Kalamazoo: Medieval Institute Publications, 1982. 177–88, 290–97.

"The Most Amusing Book in the Language [the *DNB*]." *The American Scholar* 54 (1984–85): 89–97.

"The *Canterbury Tales* III: Pathos." *The Cambridge Chaucer Companion*, ed. Piero Boitani and Jill Mann. Cambridge: Cambridge University Press, 1986. 143–58.

"*Meditationes Vitae Christi*: The Logistics of Access to Divinity." *Hermeneutics and Medieval Culture*, ed. Patrick J. Gallacher and Helen Damico. Albany: State University of New York Press, 1989. 39–50.

"Inept Chaucer [Presidential Address to New Chaucer Society]." *Studies in the Age of Chaucer* 11 (1989): 5–14.

"Pathos in Chaucer's Religious Tales." *Chaucer's Religious Tales*, ed. C. David Benson and Elizabeth Robertson. Chaucer Studies 15. Cambridge: D. S. Brewer, 1990. 39–52.

"The 'Hungry Gap,' Crop Failure, and Famine: The Fourteenth-Century Agricultural Crisis and *Piers Plowman*." *Yearbook of Langland Studies* 4 (1990): 87–104; reprinted in *People of the Plow: European Agriculture in the Middle Ages*, ed. Del Sweeney, Philadelphia: University of Pennsylvania Press, forthcoming.

Rev. of Wendy Scase, *"Piers Plowman" and the New Anticlericalism*. *Studies in the Age of Chaucer* 13 (1991): 232–35.

"Pilgrimage and Sacral Power." *Journeys Toward God: Pilgrimage and Crusade*, ed. Barbara N. Sargent-Baur. Studies in Medieval Culture 20. Kalamazoo: Medieval Institute Publications, 1992. 31–43.

The Frustration of Narrative and the Reader in *Piers Plowman*

C. DAVID BENSON

Although Bob Frank wrote the first (and still among the best) critical books on the B-text of *Piers Plowman*, much of his subsequent work has been on Chaucer. The following essay is by one who has recently made a journey in the opposite direction. The initial bafflement I felt when confronted with the narrative challenges of *Piers Plowman* after so much time with Chaucer's poetry may seem strange to experienced Langlandians, but I believe it is shared by others who approach the poem with modern conceptions of what literature is supposed to be. However preliminary and personal this study of narrative and readers may be, I am grateful for the opportunity to salute a great scholar and a good man to whom so many of us owe so much.

Despite its achievement, *Piers Plowman* may be the most unread, misrepresented, and even disliked major poem in the English language. The contrast with Chaucer is revealing. Despite the many medievalists from Skeat to Aers who have divided their work between the two poets, it is intriguing to go down the index of Derek Pearsall's recent bibliography of Langland and discover how many prominent Chaucerians are missing (including Kittredge, Root, Lumiansky, Ruggiers, Ridley, Jordan, David, and Larry Benson) or how many have only a single entry, such as Lewis, Baugh, Fisher, and Brewer.[1] Even more surprising is how much *Piers Plowman* seems to offend some students of Middle English. I am struck by how often in conversation the very mention of *Piers* elicits expressions of distaste and hostility from otherwise tolerant scholars. Even supporters of the poem admit its problems: A. C. Spearing calls it "one of the most fascinating, and also one of the most difficult, of fourteenth-century poems."[2]

In Edmund Crispin's mystery novel *Buried for Pleasure*, the detective, Gervase Fen, who is also Professor of English at Oxford, is asked by a woman taxi-

---

[1] Derek Pearsall, *An Annotated Critical Bibliography of Langland* (Ann Arbor: University of Michigan Press, 1990).

[2] A. C. Spearing, "The Art of Preaching and *Piers Plowman*," *Criticism and Medieval Poetry*, 2d ed. (New York: Barnes and Noble, 1972), 107.

driver in a remote village why he has come there to stand for Parliament. Fen finally replies:

"I felt I was getting too restricted in my interests. Have you ever produced a definitive edition of Langland?"
"Of course not," she said crossly.
"I have. I've just finished producing one. It has queer psychological effects. You begin to wonder if you're mad. And the only remedy is a complete change of occupation."[3]

It must be admitted that the resistance that Langland encounters among many contemporary academics and their students is largely his own fault. Even those who admire *Piers* find that it is almost impossible to teach. Running to over 7,000 lines (even if we ignore its three or four distinct versions), the poem is too long to suit the needs of contemporary literature courses. Nor can it easily be taught in selections; much of the power of individual passages comes from their complex links to others parts of the poem, which are lost when read in isolation. The contrast with Chaucer is striking. Good businessman that he was, Geoffrey had obviously looked far into the future and nicely anticipated the needs of the twentieth-century American university curriculum. Of course, he produced his own 7,000-line masterpiece should there be a call for it, but he also wrote *The Canterbury Tales*: a literary delicatessen with items to satisfy any pedagogical taste: long tales, short tales, funny tales, moral tales, courtly tales, ancient tales, modern tales, serious tales, and silly tales. Langland is no such obliging supplier of poetic delights: you take what he sets before you, all of it, or you leave it. Unlike so much medieval literature, *Piers* has little chivalry and few women or romance.

The poet has done very little to make *Piers Plowman* easy for many modern readers to approach or understand as poetry. Anne Middleton states that until this century "its stature has been that of an English historical monument rather than a European literary masterpiece," and she notes that an undergraduate is still as likely to encounter it in a history course as in a literary survey.[4] *Piers* is hard to classify, and there is no other medieval work much like it: Morton Bloomfield suggests that it draws from seven different genres (allegorical dream, dialogue or debate, encyclopedic satire, complaint, commentary, sermon, and apocalypse), and Geoffrey Shepherd lists nine (satire, complaint, preachment, dream allegory, meditation, apocalypse, debate, moral tract, and epic).[5]

Langland has given his poem no recognizable form, and it often seems about to collapse into incoherence. Rosemary Woolf and J. A. W. Bennett have both

---

[3] Edmund Crispin, *Buried for Pleasure* (Philadelphia: Lippincott, 1949), 12.
[4] Anne Middleton, "Introduction: The Critical Heritage," in *A Companion to Piers Plowman*, ed. John Alford (Berkeley and Los Angeles: University of California Press, 1988), 1–2.
[5] Morton W. Bloomfield, *Piers Plowman as a Fourteenth-century Apocalypse* (New Brunswick: Rutgers University Press, [1961]), 10; Geoffrey Shepherd, "The Nature of Alliterative Poetry in Late Medieval England," Gollancz Memorial Lecture, *Proceedings of the British Academy* 56 (1970): 64.

observed that *Piers*, in contrast to the orderliness of most medieval dream allegories, proceeds with the disjointed bewilderment of real dreams.[6] Instead of the "clarity, explicit organization, and comprehensiveness of form" that Middleton declares were "the entire purpose of the teaching compendia" like Mannyng's *Handlyng Synne*, Dan Michel's *Ayenbite of Inwit*, or *Cursor Mundi*, the execution of *Piers*, according to another critic, is more like the old madcap comedy film *Hellzapoppin*.[7] The seven deadly sins and the ten commandments appear in *Piers*, but they provide no central principle of organization as they do in so many other manuals or poems such as Gower's *Confessio Amantis*. When a clear allegorical schema does briefly appear, as in Piers's directions of the way to reach Truth (B.5.560ff), we are reminded of what is missing in most of the poem.[8]

Yet what most bothers literary critics about *Piers Plowman*, I believe, is its lack of narrative. *Piers* is usually taught along with poets like Chaucer and the *Gawain*-poet who, whatever else they do, are supreme storytellers. It was precisely this lack of narrative that struck me most when I began to read Langland again seriously after several years of concentrating on Chaucer. Chaucer tells wonderful stories, almost all of which have beginnings, middles, and ends – stories so strong that they can easily be adapted for children. (Imagine a child's version of *Piers*!) Chaucer is able to make the most intractable and inert material dramatic – Boethius on predestination in *Troilus*, anti-feminist arguments in the Wife of Bath's Prologue, alchemical lore in the Canon's Yeoman's Tale. We never lose the thread of the narrative or of the speaker's voice. Despite all the digressions, changes of tone, and discordant discourses in the Nun's Priest's Tale, the basic story of Chanticleer's wives, pride, dream, capture, and escape remains. The works of the other great poets of fourteenth-century England are also strong narratives – not only the romance of Gawain and the biblical tale of Jonah but also *Pearl*, despite its lack of action. In contrast to Chaucer and the *Gawain*-poet, Langland, in C. S. Lewis's phrase, "hardly makes his poetry into a poem."[9]

In other dream visions we usually know where we are, even if it is in a supernatural landscape, and who is talking, even if it is an allegorical figure.

---

[6] Rosemary Woolf, "Some Non-Medieval Qualities of *Piers Plowman*," *Essays in Criticism* 12 (1962): 111–25; J. A. W. Bennett, "Langland," in *Middle English Literature*, ed. Douglas Gray (Oxford: Clarendon Press, 1986), 430–55.

[7] Anne Middleton, "The Audience and Public of 'Piers Plowman'," in *Middle English Alliterative Poetry and Its Literary Background: Seven Essays*, ed. David Lawton (Cambridge: D. S. Brewer, 1982), 112; Christine Brooke-Rose, "Ezra Pound: Piers Plowman in the Modern Waste Land," *Review of English Literature* 2 (1961): 78.

[8] All citations to Langland are from the B-Text unless otherwise noted and taken from *The Vision of Piers Plowman*, ed. A. V. C. Schmidt (London: Dent, 1978). All citations to the C-Text are from *Piers Plowman by William Langland: An Edition of the C-Text*, ed. Derek Pearsall, York Medieval Texts, 2d ser. (Berkeley and Los Angeles: University of California Press, 1978).

[9] C. S. Lewis, *The Allegory of Love* (1936; reprint, London: Oxford University Press, 1948), 161.

Such basic requirements of narrative are frequently missing in *Piers*. Scenes shift so radically and apparently randomly that Muscatine calls the effect "surrealistic."[10] During much of the Vita we hear voices who speak at length, but we are given no sense of physical locale. Nor are these voices always clearly identified. Editors have to guess when speeches by such as Trajan actually end, for the text gives contradictory signals and the narrator or another character may at any time radically change tone and suddenly begin to adopt the mystical voice of prophecy (e.g. 3.285ff, 6.320ff). Rosemary Woolf declares that "there can be few Medieval poems in which the literal level is so tenuous and confused."[11] Attempts to summarize the plot of *Piers* often miss what is most important in the poem, rather like the television film editor who eliminated the Marx Brothers' extraordinary stateroom scene in *A Night at the Opera* because he insisted correctly and absurdly that it did not advance the plot. With *Piers* as with the Marx Brothers, plot is often beside the point. Muscatine notes that we "come away from it with something of the feeling that in it anything might have happened."[12]

Piers Plowman repeatedly lacks both the basic level of plausible fiction found in the works of Chaucer and the *Gawain*-poet (whatever their thematic complexities) and the clear programmatic structures of medieval sermons and didactic allegories. In their edition of selections from the C-Text, Salter and Pearsall counsel us to accept "that the poem has no proper narrative structure" and that "Langland is not committed to a narrative structure in any continuous way." They admit that other medieval allegories such as the *Roman de la Rose* will not prepare us for "its interrupted and suspended narratives."[13] John Chamberlin, in a recent essay whose title I wish I had used first, "What Makes *Piers Plowman* So Hard to Read?," joins Priscilla Martin in speaking of the poem's "narrative discontinuity" (34).[14]

In the rest of this paper, I want to look in more detail at the frustration of narrative in *Piers* because I believe that the explanations for it have been inadequate and ignore the crucial role of the reader. I am using a very general definition of narrative, which I think would be accepted by both Aristotle and Vladimir Propp, as the recounting of a sequence of events involving characters. For my purposes here the familiar critical distinction between story and discourse is irrelevant, and I shall use story and storytelling as synonymous

---

[10] Charles Muscatine, "Locus of Action in Medieval Narrative," *Romance Philology* 17 (1963): 121–22.

[11] Woolf, 112.

[12] Charles Muscatine, *Poetry and Crisis in the Age of Chaucer* (Notre Dame: University of Notre Dame Press, 1972), 105.

[13] Elizabeth Salter and Derek Pearsall, eds., *Piers Plowman*, York Medieval Texts (Evanston, Ill.: Northwestern University Press, 1969), 32.

[14] John Chamberlin, "What Makes *Piers Plowman* So Hard to Read?" *Style* 23 (1989): 34; Priscilla Martin, *Piers Plowman: The Field and the Tower* (London: Macmillan, 1979), notes the "narrative patterns disrupted in the interest of the argument" (39) and how readily Langland "is prepared to thwart our narrative expectations if inconclusiveness or re-statement best serve the cause of precision" (51).

with narrative. Much of what I say about narrative will also be appropriate for non-narrative elements in *Piers*. Some of Langland's most accomplished effects are not really narratives at all but two other "text-types" (to use Seymour Chatman's term) that are common in fiction: description, as in the accounts of the sins in Passus 5, and, of even more importance, argumentation, as in the debates and speeches that dominate much of the poem.[15] Part of the excitement and difficulty of *Piers* is that it is often all but impossible to separate narration from description and argumentation – each is always becoming the other. For example, in an early passage chosen at random, hermits on the field of folk are described:

> Heremytes on an heep with hoked staves
> Wenten to Walsyngham – and hire wenches after:
> Grete lobies and longe that lothe were to swynke
> Clothed hem in copes to ben knowen from othere,
> And shopen hem heremytes hire ese to have.   (Prol. 53–57)

This passage is primarily a physical description of hermits, but it also makes a sharp argument about their hypocrisy and even includes a brief narration of their pilgrimage to Walsingham. My emphasis is on narrative, but it is hard to avoid the other text types; what I say will often apply to them.

The most basic narrative frustration for readers of *Piers Plowman* is that the story does not seem to get anywhere. Instead of making linear progress, we get little sense of direction. The most extensive narrative in the poem is Will's search for Dowel, but this quest is missing from both the beginning and end of the poem, it is often attenuated, and it is not clear what is finally achieved. *Piers Plowman* is very different from the patterned circularity of *Sir Gawain and the Green Knight* whose return to Camelot emphasizes just how far Gawain and the reader have traveled. Even a poem as loosely structured as Chaucer's *House of Fame* gives the sense of a rational progression through different landscapes, events, and characters. But *Piers* is more like a literary game of snakes and ladders, in which we constantly find ourselves back at what looks very much like the place from which we started. Episodes (such as the life of Christ), points of doctrine (such as the deadly sins), and characters (such as Conscience), which we might have thought had already been dealt with fully, suddenly reappear. If the poem is generated more from theme than narrative, as Salter and Pearsall argue, these themes also are not so much developed as revisited.[16] The proper attitude toward money and beggars, for example, or the value of speech and friars are topics that keep returning.

In most narratives, we see characters experiencing the crucial events of life: they are born, marry, and die. Biographies start with their subject's birth; novels used to end happily ever after in marriage, and death concludes Shakespeare's tragedies. None of this or anything like it happens in *Piers*.

---

[15] For these three text-types, see Seymour Chatman, *Coming to Terms: The Rhetoric of Narrative in Fiction and Film* (Ithaca: Cornell University Press, 1990).

[16] Salter and Pearsall, 32–36.

Langland is capable of abandoning what story there is at any moment, as he abruptly does with one of the longest narratives in the poem, the proposed marriage of Lady Meed. Despite the plans of many, Meed never marries anyone, just as the one apparent death in the poem (that of Christ) turns out not to have happened after all. Similarly, Piers gives up plowing his half acre, Peace's accusation in Parliament against Wrong is never settled, the sins do not finally repent, and Haukyn is last seen weeping in despair. Many journeys are proposed and undertaken in *Piers*, but few are completed. The dwelling places of Truth or Dowel are not discovered (for very good reasons), and at the end of the poem, Conscience sets out on one last pilgrimage in pursuit of the increasingly elusive Piers the Plowman.

In addition to a lack of apparent progress in *Piers*, narrative frustration also results from our trying to understand why a particular incident comes after another. The poet occasionally apologizes for a digression (e.g. 11.317; C.20.357–58), but the narrative fissures I refer to are far more radical and persistent. Salter and Pearsall note that "the abruptness of the transitions" has occasioned much comment, often to the disparagement of Langland's art.[17] They list as examples the displacement of lawyers by a "route of ratons" in the prologue, the sudden switch from Piers's pursuit of the devil to the life of Christ in Passus 16, and the surprising appearance of Piers during the Feast of Patience in the C-text. These abrupt transitions may owe something to the fluidity of dream logic, but I cannot think of a contemporary parallel for the violence and frequency with which they break the narrative. The many different dreams in *Piers* (not to mention dreams within dreams), which are unparalleled in medieval literature, add to the disjointed effect by creating a variety of unconnected dream settings (from Westminster to Jerusalem by way of a half acre) and casts of characters (from laborers to intellectual abstractions). Langland seems to have no strong dedication to the story itself, which he is always willing to suspend and redirect. Anne Middleton even claims that "the disrupted episode" is Langland's "poetic signature."[18]

The most famous and among the sharpest narrative jolts in the poem are the self-introductions through dramatic speech of Piers and Trajan: " 'Peter!' quod a Plowman, and putte forth his hed" (5.537); " 'Ye, baw for bokes!' quod oon was broken out of helle" (11.140). Other characters appear or leave the story almost as unexpectedly. Why is it that Theology interrupts Meed's marriage plans in Passus 2 and where does he come from? In Passus 5, Robert the Robber disappears as abruptly as he arrived (5.462–72). After Piers's pardon from Truth is announced in Passus 7, a priest materializes to construe it (7.105) and, just as surprisingly, the Dreamer himself is now on the scene: "And I bihynde hem bothe biheld al the bulle" (7.108). At the end of the poem the

[17] Salter and Pearsall, 31.
[18] Anne Middleton, "Narration and the Invention of Experience: Episodic Form in *Piers Plowman*," in *The Wisdom of Poetry: Essays in Early English Literature in Honor of Morton W. Bloomfield*, ed. Larry D. Benson and Siegfried Wenzel (Kalamazoo: Medieval Institute Publications, 1982), 119.

Dreamer again puts himself directly into the narrative without warning, when, during a description of Elde's pursuit of Life, he says in mid-line, "And Elde anoon after hym, and over myn heed yede, / And made me balled bifore and bare on the croune" (20.183–84).

In contrast to these violent transitions but equally subversive of narrative coherence is the poet's tendency to introduce episodes and themes indirectly, almost carelessly. Bennett notes that although love is the most important word in the poem, it first appears "unobtrusively" in a brief account of those who live correctly "for the love of Oure Lord" (Prol.26).[19] The same device is used to introduce narrative in *Piers*. The dinner in Passus 13 is often called the Feast of Patience, but even though Patience will eventually dominate the scene, he has no prior invitation to the meal. When we first see him, he is standing pitifully outside the hall "in pilgrymes clothes" begging for food (13.29) until Conscience, apparently by chance and with no announced motive, invites him in to dine.

A third impediment to narrative in *Piers*, in addition to aimlessness and abrupt transitions, is its poetic and intellectual density. Langland's intricacy of argument and richness of imagery often resemble metaphysical poetry. At times, *Piers Plowman* reads less like narrative than lyric, as though it were a Donne holy sonnet extended to 7,000 lines. Rosemary Woolf has written about the subtle and complex texture of the poem's style, in which associated ideas are not set out side by side but interwoven and compressed together, and more recently Chamberlin has said that the poem is "composed of parts that call attention to themselves by their very richness" and suggests that perhaps "it is not that there are so few but so many strands of continuity, multiple, simultaneous, competing concatenations that spin out from the words of the text to be sometimes overtaken by other developments."[20] This concentration of ideas and images is very different from Chaucer's usual conversational style. An example of such metaphysical intensity is the extraordinary description of the Incarnation as plant of peace found in the midst of Holy Church's generally straightforward speech:

> "For Truthe telleth that love is triacle of hevene:
> May no synne be on hym seene that that spice useth.
> And alle his werkes he wroughte with love as hym liste,
> And lered it Moyses for the leveste thyng and moost lik to
>   hevene,
> And also the plante of pees, moost precious of vertues:

---

[19] Bennett, 436. Similarly, although the need for patience in poverty becomes a major theme in the second half of the poem, what I believe is the first linking of this alliterating pair is Scripture's casual use of the phrase "poverte with pacience" (10.338) in the midst of a debate with the Dreamer over other issues. In the notes to his edition, Schmidt says that the theme of patient poverty is introduced at 11.255, though not developed until passus 13 (p. 335).

[20] Woolf, 124; Chamberlin, 32, 39–40.

For hevene myghte nat holden it, so was it hevy of hymself,
Til it hadde of the erthe eten his fille.
And whan it hadde of this fold flessh and blood taken,
Was nevere leef upon lynde lighter therafter,
And portatif and persaunt as the point of a nedle,
That myghte noon armure it lette ne none heighe walles."

(1.148–58)

There is a narrative behind these lines, but it is almost lost in a compression of medicinal, plant, food, and military images (all of which are important in the rest of the poem) of a kind almost never found in the looser poetry of Chaucer, except occasionally in formal beginnings and endings.

Two principal explanations have been offered by critics for the frustrations of narrative that I have been discussing. Both are valuable, but neither is fully satisfactory. The first explanation is that the poet is incompetent or overwhelmed. In this popular view Langland, whatever his other achievements, is just not much good at telling a coherent story, perhaps because he is defeated by the difficult questions he raises. This I take to be Lewis's point when he said that Langland "hardly makes his poetry into a poem." Burrow has recently emphasized the autobiographical side of this position with the claim that Passus 11–12 record a genuine crisis suffered by the poet in late middle age.[21] A second kind of explanation insists that *Piers* is coherent once we recognize the medieval principles by which it is constructed. Thus Robertson and Huppé understand the poem as a working out of four-fold scriptural exegesis, Alford argues that it is built on a sequence of Biblical quotations developed from preaching concordances, and Wittig argues that Will undertakes an inward journey based on monastic psychology that gives the poem a "consistent narrative and dramatic pattern."[22]

I would not deny that there is some truth in both views, but neither is satisfactory. The autobiographical explanation makes the poem too subjective and minimizes Langland's conscious artistry, as if he were writing *The Book of Margery Kempe*. The related argument that Langland is incompetent can only be an explanation of last resort. We should always hesitate to condescend to great poets. But the strongest argument against this view is that Langland is an accomplished teller of stories when he chooses to be. The plowing of the half acre, the tearing of the pardon, the devil running away from the Tree of Charity with Piers's fruit are dramatic and memorable scenes. Langland's

---

[21] John Burrow, "Langland *Nel Mezzo Del Cammin*," in *Medieval Studies for J. A. W. Bennett*, ed. P. L. Heyworth (Oxford: Clarendon Press, 1981), 21–41.

[22] D. W. Robertson, Jr., and Bernard F. Huppé, *Piers Plowman and Scriptural Tradition* (1951; reprint, New York: Octagon, 1969); John Alford, "The Role of the Quotations in *Piers Plowman*," *Speculum* 52 (1977): 80–99; Joseph S. Wittig, " 'Piers Plowman' B, Passus IX–XII: Elements in the Design of the Inward Journey," *Traditio* 28 (1972): 211–80; Wittig, "The Dramatic and Rhetorical Development of Long Will's Pilgrimage," *Neuphilologische Mitteilungen* 76 (1975): 52–76. The quotation I use is from the summary to this last article (52).

retelling of the Crucifixion and Harrowing of Hell in Passus 18 is frequently anthologized (often the only thing from *Piers* that is anthologized) because it most closely resembles the narratives of the other great Ricardian poets. The episode has a variety of characters, much action, and a resolved plot.

Another and perhaps more original example of Langland's narrative skill is the Feast of Patience. Without denying its allegorical potential, Elizabeth Kirk stresses the novelistic qualities of the episode by not unjustly comparing Langland's eye for social behavior to Jane Austen's.[23] Kirk analyzes the subtle self-revelations of the pompous, hypocritical Doctor of Divinity and calls special attention to the poet's account of Conscience's actions after the Doctor has been rudely attacked by the Dreamer:

> Thanne Conscience ful curteisly a contenaunce he made,
> And preynte upon Pacience to preie me to be stille,
> And seide hymself, "Sire doctour, and it be youre wille,
> What is Dowel and Dobet? Ye dyvynours knoweth."
>
> (13.111–14)

In these few lines, Kirk notes, Langland has perfectly captured the reaction of a hostess in an awkward situation: "the grimace of mingled complicity and rebuke to the offender, the glance at the reliable guest that says '*Do* something'; and the flattering inquiry addressed to the offended party."[24] Each of the principal characters in the Feast of Patience is deftly characterized and the relations between them minutely observed (the Dreamer's rising irritation with the Doctor despite Patience's attempts to soothe him is particularly well done, as is the leave-taking of Conscience and Clergy). The episode is even allowed a conclusion as Conscience decides to abandon Clergy and follow Patience. Although the scene is brief (less than 200 lines), its sophistication at portraying the social and psychological interactions of a variety of characters is comparable to that in *Sir Gawain and the Green Knight* and Chaucer's *Troilus and Criseyde*. Here Langland is not at all overwhelmed by the difficulty of his material; instead he shows himself to be a master storyteller.

The second explanation for narrative frustration in *Piers* is that the poem has a coherent order if only we apply the correct medieval paradigm (exegesis, Biblical quotations, monastic psychology), but this risks making *Piers Plowman* more programmatic and less difficult than it really is, as though it were *The Pricke of Conscience*. Langland is nothing like Chaucer's Parson, who rejects "fables and swich wrecchednesse" for "moralitee and vertuous mateere" and who disdains "'rum, ram, ruf,' by lettre" (*Canterbury Tales* X.34–44).[25] Langland does not believe that one can so easily replace the deceptions of fiction with the clarity of doctrine. Narrative frustration is only a symptom of

23 Elizabeth D. Kirk, *The Dream Thought of Piers Plowman* (New Haven: Yale University Press, 1972), 148.

24 Kirk, 147.

25 *The Riverside Chaucer*, 3d ed., gen. ed. Larry D. Benson (Boston: Hougton Mifflin, 1987).

deeper literary and moral irresolutions in *Piers*. If we are able to find no sustained comfort in the storytelling, there is also none to be found in other aspects of the poem. For example, *Piers* is unusual among religious allegories in containing no reliable guide or sure authority figure. Holy Church seems to adopt this role briefly, but her teaching does not fit the Dreamer's needs and she soon disappears. Even Piers is fallible, at least in the Visio. He loses control of the plowing and gets a stomach ache from overindulgence (6.255–56). Apparent authorities in the Vita are similarly ambiguous. Husband and wife allegories bicker and give contradictory definitions of the three lives. Imaginatif corrects many of the Dreamer's more extreme views, yet he too is limited: some of his reasoning seems doubtful (such as the comparison of intellectual learning with knowing how to swim [12.161–74]), and he finally admits that there are many mysteries, such as why only one thief on the cross asked to be saved, that all the clerks in the world cannot explain (12.216). Although narrative in *Piers* constantly gives way to argumentation, these arguments are often as frustrating as the poem's storytelling.

In contrast to the many critics who find fault with the poet or his audience, I believe that Langland knows what he is doing and that the difficulties experienced by moderns are genuine. The frustration of narrative and instruction in *Piers* is neither inadvertent nor imaginary: it is real and deliberate. The object of this frustration is someone not given enough attention in Langland criticism – the reader. Critics such as Bennett and Wittig claim that the reader is meant to identify with the experiences of the Dreamer, but I would argue that our experience as readers is itself central.[26] Middleton is closer to the truth when she argues that Will is merely a function for our benefit; it is we, not Will, she argues, who must learn from the poem, even though its playful form is more equivocal than the more obviously instructional models it seems to imitate.[27] I would suggest that *Piers* offers its readers neither entertaining narrative nor direct statement but instead involves them in complex narratives and moral questions that it intentionally does not resolve.

If the narratives of the Feast of Patience and the Harrowing of Hell are exceptional in their completeness, it may be because in them good and evil are so clearly distinguished. The Doctor of Divinity represents everything Langland hates about the Established Church, and Patience is his answer. Even more obviously, the conflict between Christ and the rulers of Hell opposes truth and falsehood, light and dark, life and death. Yet even the Feast of Patience, for all its narrative skill, is less than fully satisfying as a story. The wonderfully hypocritical Doctor is not developed as much as he would be by any competent novelist (think what Trollope would have done with him) and, as so often with other characters in the poem, simply fades away. The episode is resolved in that Conscience decides to follow Patience, but the result is one

---

[26] Bennett, 439; Witting, "Dramatic and Rhetorical Development," 61.
[27] "Audience," 116–21.

more journey with no clear end. The Harrowing of Hell may be the only example of complete narrative resolution in the poem – the devils are defeated, the righteous rescued, and the Four Daughters of God reconciled – but it is also the only episode in *Piers* with God as its protagonist and the only one set in an eternal, nonterrestrial realm.

The other Ricardian poets, especially Chaucer and the *Gawain*-poet, allow great freedom of interpretation, as modern criticism has shown, but Langland's demands on his readers are more radical and unavoidable because he makes it impossible for them to enjoy an agreeable fiction. False minstrels and tellers of idle tales are repeatedly blamed in *Piers*, and its author makes sure that we will not confuse his work with mere diversion. The narrative frustrations of *Piers* produce something comparable to Brecht's alienation effect, keeping us from identifying too closely with the characters or losing ourselves in the working out of the story. It is as though the outer layer of tale telling that is so strong and appealing in Chaucer and the *Gawain*-poet had been entirely eliminated, rather like a modern building such as the Pompidou Center with all its plumbing and reinforcements exposed. Since we cannot be satisfied by the pleasures of narrative, we are forced to look elsewhere. When we do, we find that the authority figures and the statements they make are equally unresolved. Many manuscripts of *Piers* label the work a *dialogus*. Perhaps we should think of the poem as a genuine medieval dialogue or debate, like those between water and wine or spring and summer, in which neither side is wholly right or wrong and judgment remains with the reader. For all its apparent instruction, *Piers* offers few final answers to the serious questions it raises, for its poet seems to accept that true learning occurs from within rather than from without, only when we have found answers that are fitting and proper for us. Langland is the creator of the poem called *Piers Plowman*, but its meaning he necessarily leaves to the responsibility of individual readers.

In the long autobiographical passage added to the beginning of Passus 5 in the C-text, we are given a hint as to how to approach the poem. The Dreamer's account of his way of life turns into self-justification when he is criticized by Reason and then becomes a general attack by him on ecclesiastical abuses and the corruption of social hierarchy by money. But this full flight of moral and social criticism, so characteristic of *Piers*, is cut short by Reason's rebuke that such statements are beside the point ("By Crist, y can nat se this lyeth" [C.5.89]) because they do not address the Dreamer's particular failures. Admitting that he has misspent his time, the Dreamer says that he still hopes with grace to reform so that "alle tymes of my tyme to profit shal turne" (5.101). Reason not only interrupts a promising narrative, to the frustration of biographers, but he also warns us that apparently sound moral preachments, such as the Dreamer's attacks on the Church and society, may be irrelevant and self-serving. The reader is warned that he should not automatically accept the stated lessons of the poem, however plausible or apparently endorsed by the poet; instead, we must actively question them until we also find what will be profitable to our particular situation. Langland *must* trust his readers with this interpretive freedom because he does not know their individual spiritual needs;

he *can* trust them because of his confidence that whatever answers they find will be within a context of orthodox Christianity.

Piers Plowman is often treated as a didactic work, but in what way is this so? Its tone is didactic, but what exactly are the lessons it provides? It instructs us not to have sexual relations at the wrong time, not to tell tales, and not to murder. On a more significant level of teaching, the poem urges us to love our neighbors and share our goods with them; it recommends patient poverty. Yet although these latter lessons are as important as they are unoriginal, they are not easy to apply. *Piers* repeatedly shows how difficult such ideals are to understand, let alone realize in actual life. The reader must work out their meanings and applications individually. Although *Piers* insists that we should care about social justice, it does not really tell us how to go about achieving it. In contrast to Chaucer, Langland does seem to want to change his readers' lives and to save their souls, but he is not so silly to think that he can do this by fiat.

Neither Holy Church's doctrine in Passus 1, sound and often sublime as it is, nor the friar's attempt to explain sin through his parable of a man in a boat at the beginning of the Vita in Passus 8 is sufficient. By themselves they remain inert narrative and moral discourses. In response to each, Will insists that he has no "kynde knowynge" of what it meant (1.138 and 8.58). "Kynde knowynge" is precisely what the narrative design of *Piers* is intended to provide, though "kynde knowynge" not so much for Will (whatever his relationship to the real Langland, he remains a fiction) as for us. Preaching alone will not produce such knowledge, only the active involvement of the reader.

Although they have not sufficiently emphasized the role of the reader, several critics have insisted upon the importance of this kind of knowledge in *Piers*. Martin declares that the poet "demonstrates through his exhausted but indefatigable Dreamer that 'truth' must be felt as experience rather than learned as lesson."[28] More recently, James Simpson has argued that *Piers Plowman* is in the tradition of affective rather than speculative theology: in the second half of the poem especially, he says, "the modes of the poetry seem to me to be consistently designed to produce a sapiential, experiential, 'kynde' knowledge of God" (14).[29] The imperative *redde quod debes*, which dominates the end of the poem, is a demand that individual readers must answer for themselves (what do I owe?) and then practice. It is not an injunction that can be imposed by someone else, even a great poet, but is a call for self-examination and self-definition. Langland does not provide any sort of programmatic teaching (how could he know what each of us owes?) but rather offers an interactive text, as Iser might call it, whose narrative and instructional frustrations demand the reader's involvement.

Lest my argument appear to be another modern attempted assassination of the author as well as a non-medieval privileging of the reader, Beryl Smalley

---

[28] Martin, 58.

[29] James Simpson, "From Reason for Affective Knowledge: Modes of Thought and Poetic Form in *Piers Plowman*," *Medium Ævum* 55 (1986): 14.

reminds us that Gregory the Great believed that the Bible itself was adaptable to individual readers: in his *Homilies* on Ezekiel, Gregory "construes St. Augustine's teaching, that all knowledge useful to man is contained in Scripture, to mean that each text contains, or points him towards, *what is useful to any particular man at any particular moment*" (my emphasis). No unitary lesson is offered, but like the wheels of the beasts in the vision of Ezekiel (1:21), Scripture "corresponds with the state of the student; it goes, stands, is lifted up with him, like the wheels, according as he is striving after the active life, after stability and constancy of spirit, or after the flights of contemplation."[30]

What lessons there are in *Piers* are rarely direct or unitary. Among the most important moments in the Harrowing of Hell and the Feast of Patience seem to be the metaphysical, riddling wordplay by Christ in the first episode and by Clergy and Patience in the second (13.119–71), which is dismissed by the Doctor as a mere minstrel's tale (13.172). During the debate of the Four Daughters of God before the Harrowing, Mercy's poetic discourse, full of puns and paradoxes (18.136–41), turns out to be truer than the rational statements of Truth herself, though the latter, like the Doctor, at first rejects her sister's words as a "tale of waltrot" (18.142). David Aers has likewise shown that the lively narrative of the Tree of Charity is an open and suggestive allegory that cannot be reduced to paraphrase.[31] Geoffrey Shepherd has proposed that *Piers*, like Julian of Norwich's *Shewings*, may have its origin in a series of images whose meaning the poet had gradually to work out.[32] Shepherd argues that when Langland first composed the pardon scene at the end of the Visio, for example, he did not know its meaning. I would go further and suggest that the critical debate over the tearing of the pardon shows that Langland never presumed to give it one meaning. His job as poet was to make the scene exciting and dramatic; meaning he left to his individual readers. This episode and others like it are didactic only in a special way; they do not instruct us so much as they challenge us to explore their mysteries and find what is useful for us.

One explanation for why *Piers Plowman* so often frustrates moderns is that it may have originally been read in a way very different from the way we now approach literature. Robert A. Wood and Middleton have recently discussed late fourteenth-century and early fifteenth-century wills that mention manuscripts of *Piers* among the owner's possessions.[33] These documents suggest that for many, though not all, of the poem's original readers, especially clergymen, *Piers* might well have been one of few works of its kind that they possessed. One would then assume that the poem was read over and over by this early audience. If so, these readers would probably be less interested in the narrative,

---

30 Beryl Smalley, *The Study of the Bible in the Middle Ages* (1952; reprint, Notre Dame: University of Notre Dame Press, 1964), 32.

31 David Aers, *Piers Plowman and Christian Allegory* (London: Arnold, 1975), 79–109.

32 Shepherd, 73–74.

33 Robert A. Wood, "A Fourteenth-Century London Owner of *Piers Plowman*," *Medium Ævum* 53 (1984): 83–90: Middleton, "Audience," 103–04 and especially n. 6.

in finding out what happens in the story as we want to know with a modern novel, than in pondering over particular episodes – the tearing of the pardon, the Feast of Patience, the tree of charity – just as Julian did with her individual visions or as ordinary worshipers did with the wall paintings in their local churches. These original readers of *Piers* would be very different from Oscar Wilde, who in the familiar story continued translating the Bible even after he had convinced his Oxford examiners that he knew Greek because, he claimed, he wanted to know how the story came out. Serious religious readers of the Bible, medieval and modern, tend not to read it as a continuous narrative; because they are familiar with its general outline from constant reading, they can consult and meditate over individual passages. *Piers* may have often been read in the same way.

Contemporary evidence suggests that such a method of non-sequential reading was well recognized by writers in the vernacular. In the prologue to his fourteenth-century *Handlyng Synne*, Robert Mannynge of Brunne tells his readers that they can begin the poem anywhere: "Whedyr outys þou wylt opone þe boke, / Þou shalt fynde begynnyng on to loke. / Oueral ys begynnyng – oueral ys ende . . ." (121–23).[34] And he urges them to read the work often: "Wyþ ofte redyng mayst þou lere. / Þou mayst nouȝt wyþ onys redyng / knowe þe soþe of euery þyng' (126–28). The translator's prologue to the *Orcherd of Syon* is even more explicit about the way a reader must customize a didactic work:

> "in þis goostli orcherd [the work itself] . . . I wole þat ȝe disporte ȝou & walke aboute where ȝe wolen wiþ ȝoure mynde & resoun, in what aleye ȝou lyke, and namely þere ȝe sauouren best, as ȝe ben disposid. Ȝe mowe chese if ȝe wole of xxxv aleyes where ȝe wolen walke, þat is to seye, of xxxv chapitres, o tyme in oon, anoþir tyme in anoþir. But first my counceil is clerely to assaye & serche þe hool orcherd, and taste of sich fruyt and herbis resonably aftir ȝoure affeccioun, & what ȝou likeþ best, aftirward chewe it wel & ete þereof for heelþe of ȝoure soule."[35]

If this is the way that *Piers* was intended to be read, and I think it may be, it is obvious why we have trouble teaching it in English literature classes as though

34 *Handlyng Synne*, ed. Idelle Sullens (Binghamton, N.Y.: Medieval & Renaissance Texts & Studies, 1983).

35 *The Orcherd of Syon*, ed. Phyllis Hodgson and Gabriel M. Liegey. EETS OS 258. (London: Oxford University Press, 1966), I.1. Two other religious treatises also suggest that *Piers Plowman* may have originally been approached, at least by some readers, very differently from the way we now read secular literature. At the end of the *Ancrene Wisse*, the author recommends that the anchorites for whom he is writing read some of it every day, and he hopes that frequent reading will make it profitable to them (*Ancrene Wisse*, ed. J. R. R. Tolkien, EETS OS 249 (London: Oxford University Press, 1962), 221. At the beginning of *A Talkyng of the Love of God*, the author recommends that his work be read slowly and not right through, and then suggests that deeper insight will be achieved by meditating on what has been read and related subjects (*A Talkyng of þe Loue of God*, ed. M. Salvina Westra [Hague: Martinus Nijhoff, 1950], 2).

it were a novel. Yet if *Piers* can never be the purely narrative poem we sometimes try to make it, it remains an intellectual, moral, social, and poetic work of the highest quality, though more like the Bible and Julian of Norwich than conventional imaginative fiction. Because it is so different from what literature has come to mean in the twentieth century, we need new techniques to read and teach it.

Langland's Narrative Christology*

ELIZABETH D. KIRK

Christology, or the branch of theological doctrine describing what is distinctive about the nature and action of Christ, is one of the more difficult areas in which thinkers have attempted to give conceptual form to notions originally (if problematically) derived from Scripture. It attempts to explain what makes Jesus different from other great prophets and religious leaders: what, Christians assert, makes his life and death the hinge upon which the universe turns, the centrally defining moment of human history. This is an issue peculiarly incumbent upon Langland to address sooner or later in *Piers Plowman*, since he has chosen to represent the human condition as a "fair field" with Truth dwelling outside of it in his tower, separated from the human condition while defining it. Implicit in this diagram are the possibility (in Langland's drama) and the certainty (in biblical witness) that Truth has descended from his tower to act on the "fair field" and has fundamentally changed the conditions that obtain there by doing so. As early as the *Visio* of the A text of *Piers Plowman*, Langland represents this action only through the riddling metaphor of the "pardon," a document Truth, who has "heard" of the events on the fair field, has "sent" down to Piers from outside the dream world.[1]

* I am grateful to Melvin Keiser, Karen Bock, and Elizabeth Bryan and to members of the Ninth Coolidge Research Colloquium (1992) for helpful suggestions during the writing of this essay.

[1] Significantly, Langland's two most eloquent passages on the Incarnation and Atonement within the B-Visio, Holy Church's account of love as the "plante of pees" (1.148–64) and Repentance's prayer in which the Crucifixion is "meel tyme of Seintes" (5.484–500), are B insertions to the A-text and have a different stylistic character than the surrounding material. I will return to these passages later. All Langland quotations are identified in the text by passus (if not clear from the context) and line numbers. Citations to the B-text will be to *Piers Plowman: The B-Version. Will's Visions of Piers Plowman, Do-Well, Do-Better and Do-Best*, ed. George Kane and E. Talbot Donaldson (1975; rev. ed. London: Athlone Press, and Berkeley and Los Angeles: University of California Press, 1988), except where notes to *The Vision of Piers Plowman: A Complete Edition of the B-Text*, ed. A. V. C. Schmidt (1978; rev. ed. London: J. M. Dent, 1984) are specified. All citations of the C-text are to *Piers Plowman by William Langland: An Edition Of The C-Text*, ed. Derek Pearsall, York

It is not surprising that Langland's representation of this simultaneous invasion of law and grace into the world of the poem should be his single most profoundly enigmatic allegorical action, as consistently riddling to interpreters of his poem as the events of the New Testament are to theologians. Many of these problems derive from the fact that the sending of a document from outside the human world is, to say the least, an incomplete image of the immanence of God in the human condition, the very phenomenon with which the doctrines of the Incarnation and the Atonement are concerned. It is, however, in keeping with the emphasis placed by late medieval nominalism on the extreme otherness of God in his *potentia absoluta*, as distinct from his *potentia ordinata*, his acts of revelation or other arbitrarily willed interventions in the natural order.[2]

Christian doctrine has never committed itself to any one binding conceptualization of what the Atonement was and did. The struggles that dominated the early patristic church councils issued in formulations of the Incarnation, embodied in the Nicene and Apostle's creeds, which, while making theologically clear that Christ was fully God and fully man, leave this paradox as hard to grasp psychologically and experientially as ever. Explanations of the Atonement have ranged from the military metaphor of a straight-forward battle between God and the Devil, through the legally oriented notion, which receives its classic formulation in Anselm's *Cur Deus Homo*, that the Atonement is a transaction between God's justice (by which man is damned) and his mercy (by which man is saved), to Abelard's idea that God broke through the vicious circle of human entrapment in evil by making himself so irresistibly loving to us by dying for us that we cannot but fall in love with him in response.[3] Langland's enterprise of representing the world of

Medieval Texts, 2d series (1978; Berkeley and Los Angeles: University of California Press, 1979).

[2] See Heiko Oberman, "Some Notes on the Theology of Nominalism," *Harvard Theological Review* 53 (1960): 47–76, especially 56–60; and Elizabeth D. Kirk, "Nominalism and the Dynamics of the Clerk's Tale: *Homo Viator* as Woman," in *Chaucer's Religious Tales*, ed. C. David Benson and Elizabeth Robertson (Woodbridge, Suffolk: D. S. Brewer, 1990), 111–20, especially 114–15.

[3] Extremely useful overviews of the tradition as well as treatments of particular texts are found in J. A. W. Bennett, *Poetry of the Passion: Studies in Twelve Centuries of English Verse* (Oxford: Clarendon Press, 1982) – Chapter IV is on Langland – and Rosemary Woolf, *The English Religious Lyric in the Middle Ages* (Oxford: Clarendon Press, 1968); see also Vincent Gillespie, "Strange Images of Death: The Passion in Later Medieval English Devotional and Mystical Writing," in *Zeit, Tod und Ewigkeit in der Renaissance Literatur*, ed. James Hogg, *Analecta Cartusiana* 117 (1987): 11–59. For *Piers Plowman* in particular, see also Wilbur Gaffney, "The Allegory of the Christ-Knight in *Piers Plowman*," *PMLA* 46 (1931): 155–68; Raymond St-Jaques, "Langland's Christ-Knight and the Liturgy," *Revue de l'Université d'Ottawa* 26 (1967): 146–58; A. V. C. Schmidt, "The Treatment of the Crucifixion in *Piers Plowman* and in Rolle's *Meditations on the Passion*," *Analecta Cartusiana* 35 (1983): 174–96; and Bruce Harbert, "Langland's Easter," in *Langland, the Mystics and the Medieval English Religious Tradition: Essays in Honour of S. S. Hussey*, ed. Helen Phillips (Woodbridge, Suffolk:

human experience as a self-contained dream-world yet setting its story in a reconstruction of biblical history leaves him with the task of representing the Incarnation and Atonement sooner or later. What does it mean to assert that the ineffable and infinite has become finite and historical without loss of its essential nature? The long and labored history of theological discussion of this issue has subjected the notion of God's intervention in history, as represented in scriptural narrative, to increasing conceptual restriction. These restrictions are intended to protect the dogmas of God's omniscience and omnipotence – God cannot be thought of as acted on from without, whether to make him suffer or be angry or learn, without compromising them. But they do so at the expense of God's interactive relation to human existence and to the developmental character of the processes dramatized in the very biblical narrative they seek to explain. This difficulty is inherent in the central paradox of the Trinity by which it is asserted that the three distinguishable "persons" (or personas or modes) of God are both one single thing and three different things. Similarly, the notion of Jesus as the incarnate "Son" or "Word" asserts that Jesus had a divine nature "of one substance with the Father" (as the Athenasian Creed puts it) and a human nature distinguishable from it and yet that this entity with its two differentiable aspects was one entity, fully God and yet fully man, a notion which can be posited conceptually but not envisaged experientially. However fully one postulates that God is one and that Christ is one, it is impossible to discuss what these entities actually do and experience without sounding as if something could happen to one "part" of God and not another or to one "part" of Jesus and not the other.

This problem Langland addresses in its fullest narrative realization in Passus 18, in some ways the culminating section of the poem, often praised as displaying the highest development of his epic style and the most optimistic point in his analysis of human history. The implications of this scene for understanding Langland's narrative strategies, along with the question of how successful his depictions of the Crucifixion and the Harrowing of Hell are in complementing the riddling and skeletal representation of divine intervention offered in the Pardon Scene, are the concern of this essay. Langland offers a resolution of this theological problem in a paradoxical way: by a re-solution of conceptual theology into the narrative medium from which it was initially inferred. Yet he does so by a juxtaposition of devices which do not allow the issues to subside into mere pragmatic or intuitive plausibility but rather throw into relief their emergence into meaning through the use of innovative narrative strategy.

D. S. Brewer, 1990), 57–70. *Cur Deus Homo* is translated by Sidney Norton Deane in *Saint Anselm: Basic Writings* (1903; 2d ed. La Salle, Ill.: Open Court Publishing Company, 1968), 173–288; other relevant texts are in *The Prayers and Meditations of St. Anselm*, trans. Benedicta Ward, S. L. G. (Harmondsworth, Middlesex: Penguin Books, 1973). For Abelard, see Richard E. Weingart, *The Logic of Divine Love: A Critical Analysis of the Soteriology of Peter Abailard* (Oxford: Clarendon Press, 1970).

What is distinctive about Langland's approach is thrown into relief by being set in the context of representations of the Incarnation and Atonement in his time. Meditation on the crucifixion of Christ was perhaps the central element of affective piety in the later Middle Ages. This was the period of the great polychrome wooden crucifixes that are some of the few visual representations of human suffering that have not been rendered banal by what twentieth-century photography has recorded of human atrocity. The cyclical dramas which portray biblical history rightly earned the title of "the play of *corpus christi*" because they put the notion of Incarnation and Atonement at the center of this essentially civic model of God's relation to humanity. The dominant element in representation of the Crucifixion is vivid and detailed portrayal of Christ's physical suffering, sometimes but not necessarily combined with emphasis on the cruelty of those inflicting it. Central is the verse from the Lamentations of Jeremiah (1:12): "Behold and see, if there be any sorrow like unto my sorrow." The religious lyric is dominated by addresses from the cross which ask the reader either to "Look what you did to Me" or to reflect "*I* did this to Him." The object is to involve the reader in as keen a sense as possible that to sin is to be an inflicter of unspeakable degradation and pain upon the accepting and willing savior.

The visions of many mystics involve the visionary in a dialogue with Christ on the Cross. Margery Kempe's notorious storms of weeping range from her sufferings in Jerusalem where she experiences labor-like pains to other more overtly erotic responses to actual crucifixes. Langland's contemporary Julian of Norwich herself formulates the relationship she perceived between such works of art and the necessity of fully understanding Christ's suffering when, in the earlier "short version" of her book, she connects her visions, in all their scarifying visual detail, with her wish as a young woman to experience three wounds, one of which was to experience the torment of Christ in a way analogous to but fuller than that provided by paintings and crucifixes:

> . . . me thought I hadde grete felynge in the passyonn of Cryste, botte ȝitte I desyrede to haue mare be the grace of god. Me thought I wolde haue bene that tyme with Mary Mawdeleyne and with othere that were Crystes loverse, that I myght have sene bodylye the passionn of oure lorde that he sufferede for me, that I myght have sufferede with hym as othere dyd that lovyd hym, not withstandynge that I leevyd sadlye alle the peynes of Cryste as halye kyrke schewys *and* techys, *and* also the payntyngys of crucyfexes that er made be the grace of god aftere the techynge of haly kyrke to the lyknes of Crystes passyonn, als farfurthe as man ys witte maye reche.[4]

---

[4] Julian of Norwich, *A Book of Showings to the Anchoress Julian of Norwich*, ed. Edmund Colledge, O. S. A. and James Walsh, S. J., 2 vols. (Toronto: Pontifical Institute of Mediaeval Studies, 1978), 1: 201–02. For a suggestive comparison between Julian and Langland, see A. V. C. Schmidt, "Langland and the Mystical Tradition," in *The Medieval Mystical Tradition in England: Papers Read at The Exeter Symposium, July 1980*, ed. Marion Glasscoe (Exeter: University of Exeter, 1980), 17–38.

This desire to share in the agony of Christ takes its culminating form in the phenomenon of the stigmata, which begins in the era of St. Francis of Assisi and flourishes through the fifteenth century.[5]

One would expect that the closest parallels to Langland's Passus 18 would be found in the mystery cycle dramas, since both are works which, instead of evoking private and emotional meditation, situate the Passion and the Resurrection in a vast panorama of biblical history while simultaneously containing strong elements of social analysis and often biting satire. Langland's Harrowing of Hell, indeed, exhibits just the sort of resemblances we would expect to the cycle plays on that subject, whether by direct influence or only by their common dependence on the apocryphal *Gospel of Nicodemus*. But in contrast to that element – and in spite of the fact that Passus 18 in the aggregate is one of Langland's most dramaturgically conceived narrative units – Langland's representation of the Passion is fundamentally unlike what we find in the plays. In spite of their public and civic character, the plays offer much the same perspective on the Passion as the passion lyrics and meditations of the time. The portrayal of human brutality and divine suffering offered by the "York Realist" in the Pinners and Painters' Crucifixion play horrifies by the graphic torture it depicts and even more by its recognition that the soldiers are so dehumanized by their trade that their savage wrenching of their victim's body is not even malicious in the usual sense of the word but is just their work. The plays typically add to the scriptural "seven words from the cross" a speech based on the same Jeremiah verse "Behold and see" as the Crucifixion lyrics, addressing the guilt and shame of the audience in exactly the same sort of rhetoric. The Jesus of the York Butchers' Play, for example, speaks directly to the audience:

> Thou man that of mis here has mente,
> To me tente enteerly thou take.
> On roode am I ragged and rente,
> Thou sinfull sawle, for thy sake.
> For thy misse, amendis wille I make;
> My bakke for to bende here I bide.
> This teene for thy trespase I take.
> Who couthe the[e] more kindines have kidde
> Than I?
> Thus for thy goode
> I schedde my bloode.
> Manne, mende thy moode,
> For full bittir thy blisse mon·I by.   (118–130)[6]

---

[5] Note the useful comments of Elaine Scarry on pain in religious observance (*The Body in Pain: The Making and Unmaking of the World* [1985; reprint, Oxford: Oxford University Press, 1987], 34), on "the conferring of the authority of the spirit on the fact of sentience" (219), and on the implications of Doubting Thomas's need to touch the wounds of the risen Christ to be able to believe in him (215).

[6] David Bevington, ed., *Medieval Drama* (Boston: Houghton Mifflin, 1975), 584–85.

In view of the predominance of this element in late medieval religious sensibility, its almost complete absence is the more striking when we turn to Passus 18 and note that Langland's portrayal of the events of Holy Week does not correspond with the approaches to the Crucifixion and Atonement prevalent in his time. By contrast, Langland devotes only twenty-four of his 431 lines to Christ's trial and death and another twenty-two to the events immediately following his death, particularly the non-scriptural healing of Longeus's blindness. The moments that normally receive most attention are compressed to a poignant four lines:

> "*Consummatum est*," quod crist and comsede for to swoune.
> Pitousliche and pale, as a prison þat deieþ,
> The lord of lif and of light þo leide hise eighen togideres.
> The day for drede wiþdrouȝ and derk bicam þe sonne. . . .
>
> (18.57–60)

The topos of asking readers to blame themselves is completely absent. There is almost no concrete detail about Christ's suffering. The non-presence of the three Marys, John, and the other disciples (so central not only to the plays but to the religious lyric and to paintings such as those reflected in Julian's visions) is palpable, amounting to a complete erasure of the Crucifixion as an event within any community but that of Christ's judges and executioners. Even the robbers crucified with Christ are evoked only when "A Cachepol cam forþ and craked boþe hir legges / And [hir] armes after" (73–74) and the saving of the repentant thief so poignantly evoked by Robert the Robber in Passus 5 (461–76) is not there.

What is as striking about Passus 18 in the aggregate as the absence of so many elements one would expect is the fact that, except for a tiny core of representation of actual events (and even this core riddled with gaps and absences), we are primarily given not the events but the events as *witnessed*, the events as being *interpreted by observers*. The other dominant feature is the juxtaposition of so many short segments in totally different kinds of discourse, throwing each other and their implied genres and contexts into relief. Even within the short sections of representational narrative, we find these abrupt shifts of style and tone. Only a few lines away from those I have just quoted is the Hogarthian vignette of the crowd at the trial:

> "*Crucifige!*" quod a Cachepol, "[he kan of wicchecraft]!"
> "*Tolle, tolle!*" quod anoþer, and took of kene þornes
> And bigan of [grene] þorn a garland to make. . . .
> "*Aue, raby*," quod þat rybaud and þrew reedes at hym.
>
> (18.46–48, 50)

We find riddling allegory, personification allegory, theological debate, and the witness of a variety of speakers external to the gospel narrative cheek by jowl. The reader is distanced both by refraction through commenters and by the metaphorical character of most of the action, which sets us riddles. Furthermore, many of the commenters explicitly speak as *not* knowing what is happening, so that the reader is not only dependent on them for interpretation but kept in suspense by their words. It is precisely the absence of the traditional treatment of the scene that permits it to play this role and that throws the reader into a completely different relationship to the subject from that created by the more familiar rhetoric.

The net effect is that, around a brief nucleus of represented scriptural event, Langland juxtaposes a multiplicity of discontinuous but complementary images and contexts through which to view that action. The paradox of the Passion is that it is in one sense the ultimate moment of passivity and degradation, so contrary to intuitive notions of God that it remained unrepresented through the early centuries of Christianity and was a major stumbling block to potential Christian converts whose heroic warrior ethos made the voluntary submission of God to evil unacceptable. In another sense, on the contrary, it is the single decisive act by which God responds to, accepts responsibility for, and redresses the tragic dimension of the human condition. Langland attempts to capture this paradoxical character of the Crucifixion by offering a kaleidoscope of superimposed images: what the Dreamer first sees is "a knyght þat comeþ to be dubbed" (18.13) who "Barefoot on an Asse bak bootles cam prikye" (18.11), who comes to joust in Jerusalem to "fecche þat þe fend claymeþ, Piers fruyt þe Plowman" (20); for the scout Moses/Hope, the Crucifixion is putting a seal (17.5) on a "writ" (3) he received on Mt. Sinai that activates it into "a maundement . . . To rule alle Reames wiþ" (2–3); for the herald Abraham/Feith, it is the re-encounter with the knight he once met in the form of the Trinity outside his tent (16.225–29) and whom he greets on Palm Sunday "a! *fili dauid!*" (18.15); for the Good Samaritan it is riding "On my Capul þat highte *caro* – of mankynde I took it" (17.110) to fetch the salve that alone will heal the man fallen among thieves. In Passus 18's debates of the Four Daughters of God and of Christ with the devils, it is an outwitting of the effects of the Fall; for Peace it is legal "letters patent" issued by Love appointing her and Mercy as sureties for mankind ("To be mannes meynpernour" [18.185]); for the dead body disturbed in its grave it is a battle between Life and Death whose outcome is as yet unknown. It is ultimately a solution to a theological impasse which Truth initially dismisses as "but a tale of waltrot" (142) and Righteousness finds a sign that Peace is either crazy or "right dronke" (188); for the devils and their prisoners it is the triumphant invasion of hell (266–315a); for Christ himself it is the transformation of the grapes of wrath of Joel 3:2, 12 and the "I thirst" spoken from the Cross into the resurrection of the dead:

> "For I þat am lord of lif, loue is my drynke,
> And for þat drynke today I deide vpon erþe.
> I fauȝt so me þursteþ ȝit for mannes soule sake;
> May no drynke me moiste, ne my þurst slake,
> Til þe vendage falle in þe vale of Iosaphat,
> That I drynke riȝt ripe Must, *Resureccio mortuorum*."
>
> (18.365–70)

The master image under which all these specific images are grouped is announced in the first few lines of the Passus. The Dreamer among the crowd on Palm Sunday sees a knight riding barefoot on an ass, "Oon semblable to þe Samaritan and somdeel to Piers þe Plow[man]" (18.10) and asks Faith:

> "Is Piers in þis place?" quod I, and he preynte on me.
> "This Iesus of his gentries wol Iuste in Piers armes,
> In his helm and in his haubergeon, *humana natura*;
> That crist be noȝt [y]knowe here for *consummatus deus*
> In Piers paltok þe Plowman þis prikiere shal ryde. . . ."
>
> (18.21–25)

Giving Piers this central role in the Crucifixion, with the generic *humana natura* only in apposition, sharply refocuses the reader's understanding of the latter. The figure of Piers has evolved in the course of the poem far beyond the image of the wage-earning peasant farmer confident that he serves Truth "to paye" (5.549), who received a "pardon" for his efforts on the half acre. Yet that economic and class identification still gives the image its base, grounding the notion of Incarnation firmly in a non-elitist notion of human nature quite distinct from the connotations suggested when the human nature of Christ is primarily defined in the inevitably gentrified figure of Mary, the future Queen of Heaven, chosen for the purity that differentiates her not only from Eve but from generic woman. The image is both bold and serenely triumphant. Such an identification of Piers with Christ echoes the famous line of Passus 15 where the Dreamer was told that *clergie* cannot show him Charity, but only "Piers þe Plowman, *Petrus id est christus*" (15.212).

Yet there is a striking difference between these two enigmatic images. By invoking the romance topos of the Christ-knight as the earlier image does not and by speaking of Christ borrowing Piers' human nature as borrowing not only his "paltok" but his "helm" and "haubergeon," Langland creates a powerful oxymoron which cuts ironically across the class identification of Piers that has been so central to the poem. This is more suggestive of Crucifixion imagery of the high Middle Ages than of the role of paradox (though of a quite different kind) in Donne's much later portrayal. Still closer is the much earlier riddling structure of the Anglo-Saxon "Dream of the Rood," in which images of heroic action and of servitude play against each other. There the cross is alternatively represented as a blood-stained and shameful instrument of execution and as a jeweled victory sign, and God's action in accepting death as alternatively the passivity of a condemned victim and the heroism of a Germanic warrior, a young "hæleþ," mounting to the place of combat. Unlike *Petrus id est cristus*, the Passus 18 image actually works to differentiate rather than to fuse the divine and human natures of Christ and, in the larger poem, to differentiate the roles of Piers and Christ. Representing Piers' contribution as the chivalric "helm" and "habergeon" as well as the more mundane "paltok" makes Piers' participation overtly metaphorical by its dislocation of class associations. It also relegates that participation to the borrowing of things exterior to himself that can be put on and off. The image thus suggests not so much the Christ of the creeds who is fully God and fully man – the identity affirmed in the Passus 15 image – as a collaboration between two beings of independent though hierarchically subordinated status.

A third image that falls between the strategies of the Passus 15 and 18 images appears in Passus 19, where the Dreamer sees a genuinely ambiguous figure and cannot tell if it is Piers or Christ. At the Offertory of the Easter Mass, after which the Host is first displayed on the altar, the Dreamer falls asleep and dreams "That Piers þe Plowman was peynted al blody / And com in wiþ a cros bifore þe comune peple, / And riȝt lik in alle [lymes] to oure lord Ies[u]" (19.6–8). He must ask Conscience, " 'Is þis Iesus þe Iustere,' quod I, 'þat Iewes dide to deþe? / Or it is Piers þe Plowman? who peynted hym so rede?' " (10–11). Conscience assures him that ". . . þise arn Piers armes, / Hise colours and his cote Armure; ac he þat comeþ so blody / Is crist wiþ his cros, conquerour of cristene" (12–14). Thus Conscience insists that the figure which, to the Dreamer, seemed to blend Christ and Piers indistinguishably, is unambiguously Christ, with Piers' contribution reduced to the trappings he bears. In short, both the Passus 18 and 19 passages ultimately underline the disjunction between divine and human, and prepare for the independent role Piers is to play in the last segment of the poem, so that at the end Conscience in the ruins of Unity sets off to seek not the Christ whose names and nature he expounded in Passus 19 but Piers: "sende me hap and heele til I haue Piers þe Plowman" (20.385). Piers has become something one can *have*.[7] Indeed, it is clear that given the role assigned to Piers in the poem, Langland cannot portray a Christology in the traditional sense, and it is not surprising that he must shift the weight of Passus 18 away from the Crucifixion itself toward the

---

[7] This is not necessarily to suggest that Langland was in any intentional way theologically heterodox. The sections on the Trinity in 16 and 17 show the essential impossibility of finding concrete images that successfully present the notion of a thing being simultaneously and fully one thing and also at the same time something else (even the geometrical image at the end of Dante's *Paradiso* works within this limitation). The idea can only be communicated in the language of abstract assertion. The structural implications of the life that Langland's images for the Incarnation take on *within the poem* as they develop are nevertheless extremely revealing of the poem's dynamics, and the possibilities opened up by arguing through images, rather than directly through concepts, are what this essay attempts to address. See François Boespflug, "The Compassion of God the Father in Western Art," trans. Joseph Cunneen, *Cross Currents* 44 (1992–93): 487–503, for a discussion of these issues with respect to two rare but clearly established iconographic forms, one a version of the "throne of grace" emerging in the late fourteenth century in which God the Father's face bends over the crucifix he holds and shows sorrow; the other, a slightly later development, the "Pitié-de-Nostre-Seigneur," a *pietà* in which the dead Christ lies not on Mary's lap but on that of God the Father, who may or may not show signs of grief. Boespflug does not consider these works consciously heterodox, though he calls them instances of " 'figurative thinking' . . . at work in the life of forms," but does note some cases where illuminations were later altered to remove suggestive parallelism between the poses of the Father and the crucified Christ to eliminate any suggestion of "co-crucifixion" (492).

Harrowing of Hell. There Christ can be portrayed as king and conqueror in his own right, disentangled from problems of history and Incarnation; and the language of his action can shift from romance to epic majesty, the element that most sharply distinguishes Langland's treatment from the otherwise very similar Harrowing plays.

Langland does not simply juxtapose images here, however; he also superimposes contexts. Most obviously, the Passion is set in the larger context of biblical history, particularly the meetings we have mentioned with Abraham, Moses, and the Good Samaritan. He then integrates the three into a specially tailored version of the Good Samaritan parable (Luke 10:25–37), playing brilliantly with the reader's expectations by having the Samaritan reverse them at the end where the point of the parable is changed. No longer is it, as in the gospel, that the priest and Levite who "pass by on the other side" illustrate the rigidity and hypocrisy of official religion as opposed to the charity of the quintessentially despised outsider, the Samaritan, who embodies the true definition of "neighbor" required to understand the command to "love your neighbor as yourself." On the contrary, when the Dreamer complains of Faith and Hope's cowardice, the Samaritan replies that they could not have helped the man, that they and he are the only people who have ever gotten past the robbers unscathed, and that the Samaritan is on his way to Jerusalem to "fetter þe feloun" and fetch the salve which alone can heal the wounded man. In the meantime, Faith shall be "forster" in this wilderness and Hope the "Hostiler" in the inn where the man is being nursed (17.90–124) until the Samaritan returns. Furthermore, Langland uses a form of the story in which the journey is from Jericho to Jerusalem, not the reverse, as it is in the gospel account. Thus the fact that Abraham/Faith and Moses/Hope are both seeking a knight they have seen before in order to receive confirmation of their respective covenants with him, which will validate Abraham's vision of the Trinity and the "maundement" given Moses on a rock at Sinai, is made to lead directly into the action of Holy Week, at which Abraham/Faith is one of the principal commentators and (presumably in his capacity as an expert on the Trinity) explains Christ's assumption of human nature.

A second major context is provided by the liturgy, whereby the Dreamer's experience progresses (in his waking moments as well as in his dreams) from "a mydlenten sonday" (16.172) and "a lenten" (18.5) through Palm Sunday, Good Friday, and Holy Saturday, to the singing of the *Te deum laudamus* (18.424) that marks "the end of Lent and the dawning of Easter," as A. V. C. Schmidt notes.[8] The ringing of the bells for Easter Mass in the waking world of the present and the Dreamer and his family going off to join in this celebration mark his re-entry into the community of the church in the present. Of course, this liturgical

---

[8] The *Te deum* plays a comparable role in mystery plays (e.g. at the end of the Wakefield Harrowing and at the departure of the saved from hell in Chester, though the play does not end here but continues with the speech of the unsaved Mulier and the devils' response). See Schmidt's notes to 18.36, 185, and 261 for other echoes of Holy Week liturgy.

pattern and the pattern of biblical history are intimately related since the one is a re-enactment of the other. But the point is that the liturgy makes the past present in the world of Langland's and the society's "now," whereby history is (literally) re-presented in its immanence to the life of that community.

A third major context of discourse is provided by theological debate. This begins, as we have seen, with Abraham/Faith's exposition of the Incarnation, continues in the argument among the Four Daughters of God, and culminates in the exchange between Christ and the devils. The point at issue in all three arguments, but especially the latter two, is whether God's sentence on Adam and Eve after the Fall has effectively tied his own hands so that he can do nothing to help mankind escape the Devil without doing violence to his own *potentia ordinata*, his self-binding word, his righteousness and truth. The Devil tells Christ that God would be acting as a cosmic bully were he simply to over-ride his own law by using sheer force,[9] an argument that Christ lets stand unchallenged, thus underlining the strictly metaphorical role of all the images of military action used to explain the Atonement. The image of God's blazing light irresistibly breaking the gates of hell is just such an image, but the burden of Christ's argument in the debate is to show that God is entitled to rescue his own only because he can scrupulously and meticulously demonstrate that, because the Devil cheated first, he has no true title to the patriarchs and prophets. When Christ tells him, "I . . . / Graciousliche þi gile haue quyt: go gile ayein gile!" (18.356–57), the "good feiþ" (347) by which he does so is guile only in the sense of an even cleverer and stricter construction of language than the Devil's: "So leue [it] noȝt, lucifer, ayein þe lawe I fecche hem, / But by right and by reson raunsone here my liges: / *Non veni soluere legem set adimplere*" (348–49a). Thus the familiar saying of Christ, "I came not to destroy the law but to fulfill it" (Matt. 5:17), takes on an even more precisely legal sense than in its gospel context.[10]

The debate of the Four Daughters frames the debate between Christ and the Devil, being divided into two sections, one preceding and one following the Harrowing.[11] The conflict between Truth and Righteousness, who think that there is no way consonant with his own nature for God to extricate mankind from the results of the Fall, and Peace and Mercy, who have inside information he has already done so, seems irreconcilable. To Righteousness's assertion that

[9] That is, in the nominalist terms Langland does not actually use, God may not use his *potentia absoluta* to ride roughshod over his *potentia ordinata*, though he would have been free to set up a different *potentia ordinata* in the first place had he so willed (see Oberman, "Some Notes," 56–60).

[10] The amount of attention Langland devotes to the "devil's rights" problem, more characteristic of earlier discussion of the Atonement, is in striking contrast to dominant late medieval representations.

[11] Hope Travers's survey of the background for this debate (*The Four Daughters of God*, Bryn Mawr College Monographs [Bryn Mawr, Pa.: Bryn Mawr College, 1907]) notes Langland's very different treatment from that in any source she finds available to him but disclaims any attempt to examine his complex intellectual and dramatic agenda.

"it is botelees bale, þe byte þat þei eten" (18.202), Peace replies, "I shal preue
. . . hir peyne moot haue ende" (203) on teleologically oriented grounds. God,
she argues, permitted the Fall precisely so that mankind, by knowing sorrow,
would be able to experience joy. It is therefore unthinkable that the Fall is
anything but one episode in an ongoing process of creation by which God is
opening possibilities for mankind, not washing his hands of them. Perhaps the
most striking feature of Peace's speech – and, theologically speaking, of the
whole Passus – is Peace's assertion that it is not mankind alone who learns the
true nature of joy by experiencing the effects of the Fall:

> Forþi god, of his goodnesse, þe firste gome Adam,
> Sette hym in solace and in souereyn murþe,
> And siþþe he suffred hym synne sorwe to feele,
> To wite what wele was, kyndeliche [to] knowe it.
> And after god Auntrede hymself and took Adames kynd[e]
> To [se] what he haþ suffred in þre sondry places,
> Boþe in heuene and in erþe, and now til helle he þenkeþ
> To wite what alle wo is [þat woot of] alle ioye.   (218–25)[12]

God, too, has a stake in the Incarnation and the Passion; there is something in it
for him as well as for mankind. Just as in the more strictly legalistic debate with
the Devil, the key to the apparently insoluble problem of the Fall is a matter of
the internal dynamics of God's own nature. But here the terms in which the
problem is posed are much broader and the solution both more generous and
more theologically innovative. From this point of view, the Atonement is not
primarily a transaction between two separate entities, God and man or God
and the Devil; or between two aspects of God's nature, his justice and his
mercy. Rather, what the Incarnation and Atonement do for Adam is extend the
creation process itself. That the Fall is a *felix culpa* because it enables Adam to
know joy truly by having known sorrow (220–21) and because it ultimately
results in the Incarnation is a familiar topos. What is so remarkable about
Peace's argument is that it extends this notion to God himself. In Langland's
image, the Incarnation and Atonement are part of God's self-creation as
well, an extension of God's very nature. God already, in one sense, knew
"alle ioye," but by sharing in human suffering and death God actually
acquires a new mode of awareness. He, too, by coming to know not-joy
experientially, knows joy differently.[13] Thus a more intimate collaboration

---

[12] See Bennett, *Poetry of the Passion*, 111–12, for a discussion of the importance of this
point which "may be extrapolated from patristic teaching but had surely never
before been so boldly expressed," citing the somewhat different formulation in the
C-text (see C.20.208–38, which adds lines 213–18 to an otherwise close agreement
with B.18.205–29.) As I indicate below, I regard his argument that "Langland's
general doctrine was eclectic without being idiosyncratic" and "restores the balance"
after a general late medieval "drift away from the dogma of the Incarnation and
toward meditation on the Passion" (97–99) as a considerable understatement.

[13] The Hebrew scriptures attribute suffering and anger to God, and some early
Christian theologians suggest that God suffers. The notion became established in

between God and man is suggested than the image of Christ jousting in Piers' armor conveyed.

There is no question that this is, at least in the terms stated, a developmental and teleological view of God which is open to some of the same objections as "patripassianism." This doctrine asserted that God suffered in his absolute person as the ground of being, the father, as well as in the second person, the incarnated Christ; it was early ruled heretical (along with its opposite, Docetism, which argued that not only did God not suffer but that Christ did not actually suffer either, since he merely represented suffering in a body that was not fully real, in order to teach humankind).[14] There is no question that Peace's words, in stating that God himself learns from the Incarnation, are heterodox at the level of conceptual theology in Langland's time, and there is no way her words can be otherwise construed, though Langland's very language, which sees God's action as an extension of the Creation itself, has

Christian theology, however, that God's omniscience and omnipotence exclude the possibility that he can be acted upon from without and thus that he can learn or that he can suffer. Thus divine suffering was strictly delimited as happening only to the incarnate second person of the Trinity, a distinction Langland's Repentance makes clear in a passage inserted into the B-Visio (B.5.487-90). Langland's very terms open up the lines along which an orthodox resolution of the problem is possible. If the strategies of the Incarnation and Atonement are, as he represents them, part of the intrinsic nature of the Creation, then, since God is outside of time as we know it, he is no more subjected to the historical sequence he has initiated by whatever function he wills the Incarnation to provide than he was when he "opened into new loves" (*Paradiso* 29.18) by undertaking the Creation in the first place (*Paradiso: Text and Commentary,* trans. and commentary by Charles S. Singleton, 2 vols., Bollingen Series 80 [1977; Princeton: Princeton University Press, 1982], 1: 323). Strikingly, however, though this line of thought is clearly latent in the terms of Langland's argument, he does not present it at a conceptual level.

14 Bennett's point-blank assertion (*Poetry of the Passion,* 92) that Langland "clearly accepts the orthodox answer that Christ suffered in his human nature, but not in his divine," while no doubt conceptually true of Langland's own belief and probably true of the poem in the aggregate, seems to me to understate the difficulties raised by the language of this passage, with its radical exploration of what it really means to say that God can learn in one of his modes what in another of them he could not. The orthodox separation of the "Father" from the "Son" exists to protect the intrinsic nature of God, as the "I am who am" on which all being depends, from any constraint upon divine omnipotence, omniscience, and impassibility that would make God vulnerable to (or answerable to or hostage to) finite process. Nevertheless, at the same time, the notion of the "Son" or the "Word" as *not* separate from God embodies the notion of a God interactive with the creation. The resulting paradoxes are as complex as those of the wave and particle theories of light. Compare the difficulties of Anselm's argument in the *Proslogium* (Chapter VIII) as to how God can be compassionate without losing his impassibility: "thou art so in terms of our experience, but thou art not so in terms of thine own. For, when thou beholdest us in our wretchedness, we experience the effect of compassion, but thou dost not experience the feeling. Therefore, thou art both compassionate, because thou dost save the wretched and spare those who sin against thee; and not compassionate, because thou art affected by no sympathy for wretchedness" (*Basic Writings,* 13-14).

implicit in it a potential solution to the problem.[15] The point is, however, that Langland is not working at a level of discourse at which this is a problem to which any "solution" is required. What I earlier called a "re-solution" of the issues into a narrative medium allows their exploration at a level in which meditation on their meaning is not shortcircuited or constrained by interim conflict with current intellectual idiom, by the either/or alternatives into which that medium necessarily polarizes problems in its search for cerebral lucidity, sacrificing experiential understanding.

Instead of such an abstract theological discourse, Langland offers a complex concatenation of images and contexts around a tiny base of represented biblical action. He thus creates a narrative equivalent to the glossed codexes and especially to the glossed Bibles of his day. These surrounded a small unit of Scripture, itself explained by an interlinear gloss, with consecutive rectangles filled with commentary, the *glossa ordinaria* next to the Scripture, the comments of later interpreters in turn surrounding the *glossa ordinaria*, and still later commentary at the bottom. As Mary Carruthers observes:

> The most comprehensive model of the medieval view of what constituted *memoria* is the medieval book itself, especially those fully "marked up" codices. . . . [where] the compiled comments are written all around the author-text, keyed into it, *catena* fashion, via red underlinings, heuristic symbols, and other punctuation. . . .[16]

Some pages, she notes, even had painted figures of authorities such as Augustine or Jerome in the margins, pointing at the text or commentary,

---

[15] Elaine Scarry discusses the shift away from the polarization of God and man in the Hebrew scriptures (where, however, God is represented as extremely passionate) with the introduction of the New Testament notions of Incarnation and Atonement; her terms, though based on a very different philosophical context, are suggestive here:

> the phenomenon of pain repeatedly occurs in human contexts that allow its increase to be attended by an increase in the power accruing elsewhere. The altered relation in the Christian scripture between the body of the believer and the object of belief subverts this severed relation between pain and power, assuring that sentience and authority reside at a single location and thus cannot be achieved at each other's expense.
>
> The conferring of the authority of the spirit on the fact of sentience has as a second consequence the dissolution of the boundary between body and voice, permitting a translation back and forth. The body in the Old Testament belongs only to man, and the voice, in its extreme and unqualified form, belongs only to God. *Across the cross, each of these retains its original place but simultaneously enters the realm from which it had earlier been excluded* (219; emphasis mine).

Similarly, the role of the body in knowing, often though by no means only through pain, becomes an increasing element in later medieval spirituality and even in philosophy.

[16] Mary Carruthers, *The Book of Memory: A Study of Memory in Medieval Culture* (Cambridge: Cambridge University Press, 1990), 194 and 215.

perhaps with banderoles on which were written words of exhortation or warning (216). Carruthers describes one amateur manuscript of *Piers Plowman* itself with numerous drawings which sometimes illustrate the text in our sense of the term; others cue "either chief words or concepts of the text with which they are associated"; still others are figures in the margins gazing at the text or otherwise "suggesting meditation" (228–29).

It is important to remember that *memoria* is far more than a system for retrieving data in the absence of a print culture's abundant records. Beyond that and even more basically, it is a mode of interiorizing and reflecting upon material of value and finding its meaning through meditation on the material and on its connections and connotations. To understand what Langland is doing in Passus 18, we must turn back to an earlier Passus, one of the most significant scenes in *Piers Plowman*. Here the Dreamer encounters Ymaginatif, whose image-making capacity makes him part of the process of *memoria* (12.1–28). Ymaginatif challenges the Dreamer about his writing of poetry, calling it a mode of idleness and an evasion of reality. The Dreamer replies with a defense of the writing of the poem as a heuristic process, a mode of discovering as well as retaining truth:

> . . . if þer were any wight þat wolde me telle
> What were dowel and dobet and dobest at þe laste,
> Wolde I neue*re* do werk, but wende to holi chirche
> And þere bidde my bedes but whan ich ete or slepe.   (12.25–28)

Langland's Dreamer argues to Ymaginatif that there is such an intimate connection between memory and the creation of texts that to write is both to work and to discover. Put so boldly and directly, such a defense seems to suggest analogies with ideas about poetic composition that do not appear until a much later date and which, when they do appear, are predicated on Enlightenment notions entirely distinct from medieval philosophy and psychology. Yet there the statement is. More recent study, however, has been able to place Langland's figure in its intellectual milieu, so that recognition of its importance need not appear ahistorical.[17] Yet the poem's own distinctive character confirms in another way what the Dreamer tells Ymaginatif about his need to compose in order to learn. What Langland is doing in Passus 18 in particular is precisely what the Dreamer suggested to Ymaginatif: using a mode of composition that juxtaposes material drawn from different sources and contexts as a *heuristic* process, one that permits him to discover, remember,

---

[17] My formulation of the problem in *The Dream Thought of Piers Plowman* (New Haven: Yale University Press, 1972), 139–42, emphasized the importance of the figure without being able to suggest adequate historical context. See Britton J. Harwood, "Imaginative in *Piers Plowman*," *Medium Ævum* 44 (1975): 249–59; and A. J. Minnis, "Langland's Ymaginatif and late-medieval theories of the imagination," *Comparative Criticism: A Yearbook* 3 (1981): 71–103, as well as the implications for composition of the notions of memory presented by Carruthers.

and create a solution to something he cannot grasp experientially in any other way.

Seeing writing in this way as a mode not only of recording but of creating or enacting something focuses our attention on the presence of three crucial documents among Passus 17 and Passus 18's complex of witnesses. Two are "lettres patente": Love's "lettres" (18.182), "patente" (18.186), or "dede" (18.187) appointing Peace and Mercy "meynpernour" or surety (18.185) for mankind; and Moses's "maundement" (17.2), "lettres" (17.4) or "patente" (17.11) "To rule alle Reames wiþ" (17.3) received on Mt. Sinai. Both are enactments which are made efficacious by the death of Christ; Moses actually uses the figure of Christ hanging on the cross as the "seel" that will hang from his document rendering it effective and bringing the lordship of Lucifer to an end (15.5-8).[18] The third is Book, the hinge character between the debate of the Four Daughters and the Harrowing, who presents himself not only as the witness but as the guarantor of the resurrection: "And I, book, wole be brent but Iesus rise to lyue" (18.255).[19] It is significant that Book's name is Book and not, as one would expect from Langland's earlier character representing sacred writing, Scripture. Book's "two brode eiзen" (230), whether they represent the Old and New Testaments or the literal and figurative meanings of Scripture, identify him clearly enough as a Bible, but the choice of his name would appear to reflect a sense that the biblical word is a certain kind of object as well as a certain body of content. It is an enactment and a guarantee as well as a compendium of information, an effectuating agent analogous to the deeds given to Moses and Peace, something that is not just a piece of language in the abstract but a recorded entity whose material presence gives it almost the status of a relic.[20] Book's prominence, taken together with the extraordinary emphasis in the debate scenes on legally strict and precise interpretation of the binding word, makes the Passus as a whole a strong statement about the creating and constraining power of language both as a social instrument and as a heuristic tool.

Such a view of the book as not merely a selection of language whose meaning affects its recipient but as a physical object which is efficacious as such

---

[18] See Douglas Gray's discussion of the topoi of the body of Christ as a book and as a charter in *Themes and Images in the Medieval English Religious Lyric* (London and Boston: Routledge & Kegan Paul, 1972), 129-30.

[19] The precise syntax of this passage has been much debated, but its essentially enunciative discourse is clear. See R. E. Kaske, "The Speech of 'Book' in Piers Plowman," *Anglia* 77 (1959): 117-44; E. Talbot Donaldson, "The Grammar of Book's Speech in *Piers Plowman*," 1966, reprinted in *Style and Symbolism in Piers Plowman: A Modern Critical Anthology,* ed. Robert Blanch (Knoxville: University of Tennessee Press, 1969), 264-70; and Joseph Wittig, "The Middle English 'Absolute Infinitive' and 'The Speech of Book,'" in *Magister Regis: Studies in Honor of Robert Earl Kaske*, ed. Arthur Groos et al. (New York: Fordham University Press, 1986), 217-40.

[20] Carruthers, 40-41. Langland's important earlier character Scripture clearly does not represent only biblical writing, but neither the term book nor the term scripture in Langland's normal usage does so (as the modern reader might expect by analogy

is strikingly illustrated in the terms St. Margaret is represented as using in the early Middle English *Life of St. Margaret* to describe the power that she prays a book about her life and martyrdom may have in the future:

> Ich bidde 7 biseche þe . . . þ[et] hwa-se-eauer boc writ of mi lif-lade, oþer bi-ȝet hit iwriten, oþer halt hit 7 haueþ oftest on honde, oþer hwa-se hit eauer redeþ, oþer þene redere bliþeliche lusteþ, wealdent of heouene, wurþe ham alle sone hare sunnen for-ȝeuene.[21]

The power of her martyrdom and the power of the text describing it are both quasi-sacramental. Such shifting back and forth between terms that suggest composing or copying the text, those that involve reading or listening to it, and those referring to holding the book as an object or being in its presence reflect precisely the notion of book which Langland seems to have had in mind in naming his biblical witness Book.

Looking back at the Pardon Scene in Passus 7 from this vantage point, it is clearer why Langland, in his first, enigmatic attempt to link the giving of law on Mt. Sinai and the giving of pardon to humanity in the person of Piers, used the image of a document sent by Truth to Piers, a document that has to be destroyed to become effective. This attempt at a heuristic metaphor for God's intervention in the human condition is such a difficult image that scholars have never been able to agree fully as to its meaning (as well as so shocking in its portrayal of Piers actually destroying the document Truth has sent that the C-text reviser was to cut out that part of the image). But when Langland addressed the problem again in the later B-text, he kept two notions already present in Passus 7. The first is the notion that the Atonement is something like a charter, deed, or letter of appointment, a legal "word" that makes something happen; God's action in revealing himself in Christ is like God making himself into a text, a document. The idea can be seen as an extended gloss on the notion of Christ as the Word: "The word became flesh and dwelt among us" (John 1:14). The other is that the Atonement is not a unilateral action by God but a joint action on the part of God and humanity in the person of Piers. God is not merely making satisfaction *for* mankind, not just obtaining something he then makes available to human beings who may or may not appropriate it. The Atonement is something God does *with* man. God does not need human nature merely as a tool or medium to act in. By picturing Christ's *humana natura* in

with the colloquial expression "the Good Book") – see, for example, 11.277, where "the Book" is the Bible and 15.282, where it is not. Only the terms "the Bible" and "Holy Writ" seem completely unambiguous (e.g., 11.270 and 383 respectively).

[21] "I pray and beseech thee [God] . . . that who-so-ever writes [composes and/or copies] a book of my life, or commands it to be written, or holds it and has it most often in hand, or who-so-ever reads it, or listens happily to the reader, Ruler of Heaven, be all their sins forgiven soon" (*Seinte Marherete: þe Meiden ant Martyr*, ed. Frances Mack, EETS OS 193 [London: Oxford University Press, 1934 (for 1933)], 46). I am indebted to my colleague Elizabeth Bryan for calling my attention to this passage and its implications; see Bryan, "Layamon's Brut: Relationships Between the Two Versions," Ph.D. diss. University of Pennsylvania, 1990, 42.

Passus 18 not as acquired through a woman who may be passively impregnated (as he does, of course, in many other passages) but through the collaboration of a working man in a fight, Langland suggests a notion of Incarnation strikingly different from the conventional picture of an omnipotent God reaching down to mend an essentially passive humanity.[22]

What makes the Pardon Scene so hard to grasp is the absence of any but the slightest indication of a biblical, historical, liturgical, and theological context for the action, in terms of which it can be understood. This problem Langland devised bold narrative means to solve in Passus 18. He takes the elements that are so elliptically and enigmatically compressed in Passus 7 and separates them so that he can display them in a cumulative pattern of juxtapositions. The brief core of narrative representation in which Christ's death is made present has been surrounded with the narrative equivalent of the concentric glossing on a written page which makes it possible for the reader as well as the writer to use the narrative as a heuristic device by which the meaning of a key element of revelation can be explored. But because the whole thus constructed is a dramatic enactment, the narrative can say things that are not merely excluded as heterodox by fourteenth-century theology but that cannot even be thought within the conceptual terms available to Langland. Like so much else in Langland's political, economic, and ethical analysis, which received contradictory interpretations even in his own day (as instanced by the allusions to *Piers Plowman* in the documents of the Peasants' Revolt), his theology as well can make room within an essentially conservative and traditional idiom for radically innovative dimensions of thought.

If God's intervention in history in the person of the historical Jesus is to be seen under the metaphor of God rendering himself into a "text," then that text must be interpreted – and if interpreted, then interpreted in a way which is the narrative equivalent to the way in which the ubiquitous text of God's immanence, Scripture itself, is to be interpreted: by the cumulative juxtaposition of fragmentary insights, part of an ongoing discourse, in which no one insight can bear scrutiny as fully inclusive and absolute and in which each may be finite and useful without compromising the absoluteness of biblical revelation or claiming to be a substitute for it. The more probing analysis of scriptural process Langland offers in the B-text, culminating in Passus 18, has permitted him to break through the conceptual rigidity in which the A-Visio Pardon Scene remains locked. The depth of the change in the B-poet's relation to his material is reflected not only in the power of Passus 18 itself but in the two relatively short but highly significant additions he made in revising the A-Visio, his most striking metaphysical passages on the Incarnation and

---

[22] A comparable contrast to the representation of rescued humanity as passive, this time one in which the female herself is not passively acted upon, appears in the Prioress's Prologue where the Virgin Mary, virgin mother and burning bush, is pictured as she who "ravyshedest doun fro the Deitee, / Thurgh thyn humblesse, the Goost that in th'alighte" (VII.469–70; Chaucer citations follow *The Riverside Chaucer,* 3d ed., gen. ed. Larry D. Benson [Boston: Houghton Mifflin Company, 1987]).

Atonement. One is Repentance's prayer to the incarnated Christ who "yedest in oure sute" and "in oure s[u]te deidest" (B.5.496, 487), calling the Atonement, in a powerfully compressed and elliptical Eucharistic image "meel tyme of Seintes" (492). The other is Holy Church's speech on love in the B-text, which stands in even more striking stylistic contrast to its A-text surroundings:

> For truþe telleþ þat loue is triacle of heuene:
> May no synne be on hym seene þat vseþ þat spice,
> And alle hise werkes he wrou3te *with* loue as hym liste;
> And lered it Moyses for þe leueste þyng and moost lik to heuene,
> And [ek] þe pl[ante] of pees, moost *precious* of *vertues.*
> For heuene my3te nat holden it, [so heuy it semed],
> Til it hadde of þe erþe [y]eten [hitselue].
> And whan it hadde of þis fold flessh and blood taken
> Was neu*ere* leef vpon lynde lighter þerafter,
> And portatif and persaunt as þe point of a nedle
> That my3te noon Armure it lette ne none hei3e walles.
> Forþi is loue ledere of þe lordes folk of heuene. . . .
> And for to knowen it kyndely, it comseþ by myght,
> And in þe herte þ*ere* is þe heed and þe hei3e welle.
>
> (B.1.148–59, 163–64)[23]

What is achieved here through powerfully compressed metaphor becomes accessible to a comparable "kynde knowynge in herte," as Holy Church calls the liberating apprehension of truth in the next line (165), through the narrative strategies of Passus 18. Just so in history, for God as well as man, the Fall, the Incarnation, and the Atonement are the means of knowing *kyndely.*

[22] For an excellent analysis of the word play involved in this passage, see Mary Clemente Davlin, O.P., *A Game of Heuene: Word Play and Meaning in "Piers Plowman" B* (Cambridge: D. S. Brewer, 1989), 38–41.

The Debt Narrative in *Piers Plowman*

ANNA BALDWIN

A major contribution to our understanding of the narrative movement of *Piers Plowman* was made when Bob Frank linked the traditional division of the Vita into Dowel, Dobet, and Dobest, with the Trinity, and so with the three periods of human history. Frank proposed, "the Father [is associated] with the creation of the world and man; the Son with the events of Christ's life and death; and the Holy Ghost with the period after the Ascension. A kind of chronological order is achieved by making the Father dominant in *Dowel*, the Son in *Dobet*, and the Holy Ghost in *Dobest*."[1]

Since the authenticity of the subtitles themselves has now been questioned, I would point out that Frank's case rests upon the threefold division and not on the names given to its parts. I would add that chronology is perhaps less important than the distinction between the Old Testament Law of justice (which is frequently evoked in Dowel) and the New Testament Law of mercy (offered by Christ in Dobet and accepted along with a new kind of justice in Dobest). I would here like to demonstrate the fundamental usefulness of such a narrative division by looking at Langland's discussion of debt. In those parts of the poem which precede the description of Christ's Atonement, Langland's frequent debt imagery is taken almost entirely from the old laws of contract and vicarious promise which had operated in local, borough, and royal courts for hundreds of years and were still useable (largely by merchants) in Langland's day. This debt law was invented for the illiterate and relied "vicariously" on other people to validate the fact of the debt through their knowledge of the parties, their witnessing of a ceremony, or their own promise to act as sureties. Langland also uses the thirteenth-century action of Account which is vicarious in another way, since it relies on the principle of the vicarious ownership of property on another's behalf.

But in the later fourteenth century these laws were becoming obsolete. In 1352 Edward III passed a Statute allowing any creditor to imprison a debtor

[1] Robert Worth Frank, Jr., *Piers Plowman and the Scheme of Salvation* (New Haven: Yale University Press, 1957), 16. On the rubrics' authenticity, see Robert Adams, "The Reliability of the Rubrics in the B-text of *Piers Plowman*," *Medium Ævum* 54 (1985): 208–31.

from whom he had a sealed bond. The written bond was itself proof of the debt; the seal represented the actual body of the debtor over which the creditor had power until his debt was repaid. The days of personal responsibility had arrived. There are even cases, in the boroughs at least, of women contracting debts on their own account, highlighting the association between credit and personal freedom. Langland uses this distinction between the vicarious and the personal promise in the movement from the Old Law to the New, from the Dowel and Dobet to the Dobest sections of the poem. From being a metaphor of bondage, debt becomes the key metaphor to describe the freedom of the Christian. The law of *redde quod debes* is the very basis of the New Law of Christ. The whole narrative shifts from discussing the debt of sin, which only Christ can repay, to discussing the debt to love, which only man can perform. And here too, as I will show, Bob Frank has anticipated my emphasis.

There were, of course, plenty of precedents for Langland's use of the metaphor in a theological context, and these tend to have an "Old Law" emphasis even when used in a Christian context. St. Paul had spoken of the Jews as "debtors to the whole law" (Gal. 5:3), and though Christians believed that Christ had paid the debt for Original Sin, penitential writers continued to teach that breaches of Christ's law put man in debt to God. The power to bind and loose given to St. Peter was generally seen as a mechanism for releasing man from this debt for Actual Sin but only if he paid in penance something of the debt of punishment: "For the sentence of the priest absolves . . . as well as binds. To be sure, it absolves from the debt of eternal punishment, but it binds to the payment of the debt of temporal punishment."[2] In the later Middle Ages the "debt of temporal punishment" could be paid more easily than in the days of public penance, but priests were also requiring the payment of restitution as part of the debt of satisfaction. When John de Burgo revised the popular *Oculum Sacerdotis* as the *Pupilla Oculi* in 1385, he added long passages about restitution, and Nick Gray has shown in his sadly still unpublished thesis on *Piers Plowman* and the medieval penitential tradition that this was an emphasis typical of late medieval handbooks.[3] In such contexts man is seen to be bound, if not to the devil, then to God and to the fellow creatures whom he has offended by his sins, and a sense of a personal responsibility to restore ill-gotten

---

[2] Duns Scotus (d. 1308), *On the Sentences* [4 dist. 16 q. 1. 7], trans. Paul F. Palmer, *Sacraments and Forgiveness: History and Doctrinal Development of Penance, Extreme Unction and Indulgences* (Westminster, Md.: Newman Press, 1960), 217; see also 198–219.

[3] Thomas de Chobham, *Thomae de Chobham Summa Confessorum*, ed. F. Broomfield (Louvain: Editions Nauwelaerts, 1968), 491, 501–3, 514; John de Burgo, *Pupilla Oculi* (London: H. Jacobi, 1510), ff. 31r–32v (including the phrase "Nunquam dimittitur peccatum nisi restituatur oblatum"), ff. 61v–63v. On this phrase, see John Alford, *Piers Plowman: A Guide to the Quotations* (Binghamton, N.Y.: Medieval & Renaissance Texts & Studies, 1992), 46; on restitution, see Henry Charles Lea, *A History of Auricular Confession and Indulgences in the Latin Church*, 3 vols. (London: Swan Sonnenschein, 1896), 2: 47–64; Nicholas Gray, "A Study of *Piers Plowman* in Relation to the Medieval Penitential Tradition," Ph.D. diss. Cambridge University, 1984, 209–80.

gains was developing. But still the implication is generally that the debt cannot be paid without the help of God's grace administered through the Church.

Man's debt to God was seen as incurred not only through sin but also through the very benefits which he enjoys. Such a view undermines further any sense of his personal freedom and dignity. *The Pricke of Conscience* is a case in point. The author of this very popular apocalyptic poem (which seems to me to be an undoubted influence on Langland) used the action of Account to describe the legal basis for the Day of Judgment. (V. A. Kolve has shown the same metaphor, which he assumes was taken directly from the parable of the debtor, underlying the same situation in a fifteenth-century Sermon and in *Everyman*.[4]) In a long legalistic passage the poet describes the Day of Judgment as a vast Audit under the thirteenth-century Statutes of Accompte. These gave the steward a personal liability for the goods for which he had vicarious responsibility:

> Concerning Servants, Bailiffs, Chamberlains, and all Manner of Receivers, which are bound to yield Accompte, It is agreed and ordained, That when the Masters of such Servants do assign Auditors to take their Accompt, and they be found in Arrearages . . . [all Things allowed which ought to be allowed,], their Bodies shall be arrested and . . . shall be sent or delivered unto the next Gaol of the King's . . . until they have satisfied their Master fully of the Arrearages.[5]

The steward should derive no personal benefit from his lord's money, and if any is lost perhaps in the way of business, it is put to his personal charge as an "arrerage" or debt. This legal unfairness (which Langland himself points out in his brief discussion of the abuse of Spiritus Prudencie and Spiritus Fortitudinis in Passus 19.462–67) makes for a very negative conception of the relation between man and God. In *The Pricke of Conscience*, it is designed to frighten the reader into goodness. Men are but stewards of the time, the goods, the very souls which they have received from God. Their insistence on deriving personal benefit from these goods, instead of using them on God's behalf, and their tendency to sin seem to doom them to present an account consisting entirely of debits:

> Men sal alswa yhelde rekkenynge sere
> Of al gude þat God has gefen þam here,
> Als of gudes of kynde and gudes of grace,
> And gudes of hap þat men purchases. . . .
> Of al þir gudes men byhoves
> Yhelde acounte, als þe buke pruves. . . .
> I drede many in arrirage mon falle,

---

[4] V. A. Kolve, "*Everyman* and the Parable of the Talents," in *Medieval English Drama: Essays Critical and Contextual*, ed. Jerome Taylor and Alan H. Nelson (Chicago: University of Chicago Press, 1972), 316–40.

[5] 13 Edward I c. 11 (1285); cf. 52 Henry III c. 23 (1267). See *Statutes of the Realm*, ed. Alexander Luders et al., 11 vols. (London: Dawson, 1810–20), 1: 80–1, 24.

And til perpetuel prison gang
For þai despended þa gudes wrang. . . .
Forwhi God has gyfen here nathyng,
Of whilk he wille noght haf rekkeunyng.   (5.5907–917)[6]

There is little room here for notions of freedom and personal responsibility, unless it be the responsibility of a perpetual guilt.

It is appropriate, then, that when we meet the same metaphor of Account in *Piers Plowman* it is in the Dowel part of the narrative, with its Old Law emphasis on the difficulties of doing well and its apparently very restricted possibilities of salvation. In a passage strongly reminiscent of the *Pricke*, Patience is warning man of the final Audit: "I wiste nevere renk that riche was, that whan he rekene sholde, / Whan he drogh to his deeth day, that he ne dredde hym soore, / And that at the rekenyng in arrerage fel, rather than out of dette" (B.14.105–7).[7] Whereas in the *Pricke* all men were liable to heavy arrerage, here it seems to be only the rich who are in danger. The poor are excused by the very clause which offered Stewards some protection in the Statute of Account:

> Nevertheless if any Person being so committed to Prison, do complain, that the Auditors of his Accompt have grieved him unjustly, charging him with Receipts that he hath not received, or not allowing him Expences, or reasonable Disbursements, [*non allocando expensas aut liberaciones racionabiles*], . . . Justice shall be done to the Parties [before the Barons of the Exchequer].[8]

Patience claims that the poor man has had few receipts and can claim many "allowances" (the normal translation of *allocando*[9]) for his expenditure of suffering:

> Ther the poore dar plede, and preve by pure reson
> To have allowaunce of his lord; by the lawe he it cleymeth:
> Joye, that nevere joye hadde, of rightful jugge he asketh. . . .
> For to wrotherhele was he wroght that nevere was joye shapen!
>
> (B.14.108–10, 120)

---

[6] *The Pricke of Conscience*, ed. Richard Morris (Berlin: A. Ascher, 1863), 159–60 (Book 5.5894–917).

[7] Quotations from *Piers Plowman* are taken from *The Vision of Piers Plowman: A Complete Edition of the B-text*, ed. A. V. C. Schmidt (London: Dent, 1978).

[8] 13 Edward I c. 11 (1285) in *Statutes of the Realm*, 1: 80.

[9] John Alford, *Piers Plowman: A Glossary of Legal Diction* (Cambridge: D. S. Brewer, 1988), 4, defines "allowaunce" as "Credit or reimbursement for expenses (esp. those incurred in the service of another)" and quotes an early *Register of Writs*: "The auditors of the aforesaid account have unduly oppressed the said A. in respect of the said account, debiting him with receipts which he has not received, and not allowing [*non allocando*] in his favour expenses and reasonable outgoings." See also H. S. Bennett, *Life on the English Manor: A Study of Peasant Conditions, 1150–1400* (Cambridge: Cambridge University Press, 1937), 191–92.

We can see at once how the one-sided relationship between man and God in *The Pricke of Conscience* has been replaced, at least for the poor man, by a new principle of reciprocal responsibility. The rich man has received money and goods from his Lord, for which he should have paid an income in good works. Instead, he has kept what should have been spent on others and so has fallen into arrearage. (In B.10.467-71 it is suggested that the learned man is in exactly the same position.) The poor man, on the other hand, could claim he has an "allowance" to set against any debits he might have incurred – namely, the joy which God owes him in heaven in return for all he has suffered on earth. If man is in debt to God, so also is God in debt to man. This is an extraordinary statement of the rights of the poor and one that anticipates the more modern discussion of debt which I want to associate with the end of the poem. For although Langland is using the Action of Account as a metaphor, this principle of reciprocity, of a debt for a debt, was in fact an intrinsic part of medieval debt law and one which distinguishes it from the modern law. As W. R. Anson puts it in a classic work on that subject, the defendant in a medieval action of debt "would only be liable . . . if he had received some benefit or performance, a *Quid pro Quo*, in return for his promise to pay the money."[10] Langland has turned the one-sided action of Account into the reciprocal relationship of medieval debt, and as we shall see, this principle of reciprocity will be developed later in the poem into the principle which should determine man's relation to other men as well as his relation to God.

Yet even in Langland's modified version, the Action of Account depends on the recognition of the vicarious ownership of property. The Christian is still seen as a servant. This is even truer of another extended use of the metaphor of debt, again from the Dowel section of the poem, in which Will (with the endorsement of Scripture) describes the Christian as a "cherl" or serf. Such men could not buy or sell property freely, and if they ran away, their lord could claim all "their" goods and the custody of their bodies as well.[11] Will argues that God will accept his baptized "cherls" as his own but that they for their part must retain their faith or risk imprisonment for debt, having deprived God of their services:

> "For may no cherl chartre make, ne his c[h]atel selle
> Withouten leve of his lord – no lawe wol it graunte.
> Ac he may renne in arerage and rome fro home,
> And as a reneyed caytif recchelesly aboute.
> Ac Reson shal rekene with hym and rebuken hym at the laste,
> And Conscience [shal] acounte with hym and casten hym in
>   arerage,
> And putten hym after in prison in purgatorie to brenne,

[10] William Reynell Anson, *Anson's Law of Contract* (1879), ed. A. G. Guest (Oxford: Clarendon Press, 1969), 10; W. S. Holdsworth, *A History of English Law*, 3d ed., 16 vols. (London: Methuen, 1923), 3: 420-27; see also n. 18 below.

[11] Bennett, 99-150, 304-11.

For his arerages rewarden hym there right to the day of
dome. . . ."   (B.11.127–34)

We still have the sense of a reciprocal obligation, but it is weighted down by
the insistent use of the word "arrerage" or debt and the assumption that the
Christian owns goods only vicariously. We are still within the narrative
restrictions of Dowel, with its rather minimalist ethic that Christ will help
those who are too weak to help themselves. It is an ethic which will eventually
be counterbalanced by the Law of Charity.

As an illuminating parallel to the humiliating position ascribed to the
Christian here, I would like to mention the equivalent legal incapacity of a
wife, however free born, to own any property apart from her personal
"choses" or trinkets.[12] This is demonstrated, for example, in Chaucer's
Shipman's Tale, where the Monk with an ironic legal correctness conflates the
money he owes to the wife with the money he owes the husband. On her part,
the wife is unable to contract or to repay debts on her own account, except by
employing her own tail as tally or, as the Wife of Bath calls it, her "bele chose"
(Canterbury Tales III.447). During the fourteenth century both serfs and wives
(at least in boroughs) were beginning to own property and contract debts on
their own account. The Wife of Bath is an example of this,[13] and Chaucer
seems to make a deliberate contrast between her, owner of property and so of
wifely maistrie, and the merchant's wife in the Shipman's Tale, who only has
her own body to bargain with. Langland achieves something like this contrast
when he moves from the narrative of Dowel, with its imagery of tutelage and
servage, to the narrative of Dobest, where all men carry King Conscience in
their hearts and must take personal responsibility for their debts to God and
man.

Before that point is reached, however, we must look at the debt imagery in
Dobet, where Langland employs an even older debt law as a metaphor for
man's dependence on God. Whereas he had been using the principle of
vicarious ownership to describe what the Christian owes to God and God to
the Christian in the earlier part of the Vita, he now uses the principle of the
"vicarious promise" in order to describe the even greater helplessness of Old
Testament man. This was the old form of debt law used before the
introduction of written bonds in the thirteenth century, and it was still popular
in boroughs and fairs among the illiterate, who needed other people or objects
to validate the promises they could not write down. Like the later form, this
law embodies the principle of reciprocity at the heart of all medieval debt law.
Something, however symbolic, must be given by each party to the other at the

---

[12] Holdsworth, 3: 525–27, 544.

[13] Mary Carruthers, "The Wife of Bath and the Painting of Lions," PMLA 94 (1979):
210: "The customs of the bourgeoisie . . . gave propertied married women rights that
were denied them by both the common law . . . and the canon law . . . [They]
retained the ownership and control of their property and could enter into contracts
in their own names." See Borough Customs, ed. Mary Bateson, 2 vols., Selden Society
18 and 21 (London: Quaritch, 1904–6), 1: 227–28 (1327, 1411).

time the debt is contracted for it to be legally binding. Langland makes metaphoric use of this principle – and of the archaic, vicarious validation of the promises so made – to illuminate what Christ does for man at the Atonement.

Under this old system a creditor needed other people as witnesses of the debt transaction, though the debtor had the right to question their evidence by the simple production of character witnesses (this was known as "waging one's law"). The witnesses had generally seen some brief ceremony, such as the handing over to the creditor of a coin (an "earnest") or a stick (a "wed"), which by Langland's time was generally notched and sealed as a "tally" and then split in half so that each party could keep (or destroy) his evidence of the loan. The handing-over to the creditor of some token of future repayment by the debtor symbolized the important principle of a "quid pro quo." The more cautious creditor would insist either on a genuinely valuable pledge (a "gage") or a human surety (a "borw") to guarantee the loan, and to him the wed or tally would be handed to indicate that he was now committed to pay on the debtor's behalf. Those witnessing or acting as sureties in such ceremonies were thus vicariously bound on behalf of the debtor, who could not be trusted to repay the loan without their validation.[14]

We can see Langland using the somewhat archaic language of the old ceremonies quite precisely in the following passage from *Piers Plowman*,[15] where Abraham is telling Will about the souls who are lying in limbo for their debt of sin, waiting for Christ to release them from the devil's prison or "poundfold." The vicarious responsibility which Christ holds as borw to save the helpless debtors from prison is clear, as is the element of reciprocity in the bargain between God and the devil:

> "It is a precious present," quod he, "ac the pouke it hath
>   attached,
> And me therwith," quod that wye, "may no wed us quyte,
> Ne no buyrn be oure borgh, ne brynge us fram his daunger;
> Out of the poukes pondfold no maynprise may us fecche
> Til he come that I carpe of; Crist is his name
> That shal delivere us som day out of the develes power,
> And bettre wed for us [wa]ge than we ben alle worthi –
> That is, lif for lif. . . ."   (B.16.261–68)

---

[14] See Robert L. Henry, *Contracts in the Local Courts of Medieval England* (London: Longmans, Green, 1926), 241–46 for summary; *The Treatise on the Laws and Customs of the Realm of England, commonly called Glanvill*, ed. G. D. G. Hall (London: Nelson, 1965), 117–28; e.g., 118, 121: "Now when the loan is accompanied by the giving of sureties only [*plegiorum*], if the principal debt defaults, . . . recourse is to be had to the sureties. . . . Furthermore, when anything is deposited as a gage [*vadium*] for a fixed term, . . . if the debtor does not reclaim his gage it shall become the property of the creditor, [if it is so agreed]." *Vadium* is the root of *wed*.

[15] Discussed in the context of the Redemption in Anna P. Baldwin, *The Theme of Government in Piers Plowman* (Cambridge: D. S. Brewer, 1981).

The souls of the patriarchs are owed as a debt to the devil for Adam's original sin, but Christ has offered a wed in exchange – his own body – and has stood as borw or surety for the payment of the debt by his own acceptance of death. He is prepared to risk both the loss of the wed (which is far more valuable than the original debt) and going to prison.

The ordinary mercantile language of this passage indicates not only the generosity but also the credibility of Christ's bargain. Sureties who underwrote the bad debts of others might even risk imprisonment under borough law. For example, in the Staple Court of Exeter in 1428, a certain John Davy, who had stood surety for six other merchants that they would pay for some wool they had bought on tick, was actually arrested and imprisoned because they had failed to come up with the money. Objects used as gages to secure loans could also be wholly forfeit to the creditor in some boroughs, even though they were worth more than the debt. In Ipswich in 1291, for example, it was provided that a creditor whose debt was not paid could keep the whole gage "of gold or silver plate, [or] jewellery. . . ."[16] It is clearly on such principles that Christ is operating in this passage. He will, as borw, take over full responsibility for mankind's debt; he will, as the gage itself, be entirely forfeit to the devil (who will, however, find himself unable to keep his divine gage). The balance is being maintained: the devil is part of a bargain where only the supernatural generosity is abnormal.

However, this is a bargain between God and the devil on behalf of Old Testament man; the Christian's debt, by contrast, is owed directly to God. Langland moves from the Old Covenant to the New rather as the law of England was moving in the thirteenth century from the old forms of surety-promise to the written bonds in which a man sealed his own promise to pay and could not escape the penalty if he failed. Here at last the principle of freedom, of full personal responsibility is operating.

The royal courts preferred the new to the old forms simply because under the old forms debtors could evade their responsibilities. They could deny their tallies, fail to produce witnesses of the wed ceremony, and "wage their law" (produce a jury of friends to swear their innocence of debt). As early as 1313 a judge was pointing out the advantages of the new system over the old: "[F]or a tally is not a pure deed as is a writing; for what has been inscribed [on a tally] can be shaved off and something different . . . can then be put in its place . . . without any one being able to detect it, which is not the case with a writing."[17] Debt law involving "deeds" was based on the thirteenth-century Writ of Debt which had as its chief form the "debt upon obligation," meaning a debt

---

[16] *Select Cases Concerning the Law Merchant*, ed. C. Gross, 3 vols., Selden Society 23, 46, and 49 (London: Quaritch, 1908–32), 1: 117; *Borough Customs*, 147 (both cited by Henry, 194–98, 189).

[17] *Year Book 6 and 7 Edward II* (1313–14), ed. William Craddock Bolland, Selden Society 27 (London: Quaritch, 1912), 58 (see also 35, 49, 58); *Year Book 3 Edward II* (1309–10), ed. F. W. Maitland, Selden Society 20 (London: Quaritch, 1905), 47; Henry, 131–78.

recorded by a written bond.[18] Since this sealed document was itself the evidence of the debt, the old loopholes did not apply, and in particular the debtor was not allowed to "wage his law." The principle of reciprocity was conveyed by the exchange of the money for the deed itself, the seal being held to symbolize the debtor's body. After 1352 a creditor's ownership of an unredeemed bond was enough to put the debtor into prison.[19] He had been free to contract the loan, and no one need suffer on his behalf. It had become possible to make men liable for their own acts with their own bodies, and by Langland's day only merchants could still use the old tallies in the Common Law courts.[20]

When Moses comes in after Abraham, we see how dramatically the metaphor of debt has changed. Abraham had described how Christ would pay the debt of Original Sin by a wed given on man's behalf. Moses now produces an instrument which, when sealed, will give man a new but more realistic responsibility to fulfill the law of love:

> "I seke hym that hath the seel to kepe –
> And that is cros and Cristendom, and Crist theron to honge.
> And whan it is asseled so, I woot wel the sothe –
> That Luciferis lordshipe laste shal no lenger!"
>
> . . .
>
> He plukkede forth a patente, a pece of an hard roche,
> Whereon was writen two wordes on this wise yglosed:
> *Dilige Deum et proximum tuum.* . . . (B.17.5–12)

This is not a debtor's bond but a letter patent that Christ will seal with His blood (along the pattern set by the Charter of Christ texts[21]), thus releasing man from his original debt to God. But the Samaritan soon makes it clear that this New Law will also bind man to love his fellow beings: "Be unkynde to thyn evenecristene, and al that thow kanst bidde / Delen and do penaunce day and nyght evere. . . . / The Holy Goost hereth thee noght . . ." (B.17.253–57). Failure to love can be forgiven only if the sinner makes restitution to the human victim: "*Nunquam dimittitur peccatum* . . ." (17.308). Having wiped the

---

[18] *Statutes of the Realm* 52 Henry III c. 23 (1267), 1:24; 13 Edward I c. 11 (1285), 1:80; see S. J. Stoljar, *A History of Contract at Common Law* (Canberra: Australian National University Press, 1975), 7–13; Stroud Francis Charles Milsom, *Historical Foundations of the Common Law* (London: Butterworths, 1969), 235–43. For examples of "quid pro quo," see *Year Book 11-12 Edward III*, ed. A. J. Horwood, Rolls Series 31 (London: Longman, 1883), 587.

[19] Ralph Bernard Pugh, *Imprisonment in Medieval England* (London: Cambridge University Press, 1968), 46, referring to 25 Edward III, Statute 5 c. 17.

[20] See Henry, 135, citing, for example, *Year Book 4 Edward II* (1352), ed. G. J. Turner, Selden Society 26 (London: Quaritch, 1914 for 1911), 154.

[21] See Mary Caroline Spalding, *The Middle English Charters of Christ* (Baltimore: J. H. Furst, 1914), 32. On letters patent, see T. F. Tout, *Chapters in the Administrative History of Mediaeval England*, 6 vols. (Manchester: Manchester University Press, 1920–33), 5: 122–33.

slate clean of the debt of original sin, Christ will start a new reciprocal relationship with man in which payment for his love must be made in love towards other men. Moses' letter will inaugurate a new relationship of mutual debt, where the *quid* of charity will expected in return for the *quo* of salvation.

And so in Dobest this new law is established, and men are shown trying to live by it. It might be argued that Langland has been discussing the Christian life from the beginning of the poem, but these last two Passus do seem to offer a different atmosphere of freedom and personal responsibility, a new sense of hope. For one thing the narrative has a new structure. The characters in Dobest are free from the hectoring tutelage of the allegorized authorities of Dowel and Dobet but not quite within the realistic mode of the Visio with its legal and political hierarchy. The satire is aimed not at external forces like Meed and Simony but at the forces within oneself. The king now is Conscience, a fallible figure whom every man must own as his. The sense of an unnerving freedom, of being on one's own without rules or guidance, is increased when Piers himself leaves the poem. Each man seems now to be responsible for his own salvation; for the Church of Unitas is led by no authoritative clerical figure, and although the sacraments are crucial, they seem dependent on the individual's cooperation in the grace imparted through the priest.

This is strikingly true of the key sacrament of penance. In the Visio, Repentance seems able to absolve the Seven Deadly Sins without having to extract much more than a token contrition and promises of penitential acts from each of them. Even the restitution imposed on Covetise is modified and eventually paid to the priest rather than to his victims. In Dowel, Patience helps Hawkyn to cleanse his coat acting precisely as a priest in the confessional would; and in Dobet, the Samaritan makes himself wholly responsible for healing the wounds of sin:

> "May no medicyne under molde the man to heele brynge –
> Neither Feith ne fyn Hope, so festred be hise woundes,
> Withouten the blood of a barn born of a mayde.
> And be he bathed in that blood, baptised as it were,
> And thanne plastred with penaunce and passion of that baby."
> (B.17.93–97)

All through the poem God and the Church have helped with the burden of the debt for sin. But in Dobest, as the Samaritan had anticipated, the essence of penance is restitution, *redde quod debes*; and this cannot be performed by God or the priest but only by the free Christian, taking on personal responsibility for a debt he has incurred by his own actions. Moreover, when this phrase is first introduced, it is with an importance which suggests that far more than the duty to pay restitution is involved. The lines themselves are strongly reminiscent of, and even refer to, Truth's original pardon to Piers in Passus 6, which introduced the original injunction to "do wel":

> "Thus hath Piers power, be his pardon paied,
> To bynde and unbynde bothe here and ellis,

And assoille men of alle synnes save of dette one.
   "Anoon after an heigh up into hevene
[Christ] wente, and wonyeth there, and wol come at the laste,
And rewarde hym right wel that *reddit quod debet* –
Paieth parfitly, as pure truthe wolde.
And what persone paieth it nought, punysshen he thenketh,
And demen hem at domesday, bothe quyke and dede –
The good to the Godhede and to greet joye,
And wikkede to wonye in wo withouten ende."   (B.19.189–99)

The Church's power to bind and unbind, to impose and absolve from payment of the debt of sin, is evoked only to be restricted. The most important debt will not be paid through the Church. What is this debt? Is it more than the obligation to perform penance and make restitution for one's own sins, to avoid incurring a new debt to the God who has just paid off the old one to the devil?

It soon becomes clear that it is, that it extends beyond a man's obligation to himself to pay for his own sins, that in fact it defines man's proper relationship to other men as well as to God. It is an encapsulation not only of penance but of charity. And here I return to the teaching of Bob Frank. He made this same point in 1957, finding the scriptural authority for Langland's idea of debt in Romans 13:7–8 ("Reddite . . . omnibus debita" and "Nemini quiquam debeatis, nisi ut invicem diligatis") and in Jesus' repeated insistence (as in the Lord's prayer in Matt. 6:12) that if one does not forgive others one cannot expect forgiveness from God. *Redde quod debes* means, for Frank, a new attitude to other people, for "[t]he debt referred to in *redde quod debes* is man's debt of love to God and to his neighbor."[22] Frank is assuming the principle of reciprocity which I have shown to be part of the very notion of medieval debt and applying it to the religious and moral level of Langland's allegory. I would like now to take the implications of his insight into the economic world. As well as showing what charity earns from God, Langland is also concerned to show how it could change the world. He traces the human and social results of recognizing a debt to others, and he gives a surprisingly radical view of how that debt should be measured not by the extent of one's sin but by the extent of others' needs.

The first hint that these debts are not merely personal ones comes when the community in Unitas are worried by the open-ended claims which Conscience seems to be making on their purses: " 'How?' quod al the comune. 'Thow conseillest us to yelde / Al that we owen any wight er we go to housel?' / 'That is my conseil,' quod Conscience, 'and Cardinal Vertues . . .' " (B.19.394–96). It soon transpires that "[a]ll that we owen any wight" includes charity as well as personal debt; in fact, it means giving rather than taking from others. Not

---

[22] Frank, 108–9; see also B. Harbert, "Truth, Love and Grace in the B-text of 'Piers Plowman,' " in *Literature in Fourteenth-Century England*, ed. Piero Boitani and Anna Torti (Tübingen: G. Narr, 1983), 33–48.

surprisingly, the commune, the lords, the king, and even the Pope himself prefer to take from other people rather than giving or restoring what they owe, and the rest of the Passus demonstrates how they use the Cardinal Virtues to abet this covetousness. As the "lewed vicory" says: "For the comune ... counten ful litel / The counseil of Conscience or Cardinale Vertues / But if thei sowne, as by sighte, somwhat to wynnyng" (B.19.454–56). "Wynnyng" had been commended earlier in the poem; the ploughmen themselves had won rather than wasted sustenance for the commune. James Simpson points out in his recent excellent article on "Spirituality and Economics" that "the logic of Langland's economic images of reward from God [sometimes] pushes him into imagining a set of non-traditional labour relations on earth."[23] The notion of debt repayment clearly fits Simpson's category of condign reward, which Aquinas had defined as "pertaining to commutative justice, when one thing is rendered for another, [which we find] 'in contracts.'" The notion of charitable giving, however, fits Simpson's alternative of congruent reward, based on the free grace of the giver.[24] If Langland is really saying in Dobest that to pay one's debts is to obey the law of charity and so fusing both kinds of reward into one, then the economic consequences are indeed non-traditional. The commune will never be able to keep what they have won to themselves selfishly, so long as the poor need to be fed. The wealthy will never cease to owe their goods to the poor. Nothing less is demanded than a redistribution of wealth according to need.

In the next Passus Langland reinforces the point by demonstrating what happens if we fail to supply the needy but expect them to supply themselves. In the first place, the taking of others' goods will corrupt the souls of the needy themselves. Need appears in person to make this point by tempting Will to take from others rather than to give to them and so to fail to *reddere quod debet* in economic terms: "And nede ne hath no lawe, ne nevere shal falle in dette" (20.10).[25] This was precisely the justification used by the King in 19.476–79 to avoid the legal limits on taxation. People may not use their own needs as an excuse to violate the principle of *redde quod debes*. Instead, Kynde invites Will to enter Unitas and promises him a "fynding" of food and clothes if he will

---

[23] James Simpson, "Spirituality and Economics in Passus 1–7 of the B-text," *Yearbook of Langland Studies* 1 (1987): 102.

[24] Thomas Aquinas, *Commentum in Librum II Sententiarum* (d. 27 q. 1 a. 3), in *Opera omnia* 8.366–67, cited by Simpson, "Spirituality and Economics," 96, see also his *Piers Plowman: An Introduction to the B-text* (London: Longman, 1990), 75–88.

[25] On *necessitas non habet legem*, see Alford, *Guide to Legal Diction*, 102, citing canon law and *Dives and Pauper*, ed. Priscilla Heath Barnum, 2 vols. EETS OS 275, 280 (London: Oxford University Press, 1976–80), 2: 141: "for ȝif ony man or woman ... take so onyþing in peryl of deth ... nede excusith hym from þefte & fro synne ... for nede hat no lawe." Robert Adams, who sets Need in an apocalyptic context, sees him as morally neutral but able to corrupt Will; see "The Nature of Need in 'Piers Plowman' XX," *Traditio* 34 (1978): 273–301. Neither of these critics discusses Need's relation with *redde quod debes*, which is discussed from a political perspective in Baldwin, *Government*, 9–10.

"[l]erne to love" (20.208). If beggars were offered food, they could avoid both theft and begging. Is this an appeal for a welfare state?

The second reason why the needy should not be forced to take what they need is that in so doing they may corrupt others besides themselves. Here the Friars epitomize the problem.[26] Because society has not paid what it owes them, has not found them a "fynding," they have learnt to flatter for alms. The lawless character of Need, of course, acknowledges no responsibility towards them, but Conscience makes them the same offer that Kynde made to Will: "And I wol be youre borugh, ye shal have breed and clothes" (20.248). The wording of this line recalls a similar promise made to the true beggars in Passus 7. There Langland had anticipated his later principle that no one can evade his debt to God, but promised that God himself stood surety for the beggars' debt to society: "And he that biddeth, borweth, and bryngeth hymself in dette. / . . . and hir borgh is God Almyghty" (7.79–80). But whereas God had stood surety for those beggars' debt to society, Conscience now stands surety for society's debt to the begging Friar: "And I wol be youre borugh, ye shal have breed and clothes / And othere necessaries ynowe – yow shal no thyng lakke, / With that ye leve logik and lerneth for to lovye" (20.248–50). The condition is the same as it was for Will; the poor man must love the commune which supports him. A reciprocity of love should follow on from acknowledging the reciprocity of debt.

This golden age never appears. Envy sends the friars to school (20.273, 296) where they apparently learn to justify covetousness and to corrupt penance. Most appropriately, this is expressed as a corruption of debt law: friars who keep the money which sinners give them in restitution are compared to executors of other men's wills who take the inheritance into the Westminster Sanctuary and use it to support themselves longterm, so preventing the dead from making restitution and leaving them "in dette to the day of doome" (294).[27] I need not dwell on the way the Friars corrupt penance inside Unitas itself and so expose all Christians to the attacks of their inner enemies. But the economic basis of the disaster is insisted on to the end. If society had listened to its Conscience and recognized the debt of a "fynding" which it owed the Friars, they would not need to prey on the very sacrament which should remind men of their duty towards others. This is why Conscience seeks an economic solution (a "fynding" for the friars and the other needy) as well as a moral one (the presence of Piers Plowman to teach men Truth and Charity) and a religious one (the infusion of Grace) to the problems of society.

Throughout the final two Passus man's acceptance of the debt of sin has been the sign of his new freedom to participate in his own salvation. In return for Piers' pardon of his sins, man must render what he owes to man (in restitution and in charity) and to God (in penance). The relevance of the parable of the

---

[26] Wendy Scase, *Piers Plowman and the New Anti-Clericalism* (Cambridge: Cambridge University Press, 1989), ch. 3, discusses Friars and Poverty.

[27] Anna P. Baldwin, "A Reference in *Piers Plowman* to the Westminster Sanctuary," *Notes and Queries* n.s. 29 (1982): 106–8.

debtor, from which the phrase *redde quod debes* is taken (Matt. 18:28) is frighteningly clear. The lord saved his debtor from prison for failing to *reddere quod debet* but threw him into it when he failed to be charitable to his fellow servant. God will save man from the prison of hell for failing to pay his own enormous debt of sin but will send him there if he fails to be charitable to his fellow men. And the debt of charity is not to be measured by the quantity of one's sins but by the urgency of others' needs. In Langland's poem the reciprocity and freedom of English debt law has proved a most precise parallel to the law of Christ.

The Chilling of Charity: Eschatological Allusions and Revisions in *Piers Plowman* C.16–17★

M. TERESA TAVORMINA

During his discussion of practical charity in *Piers Plowman* C, Liberum Arbitrium urges churchmen to be like the early eremitical saints, who neither borrowed nor begged, but lived on the food brought to them by "mild" creatures like St. Giles's hind or the birds that fed Sts. Anthony and Arsenius. Although the fiercer beasts "faire byfore tho men faunede," the saints received no food from them, thereby signifying that religious men should not accept gifts originally won by violence. Liberum Arbitrium heavy-handedly implies that the willing acceptance of ill-gotten alms is widespread in the contemporary Church; moreover, that it leads powerful laypeople to take "more then treuthe wolde" from weaker folk and give some of those takings to the Church, perhaps in the false hope of getting spiritual benefits from their action. If ecclesiastics refused to receive "raueners offrynges," he argues, then lords and ladies would be "loth for to agulte" and merchants and lawyers would become merciful (C.17.1–47).[1]

Liberum Arbitrium's assertions run roughly parallel to Anima's treatment of the issue in the B text (B.15.257–312), but his argument then goes on to an interesting new metaphor that adds significant eschatological overtones to the passage and relates it to an important image earlier in the discourse, the long Latin description of the partially infected tree of the Church (C.16.271–71a; B.15.117–18). The metaphor in question occurs at C.17.48–50; once the religious orders start refusing "rauenours almesses," we are told,

★ My initial interest in the challenges presented by the Anima/Liberum Arbitrium episodes of *Piers Plowman* began in research undertaken at the National Humanities Center, whose support I am happy to acknowledge.
[1] Quotations of *Piers Plowman* C in this essay are taken from *Piers Plowman: An Edition of the C-text*, ed. Derek Pearsall (London: Arnold, 1978); quotations from *Piers Plowman* B from *Piers Plowman: The B-Version*, ed. George Kane and E. Talbot Donaldson (London: Athlone, 1975), with editorial brackets suppressed. Translations of Latin texts are my own unless otherwise noted.

51

> thenne grace sholde growe ȝut and grene-leued wexe
> And charite þat chield is now sholde chaufen of hymsulue
> And conforte alle cristene, wolde holy churche amende.[2]

These new lines bring to the C text a scriptural allusion that to the best of my knowledge has not yet been noted. The phrase "charite þat chield is now" describes a state of affairs that Christian tradition regularly associated with the Last Days: "et quoniam abundabit iniquitas refrigescet caritas multorum," or, as the Wycliffite Bible translates it, "And for wickidnesse schal be plenteuouse, the charite of manye schal wexe coold" (Matt. 24:12).[3] These words, spoken by Christ himself, occur in the Matthaean version of a discourse sometimes called the Little Apocalypse or the synoptic Apocalypse (Matt. 24; cf. Mark 13, Luke 21). Langland also evokes the Little Apocalypse with his images of grace growing green-leaved and of charity warming itself up so as to "conforte alle cristene": in Matt. 24:32–33, Christ compares the signs of imminent Judgment to the budding fig leaves that foretell the coming of summer.[4] The following essay will first examine the relation of Langland's images of cooling and budding to the Little Apocalypse and its exegesis; it will then explore the connections of those images with other elements of Liberum Arbitrium's speech, and with their precedents in B. In doing so, I hope to extend our understanding of the processes and aims of Langland's revisions in the first half of Will's encounter with Liberum Arbitrium in C – a passage of particular interest both for its historically-grounded treatment of ecclesiastical obligations and corruption, and for its role as the bridge from Will's relatively personal explorations of learning and patient poverty to the pilgrimage through salvation history that begins at the Tree of Charity.[5]

---

[2] Pearsall's base text reads "loue" instead of "leued" in line 48, which he emends on the basis of MS P and the phrase "grene yleued" in C.16.249; "leued" also makes better sense, and the allusion to Matt. 24:12 in "charite þat chield is now" indirectly supports the emendation as well, thanks to the budding fig leaves in Matt. 24:32–33. The alliteration in line 50 suggests that the original form of *churche* there was "kirk."

[3] *The New Testament in English, according to the Version by John Wycliffe . . . and Revised by John Purvey*, ed. Josiah Forshall and Frederic Madden (Oxford: Clarendon, 1879), 53. Translations of the New Testament in this essay are taken from Forshall and Madden, translations of the Old Testament from the Douay version of the Bible; quotations of the Vulgate are from *Biblia Sacra iuxta Vulgatam Versionem*, ed. Robert Weber, Boniface Fischer et al., 3d ed., 2 vols. (Stuttgart: Deutsche Bibelgesellschaft, 1983), with punctuation added and capitalization normalized after the Clementine edition (Madrid: Biblioteca de Autores Cristianos, 1965).

[4] B.15.424 offers an earlier version of the image of grace becoming green ("Grace sholde growe and be grene þoruȝ hir [ecclesiastics'] goode lyuynge"), but it does not mention leaves, and thus does not echo the synoptic Apocalypse in the way that "growe ȝut and grene-leued wexe" does. See below, section 2, "The Greening of Grace."

[5] This bridging function may in part account for the structural fuzziness reflected in the various rubrics, found in eight B manuscripts and the Crowley print (WLHmYBmBoCotC and Cr), indicating both the end of "Dowel" and the beginning of "Dobet" in B.15; this variety is adduced by Robert Adams as part of his

The Chilling of Charity

The probability that Langland's words "charite þat chield is now" refer to Matt. 24:12 is very high, as an examination of the entries in the *Middle English Dictionary* under *chillen, kelen, colden, colding,* and *cold* will show. All these words have a figurative sense in which they can be applied to love, kindness, devotion, and similar "warm" affections; the meaning is generally that of losing or lacking fervor. Not surprisingly, when used in this sense, the words usually appear in religious texts; several of the *MED*'s instances of the words are drawn from texts with eschatological dimensions – paraphrases of the Little Apocalypse, or complaints and polemics that use apocalyptic rhetoric to heighten their affective impact.

Thus we have:

> Wickidnesse schal kele or make coolde þe charite of many.
> (Lanterne of Li3t 2.10)

> Wykkednesse sal wax many falde,
> And charite of many sal wax calde.   (*Pricke of Conscience* 4040)

> þis is cause whi þe world peyreþ, and charite of many cooldiþ.
> Þe ground of þis malice stondiþ in prestis, þat ben þus cooldid
> wiþ temporal goods.   (*De Apostasia Cleri*; Arnold, 3:438)[6]

argument for taking such rubrics as scribal rather than authorial. See "The Reliability of the Rubrics in the B-Text of *Piers Plowman*," *Medium Ævum* 54 (1985): 208–31, esp. Chart II, 216–31. For a different analysis of the source of the rubrics and their variations, see Lawrence M. Clopper, "Langland's Markings for the Structure of *Piers Plowman*," *Modern Philology* 85 (1988): 245–55.

Even without consideration of external structural markers, of whatever origin, the teachings of Anima and Liberum Arbitrium in B.15 and C.16–17 do seem to begin as one kind of revelation – another didactic discourse, with occasional interruptions from the dreamer, like the previous six or seven passus – and to end as something very different, more visual and set against a far broader temporal and cosmological backdrop. As Elizabeth Kirk points out, the effect of these passus is like "the sensation one has in climbing that, as the view widens, the very geography of the climb itself becomes clear for the first time only when it is seen in retrospect"; the episode draws us forward almost imperceptibly, until "we are, poetically speaking, in a new world." Here the poem begins in earnest the expansion of vision that eventually "achieves the scope and the momentum Bloomfield has so rightly called 'apocalyptic.'" *The Dream Thought of Piers Plowman* (New Haven: Yale University Press, 1972), 159. Cf. James Simpson, *Piers Plowman: An Introduction to the B-text* (London: Longman, 1990), 171 (on the "large new subjects" raised in the poem at this point); and Anne Middleton, "William Langland's 'Kynde Name': Authorial Signature and Social Identity in Late Fourteenth-Century England," in *Literary Practice and Social Change in Britain, 1380–1530*, ed. Lee Patterson (Berkeley and Los Angeles: University of California Press, 1990), 46 (on the "long and sublime narrative sequence" and "unbroken thematic path" initiated in the encounter with Anima/Liberum Arbitrium).

[6] *Select English Works of John Wyclif*, ed. Thomas Arnold, 3 vols. (Oxford: Clarendon, 1869–71).

Deuocyone is slaked, charite is coldid.

(*Orologium Sapientie* 355/11)

Er charitee in hert wexe cold. ("Eche man be war" 159; Kail, 6)[7]

Additional instances, not given by the *MED*, include the following:

Caldore of charite.   (*A Talking of the Love of God* 18/7)

... And ffor wikkede dede
To moche worþ among ham [in the Last Days,] loue & godhede
Of meni worþ al akeled.   (*South. Pass.* [Harl. MS] 416–18)

[The flight in winter (Matt. 24:20)] falliþ ... to men þat ben among siche breþeren þat han her charite a cooldid, and wanten love of Goddis lawe, and tellen more bi þe popis lawe þan bi þe lawe of Jesus Crist.

("Of Mynystris in þe Chirche"; Arnold, 2:399–400)[8]

These Middle English examples clearly demonstrate that Langland's reference to the chilled state of charity would have quickly called to mind Christ's prophecy of the signs of the Last Days. This vernacular evidence is itself a reflection of traditional Latin usage, both in exegetical contexts and in eschatological and polemic literature. Exegesis of the phrase "refrigescet caritas multorum" is typically brief and straightforward. Paschasius Radbertus, for instance, simply notes that the betrayals, scandals, and spiritual seductions of the end of time (Matt. 24:10–11) will be far worse than those experienced by the Church up till then: "Sed tunc tam maxime tradent quia refrigescet caritas multorum et tam plurimos seducent quemadmodum numquam" ["But then as never before they will betray (each other) most greatly and lead so many more astray, because the charity of many will grow cold."][9] With similar brevity, but slightly more interpretation, the *Glossa Ordinaria* remarks that charity will *seem* to be warm before the tribulations to come, or even *be* warm as long as there is peace, but that it will cool once those tribulations begin.[10]

---

[7] *Twenty-Six Political and other Poems*, ed. J. Kail, EETS OS 124 (London: Kegan Paul, Trench, Trübner, 1904).

[8] This Wycliffite text is an "exposicioun of" Matt. 24. The Middle English examples given here are no innovation in English religious literature; see for example Ælfric's "Sermo de Die Iudicii" 326–37, which associates the winter-time flight of Matt. 24:20 with the cooling of charity (*Homilies of Ælfric*, ed. John C. Pope, EETS OS 260 [London: Oxford University Press, 1968], 2:605). For further Old English examples, discussed in the context of the "senescence of the world" motif, see J. E. Cross, "Aspects of Microcosm and Macrocosm in Old English Literature," *Comparative Literature* 14 (1962): 12 (the "Rhyming Poem") and 16 (*Guthlac A* and a Wulfstan sermon). On the *Guthlac* passage, see also Thomas D. Hill, "The Age of Man and the World in the Old English *Guthlac A*," *Journal of English and Germanic Philology* 80 (1981): 18.

[9] *Expositio in Matheo Libri XII* (Turnhout: Brepols, 1984), 11.430–38; *Corpus Christianorum, Continuatio Medievalis* (*CC-M*) 56B:1162–63.

[10] *Biblia Sacra cvm Glossa Ordinaria ... et Postilla Nicolai Lirani*. 6 vols. (Douai and Antwerp, 1617), 5:393–94. The *Glossa* takes the immediate referent of Christ's

Hugh of St. Cher defines the cooling of charity as a loss of fervor, and compares it to the tepidity of which the Laodiceans are accused in the Apocalypse ("quia tepidus es, et nec frigidus, nec calidus, incipiam te evomere ex ore meo"; Rev. 3:16).[11] Nicholas of Lyra explains the phrase literally as a description of a loss of fervor among the early Christians because of the abundance of iniquity in false Christians. More interesting in connection with Langland's allusion is Lyra's tropological interpretation of the phrase and its surrounding verses. He identifies the persecutors and pseudo-prophets mentioned in Matt. 24:9–11 as "clerici peruersi" and false preachers; the former attack "pauperes religiosi" with their sharp, detracting tongues, while the latter seek only their own good, seducing many simple folk – "& sic frigescente charitate abundat iniquitas."[12]

When Lyra associates the persecutions, false prophecy, abundant iniquity, and cooling charity of the Last Days with wicked churchmen, he is treading one of the well-worn paths of medieval eschatology. As Richard K. Emmerson notes in his study of the medieval Antichrist tradition, eschatological writers frequently asserted that moral decay among ecclesiastics would be particularly prevalent in the period preceding Antichrist's appearance, at which time there will be a "general 'cooling of love' (Matt. 24:12)"; evil churchmen are often seen as precursors of Antichrist, as well as his supporters during his life.[13] In fact, among writers of antifraternal polemic, Matt. 24:12 was particularly popular, along with many other verses from the synoptic Apocalypse and the diatribe against the Pharisees that precedes it (Matt. 23–24).[14] Latin complaints on the evils of the times, which often drew on eschatological language, likewise connect the chilling of charity with ecclesiastical corruption and sometimes with general social decay as well. Thus, a thirteenth-century song on clerical venality begins with the following two stanzas:

prophecy to be the destruction of Jerusalem but also notes that the disciples had asked Christ about the end of the world as well as the fall of Jerusalem and the Temple, and the anagogical parallels between the end of the world and the destruction of Jerusalem would have been easily seen.

11 *Vgonis de S. Charo Opera Omnia in universum Vetus et Novum Testamentum*, 8 vols. (Venice, 1600), 6:75r.

12 *Biblia Sacra cvm Glossa . . . et Postilla Nicolai Lirani*, 5:393–94.

13 *Antichrist in the Middle Ages: A Study of Medieval Apocalypticism, Art, and Literature* (Seattle: University of Washington Press, 1981), 84; see also 43: "The general sign of the end most popularly explained is the great increase in evil (verse 12) and subsequent cooling of love ('refrigescet caritas'). Commentators especially recognized this condition when they complained of contemporary evils and compared them to those expected in the last days."

14 See R. E. Kaske, "Holy Church's Speech and the Structure of *Piers Plowman*," in *Chaucer and Middle English Studies in Honour of Rossell Hope Robbins*, ed. Beryl Rowland (London: Allen and Unwin, 1974), 320–27, esp. 325 and n. 16; for more detailed evidence of the polemic use of the verse by antifraternal writers, see Penn R. Szittya, *The Antifraternal Tradition in Medieval Literature* (Princeton: Princeton University Press, 1986), 24, 56, 121, 161, 186, 190 n. 25.

Frigescente caritatis
  In terris igniculo
Universae vanitatis
  Fons inundat saeculo,
  Brevi sub articulo
Audietur vastitatis
  Gemitus in populo.

Ecce, florent venditores
  Spiritalis gratiae,
Antichristi praecursores,
  Pastores ecclesiae,
  Fures eucharistiae,
Novi Judae successores
Christum vendunt hodie.[15]

[As the spark of charity grows cold on earth, the fountain of universal vanity overflows the world; in a brief moment, the groan of desolation will be heard among the people. Lo, the sellers of divine grace flourish, the forerunners of Antichrist, the pastors of the Church, the thieves of the Eucharist, the new successors of Judas, they sell Christ today.]

A late fourteenth-century poem of English provenance uses the same motif in its complaint against moral decay in several classes of society:

En! amor et caritas regnis refrigescunt;
Livor et severitas gentibus ardescunt;
Cleri, plebis veritas et fides tepescunt.
Hinc regni nobilitas et fama quiescunt.[16]

[Look! Love and charity grow cold in the realm;
Malice and harshness are inflamed among nations;
The truth and faith of clergy and people grow lukewarm;
For this reason, the nobility and glory of the kingdom fall dormant.]

Another Latin poem, "Caritas Castitas Compassio refrigescunt" (translated into Middle English in MS Harley 7322 as the four-stanza piece "Charite, chaste, pite arn waxin al colde"), laments the corruption of law, marriage, and other institutions.[17]

From Latin sources such as these – the Bible and its exegesis, eschatological literature, satire and complaint, and so on – the association of clerical degeneracy and the chilling of charity moved easily into vernacular works, as shown by the Middle English examples listed above.[18] Langland's reference to "charite þat chield is now" in a passage calling for the reform of "men of holy churche" fits well into this tradition. By making such a clear allusion to Matt.

---

[15] Guido Maria Dreves, ed., *Analecta Hymnica Medii Aevi*, vol. 21: Cantiones et Muteti (Leipzig, 1895; reprint, New York: Johnson Reprint, 1961), 151.

[16] "On the Pestilence" 57–60, in *Political Poems and Songs*, ed. Thomas Wright, 2 vols., Rolls Series 14 (London: Longman, Green, Longman, and Roberts, 1859), 1: 281.

[17] Joseph R. Keller, "The Triumph of Vice: A Formal Approach to the Medieval Complaint against the Times," *Annuale Mediaevale* 10 (1969): 125.

[18] Not to mention works in other vernaculars, such as those noted by Szittya (see n. 14 above) or Rutebeuf's "Les Ordres de Paris" 7–9: "J'ai coumencié ma matire / Sus cest siecle qu'adés empire, / Ou refroidier voi charité" ["I have begun my subject / In this age that grows ever worse / When I see charity grow cold"], in *Oeuvres complètes*, ed. and trans. Michel Zink, vol. 1 (Paris: Garnier, 1989), 226.

24:12, and thus to the Little Apocalypse in general, the poet underscores the apocalyptic urgency of his recommendations for reform. His readers are reminded of and rebuked for the iniquity and spiritual frigidity of the times, while that frigidity itself is an ominous warning of the impending Eschaton in which all iniquity will be judged and punished.

The Greening of Grace

Yet Langland's reference to "charite þat chield is now" is more than a flatly minatory reminder of the evil of the Last Days. The threatening implications of the allusion are balanced by its hope, even its promise, of subsequent change. The tribulations of the End will purify the Church, according to eschatological writers, so that she will at last be "amended" through her sufferings. If Holy Church "wolde . . . amende" – or rather, when she does, since the purging is unavoidable – then grace will truly "growe ȝut and grene-leued wexe / And charite . . . chaufen of hymsulue / And conforte alle cristene" (C.17.48–50).

Considered most generally, the green-leaved grace and soul-warming charity in these lines derive from the agricultural and seasonal metaphors through which Judeo-Christian culture has long expressed spiritual events, and by which *Piers Plowman* is so deeply informed.[19] If these two images occurred by themselves, with no nearby allusion to the Little Apocalypse, then we might simply explain their presence and effects in the poem in terms of this rich symbolic network and take them no further. However, by clearly referring to Matt. 24:12 with the phrase "charite þat chield is now," Langland creates an allusive context that encourages a far more specific interpretation of the green leaves of grace and charity's warm comfort. This interpretation, as I have already suggested, would take those images as direct references to the *parabola fici* near the end of Christ's eschatological discourse (Matt. 24:32–33; Mark 13:28–29; Luke 21:29–31). The Matthaean version reads:

> ab arbore autem fici discite parabolam: cum iam ramus eius tener fuerit, et folia nata, scitis quia prope est aestas: ita et vos cum videritis haec omnia, scitote quia prope est [adventum filii hominis] in ianuis.[20]

> [And lerne ȝe the parable of a fige tre. Whanne his braunche is now tendir, and the leeues ben sprongun, ȝe witen that somer is nyȝ; so and ȝe whanne ȝe seen all these thingis, wite ȝe that it is nyȝ, in the ȝatis.]

---

19 For a thorough discussion of these metaphors, see Stephen A. Barney, "The Plowshare of the Tongue: The Progress of a Symbol from the Bible to *Piers Plowman*," *Mediaeval Studies* 35 (1973): 262–76.

20 Luke's version of this parable was part of the Gospel for the Second Sunday in Advent (Luke 21:25–33), in several English uses as well as in the Roman Missal; thus it was likely to be fairly familiar to medieval audiences as a sermon subject. See *The Sarum Missal*, ed. J. Wickham Legg (Oxford: Clarendon, 1916), 17; *Missale ad Usum Insignis Ecclesiae Eboracensis*, ed. W. G. Henderson, Surtees Society 59–60 (Durham: Andrews, 1874), 1:4.

Whereas the chilling of charity in Matt. 24:12 suggests a spiritual winter, the budding fig tree and approaching summer can obviously signify the advent of a far more comforting season of being. Langland himself uses the literal contrast between winter's wretchedness and summer's comfort as a stepping-stone to the metaphor of heaven as eternal summer, which the honest poor have in some sense earned by their year-round suffering (C.16.10–18; cf. B.14.157–80a), and similar seasonal metaphors can be found among the commentators. To be sure, in Matthew and Mark, Christ explicitly interprets the *parabola fici* as a simile for his coming in judgment, but the intrinsically positive connotations of new growth and summertime reminded medieval exegetes that the truly faithful could look beyond their fear of Doomsday to the joys of heavenly reward. This more optimistic reading was also encouraged by the parallel passage in Luke, in which Christ glosses the *aestas* as the *regnum Dei*. Thus, the impending *aestas* could be read as a figure for both the terror of the Last Days and the bliss of the Kingdom to come.

For instance, in his commentary on Matthew, Jerome interprets the coming of summer as the "consummationis [mundi] aduentum." Although the consummation of the world might be viewed with either fear or hope, Jerome colors the reading positively by adding a brief *reverdie* of spring, buds, flowers, stalks, leaves new born from bark, and a gentle west wind (Favonius) to Christ's seasonal metaphor.[21] Ambrose, commenting on Luke's version of the simile, offers a more explicitly two-fold reading:

> Verum siue cum fructus in omnibus uirescit arboribus et ficulnea fecunda iam floret, ut omnis lingua confiteatur deo confitente etiam populo Iudaeorum, sperare *domini* debemus *aduentum, quo tamquam temporibus aestiuis resurrectionis fructus metentur*, siue cum leuem fragilemque iactantiam homo iniquitatis tamquam folia synagogae ramus induerit, *conicere debemus adpropinquare iudicium*; nam *remunerari fidem* dominus et *delinquendi finem adferre* festinat. Duplicem igitur habet figuram hic ficulnea, uel cum dura mitescunt uel cum peccata luxuriant. (My emphasis.)[22]

> [Indeed, when the fruit in all the trees grows green and the fertile fig tree already flowers – so to speak, when every tongue should acknowledge God, with even the people of the Jews acknowledging him – we ought to hope for the coming of the Lord, in which the fruits of the resurrection will be reaped as if in summertime; or when humankind puts on the light and fragile display of sin as the branch of the Synagogue puts on leaves, we ought to conclude that the Judgment approaches; for the Lord hastens to reward faith and to bring about an end of wrongdoing. Therefore this fig tree has a double meaning, either when hard things soften or when sins run riot.]

---

[21] *Commentariorvm in Mathevm Libri IV* (Turnhout: Brepols, 1969), 4.571–80; *Corpus Christianorum Series Latina (CC)* 77:231.

[22] *Expositio Evangelii secvndvm Lvcam* (Turnhout: Brepols, 1957), 10.44–45; *CC* 14:357–58.

One of the most influential interpretations of the *parabola fici* was Gregory the Great's *Homilia I in Evangelium*, a homily for the second Sunday in Advent, which made its way into later homiliaries and thus circulated widely. The Gospel for this Sunday contains the Lucan version of the parable, comparing the approaching summer to the kingdom of God; for Gregory, the comparison is particularly apt: "Bene autem regnum Dei aestati comparatur, quia tunc moeroris nostri nubila transeunt, et vitae dies aeterni solis claritate fulgescunt" ["The Kingdom of God is well compared to summer, because then the clouds of our grief pass away and the days of eternal life shine with the brightness of the sun"] (*PL* 76:1080).

The *Glossa* itself defines the *aestas* in Matt. 24:32 as the "aeterna serenitas & renascentium desiderata nouitas" ["the eternal serenity and desired newness of those who are born again"]. The gloss on Mark 13:28, quoting Jerome, combines the hopeful picture of an eternal, green, and Edenic summer with the monitory equation of summertime and Judgment Day: "Aestas vero proxima dies est iudicij, in quo vnaquaeque arbor manifestabit quod intus habuit an aridum ad comburendum, an viride ad plantandum in eden cum ligno vitae" ["Now the summer is the impending day of judgment, in which every tree will show what it has within: whether something dry for the burning or green for planting in Eden with the tree of life"]. For the parallel passage in Luke, the *Glossa* gives a slightly modified version of Gregory's comment, "Regnum Dei aestati comparat, quia tunc moeroris nostri nubila transibunt, & aeterni dies vitae sub claritate solis fulgebunt" ["He compares the Kingdom of God to summer because then the clouds of our sorrow will pass away, and the days of eternal life will shine under the brightness of the sun"] (5:402, 621, 957).

For Hugh of St. Cher, the *aestas* is to be read as the "feruens persecutio," "imminens iudicium," and the "propinqua consummatio," that will test the Church in the Last Days; it also signifies the "feruor deuotionis," the "aestas aeternitatis," and the "proxima beatitudo," and it can serve as an "animarum iocunditatis exemplum" (6:76v, 115r, 256r). His longest comment on the word expands on its joyful sense in Gregorian terms similar to those of the *Glossa Ordinaria*:

> aestas: id est futurum saeculum, in quo cum Deo regnetis, quando erit plena serenitas, quia tunc transibunt nubila moeroris & doloris & laboris quo ad bonos, qui hic quasi in hyeme tempestatem & pluuiam atque grandines persecutionum patiuntur. [Here are cited Rev. 21:4 and Is. 25:8.] Illi autem qui hic habent aestatem terrae, transibunt in hyemem perpetuam. (6:256v; cf. the summer-winter metaphor for reward in *Piers Plowman*, cited above.)[23]

---

[23] Ludolph of Saxony plays on a similar summer-winter conceit in his *Vita Christi siue meditationes secundum seriem evangelistarum* (Nürnberg, 1495), 2.44: "regnum dei quod estas erit iustis ex hyeme et peccatoribus hyems ex estate" ["the kingdom of God, which will be a summer out of winter to the just and winter out of summer to sinners"] (sig. e3r, col. 1).

[The summer: that is, the age to come, in which you may reign with God, when there will be full serenity, because then the clouds of sorrow and grief and labor will pass away for the good who suffer the storm and rain and hail of persecutions here as if it were in winter. But those who have here the summer of the world, will pass into perpetual winter.]

Similar exegesis occurs in the vernacular as well: for instance, Robert of Gretham's Sunday sermon-cycle, the *Miroir*, and its Middle English translation read the *aestas* of the parable as heavenly joy. In the words of the translation,

> Þe somyr [*var.* sunne; OF *este*] is wel lykened to þe heuen. Ffor þe sunne, þat [*var.* þan] aryseþ on hy & doþ away þe cloudes & makeþ hete. & þey þat ben in þe kyndome [*var.* kyngdom] of heuene han þe hete of loue and charyte. Þey schul no3t haue no sorwe, ne heuynnesse, ne derkenesse, for þey ben wyþ þe Lord of blysse þat neuer ne schul haue ende. & þat, wyte 3e wel, þat in helle is euer more ny3t & strong wyntur, stynke & drede, & fuyr brennand, & derkenes & gret colde, & schal neuer þe fuyr of helle for þe cold be þe lesse, ne þe hete for þe colde [*var.* colde for þe hete].[24]

The other half of the *parabola fici* – the fig tree itself – also receives a relatively consistent set of interpretations; as we will see, these interpretations are of particular interest in the light of other arboreal images in Liberum Arbitrium's speech. The newly sprouting tree is frequently identified with the *ficus arefacta*, the barren fig, which Christ had cursed for bearing leaves but not fruit, withering it *a radicibus* as a sign of God's hatred of hypocrisy (Matt. 21:18–22; Mark 11:12–14, 20–24).[25] Both fig trees were most often said to stand for the synagogue; the ultimate conversion of the Jews to Christianity, traditionally seen as an event that would occur shortly before Doomsday,[26] was thought to be signified by the dry and leafless tree sending forth new shoots. The *Glossa*, for example, explicates "ab arbore" thus:

> A populo Israel, in quo caecitas ex parte contigit [Rom. 11:25]: & fuit ficus damnata. Sed cum de arido ligno ramus fidei & charitatis in eo viruerit, & folia, id est, verba praedicationis exorta fuerint, prope est aestas, quae expectatur. (5:402)

[From the people of Israel, in whom there was blindness in part; and this was the accursed fig. But when the branch of faith and charity grows green in itself from the dry wood, and the leaves – that is, the words of preaching – have arisen, the summer that is awaited is near.]

---

[24] "The Middle English *Mirror*: An Edition Based on Bodleian Library, MS Holkham Misc. 40, with Introduction and Glossary," ed. Kathleen Marie Blumreich Moore, Ph.D. diss., Michigan State University, 1991, 42–43.

[25] These two fig trees are sometimes also equated with the unfruitful fig of Luke 13:6–9.

[26] Emmerson, *Antichrist*, 99–101.

A complementary reading occurs in the Interlinear Gloss on Matt. 21:19, explaining that the *ficus arefacta* will eventually bud anew: "folia & truncus aruit, sola radix viuit, quae in fine mundi pullulabit" ["the leaves and trunk dried up; the root alone lives, which will sprout at the end of the world"] (5:349–50). (Obviously, some of the glossators were willing to read Mark's "aridam ... a radicibus" as non-inclusive – from the roots up, but not including them – or as being remediable at the end of time.)[27] Thus the barren and withered fig of Israel, when associated with Christ's *parabola fici*, is yet another sign of the Eschaton, still partially latent since it has not yet begun regerminating, but nonetheless a visible reminder of what is to come.

However, there also existed a common secondary reading of the fig-tree simile and the barren fig with which it was regularly associated. Under this interpretation, the two trees were compared to barren elements in the Church herself – especially wicked prelates, clergy, and religious. After commentators explained the barren fig as a figure for the Synagogue, with its hypocritical priests and doctors who had the leaves of good words but not the fruit of good works, they often went on to extend the analogy to hypocritical priests, teachers, and preachers in the Church. Pseudo-Chrysostom, for instance, applies the details of his exegesis on the passage first to the Jews and then tropologically to the *homo religiosus* or *fidelis*.[28] Lyra sternly remarks that the fig represents the

> doctor vel praedicator vanus & curiosus, quaerens auditorum applausum, & non fructum, propter quod Dei maledictionem incurrit, & per deuotionis defectum exsiccatur & igne gehennae finaliter concrematur.
>
> (5:349–50)

> [vain and curious teacher or preacher, seeking the applause of hearers, and not the fruit, on account of which he incurs God's curse, and dries up through the lack of devotion and in the end is burned up in the fire of Gehenna.]

Since the cursing of the barren fig is narrated in conjunction with the driving of the buyers and sellers from the temple (Matt. 21:12–13; Mark 11:15–18), it was easy for commentators to relate spiritual barrenness to simony and

---

[27] Thus Bede, though he insists that the root as well as the trunk and limbs of the barren fig was withered (*In Marcvm* 3.1495–97; *CC* 120:580), just as strongly affirms Paul's prophecy of the conversion of the Jews (Rom. 11:25–26), corroborating it with Job 14:7–9: "Lignum habet spem, si praecisum fuerit, rursum uirescit, et rami eius pullulant; si senuerit in terra radix eius et in puluere mortuus fuerit truncus illius, ad odorem aquae germinabit et faciet comam quasi cum primum plantatum est" ["A tree hath hope: if it be cut, it groweth green again, and the boughs thereof sprout. If its root be old in the earth, and its stock be dead in the dust: at the scent of water, it shall spring, and bring forth leaves, as when it was first planted"] (*In Marcvm* 4.261–74; *CC* 120:601–2).

[28] *Homilia 39 in Matthaeum*, PG 56:844–45.

ecclesiastical avarice, as well as to hypocrisy.[29] Indeed, the *Glossa Ordinaria*, paraphrasing Bede, goes so far as to say that in driving out the sellers in the temple, Christ "ostendit quod per figuram in ficu fecit" (5:600; cf. Bede, *In Marcvm* 3.1418–20, *CC* 120:578). The connections made by medieval exegetes between the eschatological *parabola fici*, the barren fig, and venal clerical hypocrisy are strikingly similar to the connections between Langland's own allusion to the Little Apocalypse in C.17 and his most memorable image of arboreal barrenness, the comparison of the Church to a partially infected tree in C.16 and B.15. This similarity may be most clearly visible in Hugh of St. Cher's brief remarks on the *parabola fici* and his more elaborate explication of the barren fig. Hugh reads the two trees as representing synagogue, church, and cloister, *inter alia*; most interestingly, his commentary includes passages from the same pseudo-Chrysostom homily that Langland quotes at B.15.118/C.16.271a. Commenting on the *parabola fici* in Matt. 24:32, Hugh notes that

> Per ficum hanc intelligitur peruersa Iu[d]eorum ariditas, quae fuit tempore Christ. Haec enim est sterilis illa ficulnea cui maledixit Dominus, & statim exaruit, & adhuc in eadem ariditate manet. De hoc super [cap.] 21.b. Chrys[ostomus:] Quare plus de ficu, quam de alia arbore ponit similitudinem? Quia pene post omnes arbores vernat, & difficile frigus post ficum vernantem venit. Item Chrys[ostomus:] Ecclesia per ficum significatur, quia sub vno cortice multa grana inter viscera dulcedinis habet inclusa [*Hom. 49 in Matt.*; *PG* 56:920]. . . . Rami proximo adhaerentes stipiti, sunt praelati. . . . Folia sunt doctores, & praedicatores: Modo sunt multa folia, quia multa verba. (6:76v)

> [By this fig is meant the perverse aridity of the Jews, which there was at the time of Christ. For this was the unfruitful fig that the Lord cursed, and it immediately dried up, and it still remains in the same aridity. Concerning which, see above, chapter 21b. Thus Chrysostom: "Why does he present a similitude of the fig rather than of another tree? Because it blooms after almost all the [other] trees, and frost comes after the blooming fig with difficulty." Again, Chrysostom: "The Church is signified by the fig, because under one skin it holds many seeds enclosed within the pulp of sweetness." . . . The branches clinging close to the stock are prelates. . . . The leaves are teachers and preachers: Now there are many leaves, because there are many words.]

In his analysis of the barren fig in Mark 11 (much lengthier than the comments on the synoptic passage in Matt. 21, and thus more convenient for my purposes here), Hugh comments:

[29] The charge of hypocrisy among the clergy was yet another eschatological commonplace, enthusiastically adopted by the antifraternal controversialists, who equated the friars with the Pharisees (*inter alia*). See Szittya, 34–41, 90–91, 149–51, 159–60, 166, 170–71, 179–80, etc.

Ficus est synagoga vel ecclesia, vel claustrum, quia sicut ficus sub vna cortice multa grana continet, sic Synagoga, ecclesia, vel claustrum sub vno iure viuendi multos homines habet. . . .

Ficus vbi bona est, optima est, vbi mala, pessima est, sic de viris ecclesiasticis, & maxime claustralibus. . . .

Radices ecclesiae sunt prelati & doctores, a quibus debet procedere humor fidei, morum & intelligentiae ad ramos, per quos debet totum corpus ecclesiae viuificari, & in terram viuentium radicari. Sed heu ficus arefacta est a radicibus, & a radicibus ascendit vsque ad ramos. . . . Chrys[ostomus:] Cor & stomachus ecclesie sunt sacerdotes, *qui si peccauerint, totus populus conuertitur ad peccandum*. Vnusquisque enim christianus pro suo peccato reddet rationem, sacerdotes autem non tamen pro suis, sed pro omnium subditorum peccatis. *Quemadmodum videns arborem pallentibus folijs marcidam, intelligis quia aliquam causam habet circa radicem, ita cum videris populum indisciplinatum, sine dubio cognoscis quia eius sacerdotium non est sanum* [*Hom. 38 in Matt.*, PG 56:839].

(6:110r–v; my italics, indicating material also used in *Piers Plowman*)

[The fig is the synagogue or the church or the cloister, for as the fig contains many seeds under one skin, so the synagogue, church, or cloister has many people living under one law. . . .

When the fig is good, it is the best; when it is bad, it is the worst; and so likewise for churchmen and especially the cloistered ones. . . .

The roots of the church are prelates and teachers, from whom the sap of faith, morals, and intelligence should proceed to the branches, through whom the whole body of the church should be given life and rooted in the land of the living. But alas, the fig is dried up from the roots, and from the roots it ascends even to the branches. . . . So Chrysostom: "The heart and stomach of the Church are the priests, who if they should sin, the whole people is converted to sinning. For each Christian renders an account for his own sin; but priests do so not only for their own but for all the sins of their flock. For just as when you see a withered tree with faded leaves you know that it has some cause near the root, so when you see an unruly people you recognize without a doubt that their priesthood is unsound."]

The passage from pseudo-Chrysostom's *Homilia 38 in Matthaeum* did not originally refer directly to the cursing of the fig tree (Matt. 21:18–22), which is explicated in his *Homilia 39*, but to the ejection of the buyers and sellers from the temple (Matt. 21:12–13). In Hugh's own comment on Matt. 21:12–13, he offers remarks similar to but briefer than those in the gloss on Mark quoted here, including parts of the pseudo-Chrysostom quotation (6:68r). Despite the original appearance of that quotation in connection with the Temple-episode, Hugh obviously found it an apt comment on the barren fig as well.

From exegesis like this, it is an easy step to Langland's Tree of the Church, partially barren and infected with corrupt, hypocritical clergy, who give evil example to the faithful by their lechery, their avarice, and their willingness to accept tithes from usurers, whores, and tyrants. In their iniquitous, loveless state, they are "bowes þat bereth nat and beth nat grene yleued" (C.16.249; not in B). Langland's own excerpts from pseudo-Chrysostom overlap Hugh's quotation, but are not identical with it. However, the similarity of their metaphors for ecclesiastical corruption and hypocrisy, ultimately both deriving from pseudo-Chrysostom, can easily be seen by comparing the preceding excerpts from Hugh with the following passage in *Piers*. In anticipation of the next two sections, I have marked C-revisions in the passage; lines in boldface are new in C, while the lines preceded by an asterisk are significantly revised from the B original:

> As holiness and honestee out of holy churche
> **Spryngeth and spredeth and enspireth þe peple**
> **Thorw parfit preesthoed and prelates of holy churche,**
> Riht so oute of holy churche al euel spredeth
> There inparfit preesthoed is, prechares and techares.
> And se hit by ensample in somur tyme on trees,
> Þere som bowes bereth leues and som bereth none;
> **Tho bowes þat bereth nat and beth nat grene yleued,**
> There is a meschief in þe more of suche manere stokkes.
> Riht so persones and prestes and prechours of holy churche
> Is þe rote of rihte fayth to reule þe peple;
> Ac þer þe rote is roton, resoun woet þe sothe,
> Shal neuere floure ne fruyt wexe ne fayre leue be grene.
>   For wolde ȝe lettered leue þe lecherye of clothyng
> *And be corteys and kynde of holy kyrke godes,
> **Parte with þe pore and ȝoure pruyde leue**
> And þerto trewe of ȝoure tonge and of ȝoure tayl also
> And hatien harlotrie and to vnderfonge þe tythes
> *Of vsererus, of hores, of alle euel wynnynges,
> Loeth were lewed bote they ȝoure lore folweden
> And amenden of here mysdedes more for ensaumples
> Then for to prechen and preue hit nat – ypocrisye hit
>   semeth.
> **Ypocrisye is a braunche of pruyde, and most amonges**
>   **clerkes,**
> And is ylikned in Latyn to a lothly dong-hep
> That were bysnewed al with snowe and snakes withynne,
> Or to a wal ywhitlymed and were blak withynne;
> Riht so many prestes, prechours and prelates,
> That ben enblaunched with *bele paroles* and with *bele* clothes
> *And as lambes they loke and lyuen as wolues.
> Iohannes Crisostomus carpeth thus of clerkes:
> *Sicut de templo omne bonum progreditur, sic de templo omne malum*
> *procedit. Si sacerdocium integrum fuerit, tota floret ecclesia; si autem*
> *corruptum fuerit, omnium fides marcida est. Si sacerdocium fuerit in*
> *peccatis, totus populus conuertitur ad peccandum. Sicut cum videris*
> *arborem pallidam et marcidam, intelligis quod uicium habet in radice, ita*

*cum videris populum indisciplinatum et irreligiosum, sine dubio
sacerdocium eius non est sanum.*

(C.16.242–71a; cf. B.15.92–118)

Hugh's commentaries on Matt. 21 or Mark 11 are not the immediate source
of Langland's Latin lines here, but they do suggest that the poet may have run
across the material in an exegetical context, and perhaps in specific connection
with venal churchmen and the cursing of the barren fig.[30] Certainly, the
infected Tree of the Church depicted in B.15 and C.16 has the hypocritical
characteristics represented by the leafy, fruitless fig: *bele paroles* covering bad
example, preaching without practice, lamb-like appearance and wolvish
living.[31] The picture is not completely identical to the biblical fig tree, either
before or after Christ's curse – "some bowes ben leued and some bereþ none"
(B.15.97/C.16.248) – but then the Church is only corrupt in some of her
members, and thanks to the comforting heat of grace – or more literally, to the
power of the Holy Spirit – will never be rendered completely sterile.

The role of the Holy Spirit in preserving and nurturing the Church's
spiritual fruitfulness is an important final point to be noted before we turn our
attention more fully to the connections of ideas and images in C.16–17 and
their antecedents in B. When Langland speaks of the action of grace and charity
in terms of growth, greenness, warmth, and comfort, he is clearly signalling
the special activity of the Holy Spirit within the Christian community. The
name "Grace," of course, is applied to the Holy Spirit later in the poem, and the
association of the Spirit with loving and vivifying warmth appears forcefully
in the comparison of the Trinity to a taper and in C's version of the Tree of
Charity scene (B.19.200–334/C.21.200–335; B.17.204–84/C.19.167–260;
C.18.72–75). Both the Spirit and grace are signified elsewhere in *Piers* by the
shooting forth of blades of wheat and grass, "spires" that "spring forth and
speak," animated by the divine breath of life and eloquence (cf. B.9.101–4;
B.12.59–63a/C.14.23–27a; C.18.230–33). Furthermore, the Holy Spirit's
operation in the Church is especially a work of "comforting," both in the
etymological sense of strengthening and in the sense of consoling. The word
"paraclitus" in John 14:26, 15:26, and 16:7 is translated as "comforter" in the
Wyclif Bible; a glance at the words "comforten" and "comfortour" in the *MED*
shows the frequent application of those terms to the Holy Ghost throughout
Middle English religious literature. Liberum Arbitrium himself describes the
Spirit as "the sonne of al heuene, / [Who] conforteth hem in here continence þat
lyuen in contemplacoun" (C.18.72–73).

---

[30] Another author who quotes pseudo-Chrysostom in a similar context is Ludolph of
Saxony, in his *Vita christi* 2.29, where he comments on the ejection of the buyers and
sellers. His excerpts from *Homilia 38* are somewhat more extensive than Hugh's or
Langland's and include all the material found in *Piers* plus substantially more of the
original homily (sig. b7v, col. 1).

[31] On Langland's powerful antagonism to hypocritical abuses of language, with
particular reference to the clergy and the Tree of the Church in B.15, see A. V. C.
Schmidt's "*Lele Wordes* and *Bele Paroles*: Some Aspects of Langland's Word-Play,"
Review of English Studies n.s. 34 (1983): 140–41.

That Liberum Arbitrium's hopeful warning employs fitting language for describing the third person of the Trinity can also be seen by comparing that language with Stephen Langton's well-known sequence, "Veni, sancte spiritus." Addressing the Spirit as "Consolator optime," among other titles, Langton writes:

> Lava quod est sordidum,
> riga quod est aridum,
>   sana quod est saucium;
>
> Flecte quod est rigidum,
> fove quod est frigidum,
>   rege quod est devium.[32]

Both Langton and Langland imply that many Christians are locked in a cold, dry, stiff winter of the soul, but that they can be warmed, watered, and softened by the spring and summer of the Holy Spirit, the divine Grace who aids Piers in preparing the ground for his spiritual agriculture.[33] As we will see below, Liberum Arbitrium's discourse pays added attention to the relation between the work of the Spirit and the ecclesiastical reform needed to bring the comforting warmth of charity back to the world.

From Anima to Liberum Arbitrium

The language describing the Tree of the Church in C.16 is echoed, probably by design, in the new passage on grace and charity growing green-leaved and warm in C.17. Like the B text, the C version introduces its arboreal simile for the Church with the injunction, "se hit by ensample in somur tyme on trees" (C.16.247/B.15.96); two lines later, Langland inserts a new line (in bold print below) that specifies precisely which branches have rotten roots:

> Þere som bowes bereth leues and som bereth none;
> **Tho bowes þat bereth nat and beth nat grene yleued,**
> There is a meschief in þe more of suche manere stokkes.
>   (C.16.248–50; cf. B.15.97–98; my emphasis)

---

[32] *The Oxford Book of Medieval Latin Verse*, ed. F. J. E. Raby (Oxford: Clarendon, 1959), 375–76. See also A. Wilmart, "L'Hymne et la séquence du Saint-Esprit," *La Vie et les arts liturgiques* 112 (1924): 400, who describes the content of these two stanzas as "les bienfaits spécialement sollicités [par la séquence,] qui sont les manifestations diverses de la grâce"; and Herbert Thurston, "The *Veni, Sancte Spiritus* of Cardinal Stephen Langton," *The Month* 121 (Jan.–June 1913): 602–16.

[33] The fact that Pentecost necessarily falls in late spring (ME "sumor") would not have been lost on Langland or on medieval liturgists, who were well aware of the spiritual implications of the seasons of the year: Christmas at the time when the days begin to lengthen, Easter in the season of vernal renewal, the blessing of fields at spring Rogation Days, the English feast of Lammas at harvest, and so on.

Later on, when Langland describes a reformed, regenerated Church in terms of the green-leaved growth of grace and the change from spiritual winter to summer, he may well be harking back to his own tree-parable, his "ensample in somur tyme on trees . . . [with] bowes þat . . . beth nat grene yleued." The two passages are about two hundred lines apart, but the process of revising Anima/Liberum Arbitrium's discourse could easily have brought them together in the poet's awareness, possibly even more closely than in the original act of composing.

Green leaves and green growth can be found elsewhere in the B version of Anima's discourse on charity and clerical responsibilities, in contexts that suggest they played a role in Langland's revisions of that discourse in C. For example, the B text's description of the Tree of the Church contains the warning "þer þe roote is roten, . . . / Shal neuere flour ne fruyt wexe ne fair leef be grene," which C retains and reinforces with the new line on boughs that are not "grene yleued" (B.15.101–2; C.16.253–54, 249). More interesting are lines that come later in Anima's speech, at B.15.417–28a, but are omitted in C.[34] Here Anima asserts that the proper role for religious orders and solitaries is to "Peeren to Apostles" by their perfection of life. They should not take alms "of tirauntʒ þat teneþ trewe men," but rather imitate Sts. Anthony, Dominic, Francis, Benedict, and Bernard, and live humbly "by lele mennes almesse." If they would do so, says Anima, then

> Grace sholde growe and be grene þoruʒ hir goode lyuynge,
> And folkes sholden fynde, þat ben in diuerse siknesse,
> The bettre for hir biddynges in body and in soule.
> Hir preieres and hir penaunces to pees sholde brynge
> Alle þat ben at debaat and bedemen were trewe.   (B.15.424–28)

These lines, of course, repeat the subject matter of Anima/Liberum Arbitrium's earlier comments on religious orders not accepting alms gained by violence, the passage in which C but not B alludes to the "chilling of charity."

---

[34] Langland's cancellation of these lines is part of a much larger deletion, from B.15.417 to B.15.491, whose imagery is simultaneously "homely" (Pearsall C.17.187n) and almost metaphysically extravagant. Langland may have omitted it in C because of the digressive effects of its virtuosity or, as G. H. Russell suggests, because he had changed his mind on the necessity of baptism for virtuous non-Christians. See "The Salvation of the Heathen: The Exploration of a Theme in *Piers Plowman,*" *Journal of the Warburg and Courtauld Institutes* 29 (1966): 111–12; for a different view, see Gordon Whatley, "The Uses of Hagiography: The Legend of Pope Gregory and the Emperor Trajan in the Middle Ages," *Viator* 15 (1984): 62–63.

The omission of B.15.417–91 may also have been influenced by a larger compositional problem at the end of Anima's speech. Kane and Donaldson argue that major textual dislocations in the archetype of B.15.504–69 triggered several revisions in the last half of C.17 (*B-Version,* 176–79). The intense revising activity demanded by this textual corruption may have led on to the deletion of B.15.417–91 and the insertion of the new passage C.17.125–64 as well (the latter includes certain foreshadowings of themes in the dislocated later text).

In B, the two passages on the source of alms are fairly close together (about 110 lines apart), and Langland may have come to feel that returning to the topic of ill-gotten donations was unnecessary, as well as something of an interruption to the discussion of Mahomet and the conversion of the Saracens. Perhaps he realized, like Will in B.11.318, that his "lokynge" on greedy religious "hadde doon him lepe" from his principal topic. At any rate, in C Langland eliminates the digressive repetition. However, he saves the beautiful phrase "Grace sholde growe and be grene" for use in a modified form in C.17.48–50, and adapts the line about effective prayers and penance bringing about peace in another eschatological addition near the end of C.17.

Let us look first at the changes in "Grace sholde growe and be grene." The modifications by which Langland turns B.15.424 into C.17.48 have several noteworthy results. First, the image of grace becoming green is given a concrete embodiment and a specific, scripturally-based implication: the green-leaved tree budding forth as summer nears, signifying the fast-approaching eschatological moment. Second, the phrase "grene-leued" connects the line and its context in C.17 with the earlier image of the Tree of the Church and its various green-leaved and leafless branches. That tree, with its unmistakable symptoms of a corrupt clergy producing an infected crop of layfolk, is itself an eschatological sign, like the *caritas refrigescens* that leads the laity to oppress the weak and to give ill-gotten wealth to undeserving religious, who spend it in turn on "aparayl and on Purnele" (C.17.71) instead of on the poor who need it. Even love of kin, the love in which charity begins, is overturned by the insatiable alms-grubbing of the religious orders (C.17.55–63). A third important aspect of Langland's allusion to the newly sprouting tree is its exegetical association with the conversion of the Jews – a topic that Langland subordinates to the conversion of the Saracens, but is careful to stress at the climax of Anima/ Liberum Arbitrium's speech in both B and C:

> Iewes lyuen in þe lawe þat oure lord tauhte
> Moises to be maister þerof til Messie come,
> And on þat lawe they leue and leten hit for þe beste.
> And ȝut knewe they Crist þat cristendom tauhte
> And for a parfit profete that moche peple sauede
> And of selcouth sores saued men fol ofte.
> By þe myracles þat he made Messie he semede
> Tho he luft vp Lasar þat layde was in graue
> *Quadriduanus* coeld, quyk dede hym walke.
> . . .
> And ȝut they seyen sothly and so doen þe Sarrasynes
> That Iesus was bote a iogelour, a iapare amonges þe comune,
> . . .
> And hopen þat he [the Messiah] be to come þat shal hem releue;
> Moises oþer Macometh here maystres deuyneth,
> And haen a suspectioun to be saef, bothe Sarresynes and Iewes,
> Thorw Moises and Macometh and myhte of god þat made al.

> And sethe þat this Sarresynes and also þe Iewes
> Conne þe furste clause of oure bileue, *Credo in deum patrem,*
> Prelates and prestes sholde preue yf they myhte
> Lere hem littelum and littelum *et in Iesum Christum filium,*
> Til they couthe speke and spele *et in Spiritum sanctum,*
> Recorden hit and rendren hit with *remissionem peccatorum,*
> *Carnis resurrectionem et vitam eternam. Amen.*
> (C.17.297–305, 309–10, 313–22; cf. B.15.582–613)

The other line salvaged from Anima's second discussion of proper almsgiving and receiving is B.15.427, on the potential power of the religious orders to bring about peace through prayer, if only they would live perfectly, as in their founders' days. This line reappears towards the end of C.17, where Langland develops two brief B-text allusions to the duty of prelates to work and pray for peace. The B text simply refers in passing to the "plentee and pees amonges poore and riche" in the idealized primitive Church, and to prelates who "sholden preie for þe pees" (B.15.538, 563/C.17.199, 226). The C text, in contrast, spends seventeen additional lines on the Pope's special duties to maintain peace on earth, rather than armies, and to bring about, through the prayers of a perfect priesthood, a "perpetuel pees" between "þe prince of heuene / And alle maner men" (C.17.233–49).[35] Here, in the reference to the Pope's potential spiritual power, we find the line from the passage on perfect living among monks, hermits, and friars. "Were presthode more parfyte, that is, þe pope formost," says Liberum Arbitrium, "His [the Pope's] preyeres with his pacience to pees sholde brynge / Alle londes into loue." The phrasing clearly echoes Anima's remark on the potentially effective prayers of the religious orders: "Hir preieres and hir penaunces to pees sholde brynge / Alle þat ben at debaat" (C.17.233, 236–37; B.15.427–28). Once again, Langland underscores an eschatological motif – perpetual peace among men and with God – in the process of revising B to C. One of the interesting things about this instance of that process is the way lines from a single passage in B resurface in quite distinct new passages in C, and provide eschatological language for both.

One final comment on arboreal aspects of Liberum Arbitrium's speech is in order. Like Anima, Liberum Arbitrium anticipates the Tree of Charity with his picture of the Tree of the Church. Both the Tree of the Church and the Tree of

---

[35] Kane and Donaldson point out that Langland's initial reason for adding this passage may have been "to smooth an awkward transition" in his B manuscript, which appears to have been severely corrupted by dislocations of lines here (*B-Version*, 177). But this explanation does not diminish the fact that the transitional topic Langland actually chose from the preceding B lines was that of an ideal and lasting peace – another allusion to the Last Days and the Kingdom beyond them. As Russell observes, "having begun with immediately urgent repair, [Langland] does on a number of occasions allow craft to become technique, in Seamus Heaney's distinction, repair to become recreation." See "'As They Read It': Some Notes on Early Responses to the C-Version of *Piers Plowman*," *Leeds Studies in English* n.s. 20 (1989): 174.

Charity represent comprehensive communities – the entire Church, and the entire human race. Both have better and worse fruits, limbs, and leaves; both have their imperfections and infections, either from within or without. The Tree of Charity is obviously the richer of the two images, and the one that drew most of Langland's poetic energies, but we can better understand its more narrowly-defined precursor by exploring one or two of the similarities and differences between the two trees.[36]

It is important to recognize that both trees represent aspects of charity – both are part of what in B is Will's fifth dream, whose central concern is charity, as discussed by Anima/Liberum Arbitrium and as illustrated by the Tree of Charity itself and by the Good Samaritan. The Tree of the Church appears just before (and in some sense triggers) Will's question "What is charite?" (B.15.149; paralleled in C.16.284–85 by the question, "Charite . . . where may hit be yfounde?"). But the brand of charity represented by the Tree of the Church is of a particularly clerical nature: it is in effect a tree of teaching, both in word and deed. The Tree of Charity, despite its eclecticism, does not make much of priestly duties. Instead it focuses on the generation of virtue in the individual soul, and on the generation of the three virtuous states of individual life within the whole human race. This emphasis on states of life is especially clear in C, with its image of the apples of virginity being the sweetest and largest because they are nearest to the comforting heat and light of the Holy Spirit (C.18.64–66, 71–75). Clerics and regular religious would be included in two of those states (virginity or widowhood), but the emphasis is not on ecclesiastical responsibilities to fellow humans but on the relative closeness of the three states to God.[37]

True teaching and preaching, however, are also instances of charity, and very important ones. The failure of natural knowledge – weather wisdom, astronomy, grammar, philosophy, and physic – that Langland laments in B.15.347–92/C.17.72–124 is said in C.17.85 to be a punishment for "werre and wrake and wikkede hefdes." But these evils are themselves the result of a failure among "þe folk þat þe feiþ kepeþ," "techares" and "looresmen" who should "lyue as þei leren vs" but in fact "worcheth nat as [þei] fynde[n] ywryte" (B.15.347, 391; C.17.78, 84). A major theme of Anima and Liberum Arbitrium's speech is charity *as expressed by ecclesiastics* – whether secular or religious, whether called to the cure of souls or to exemplary "parfit lyuynge"

---

[36] Schmidt comments briefly on the Tree of the Church as a preparation for the Tree of Charity, both as an allegorical, arboreal "image in which the fruits are human souls" and in carrying leaves of speech that may either be *lele* or hypocritically *bele* ("*Lele Wordes*," 140). Simpson discusses the "intimately related" subjects of the Church and charity, and their two trees in *Piers Plowman: An Introduction*, 173–85, esp. 173–75.

[37] The movement from the Tree of the Church to the Tree of Charity might be read as a movement from the institutional to the individual – a strategy found elsewhere in Langland's poem, as in the movement from the first to the second dream; or from the second dream to Will's personal pilgrimage; or from the perversions of the virtues in passus 19/21 to Need's tempting of Will in passus 20/22; or from the general attacks of Kynde's allies against Antichrist's forces to Elde's very personal attack on Will.

in prayer and penance or to both.[38] Will's flatfooted joke about Anima's names and the heap of titles borne by bishops – *Presul, Pontifex, Metropolitanus, Episcopus,* and *Pastor* – introduces the subject obliquely; his misguided craving for knowledge then allows Anima and Liberum Arbitrium to criticize clergy who seek and use knowledge for pride rather than love, thereby leading to the Tree of the Church image and eventually to Will's question about charity. And the answer to that question keeps returning to the charity that should be, but so often is not, manifested by contemporary clergy and religious.

Langland's concern over preachers who seek their own glory, even at the risk of their hearers' faith, gives him the opportunity to allude to yet another tree image in the B text, just before the Tree of the Church passage: the Tree of Vices so loved by medieval homilists. To fulfill their vocation as clergy and preachers, says Anima, friars and doctors should tell "þe lewed peple" about "þe braunches þat burioneþ" from the seven sins, and about the ten commandments and five wits, rather than preaching about "materes vnmesurable ... of þe Trinite ... / Moore for pompe þan for pure charite" (B.15.70–79). C retains the warning against overly-intellectual preaching "for pompe and pruyde" (C.16.230–37), but moves B's branches of sin, grafting them onto the Tree of the Church itself, with special application to the clergy: "Ypocrisye is a braunche of pruyde, and most amonges clerkes" (C.16.264; not in B). Thus in both texts we get a juxtaposition or superposition of the image of the Tree of Vices (associated with proper preaching in B) and the Tree of the Church – whose clerical members should be preventing the growth of vicious branches but all too often are the very root of such growth. Though it should not and ultimately will not be so, the present Tree of the Church on earth stands as a *tertium quid* between the Tree of Vices and the Tree of Charity.

The eschatological theme of hypocritical preaching and clergy will recur throughout Anima and Liberum Arbitrium's discourse, although arboreal metaphors are left behind after the Tree of the Church passage (BC) and the reference to grace growing green-leaved (C only). We have already seen the theme in connection with the lament for the failure of learning, and it is equally visible in the long description of Mahomet preaching schism out of covetousness and resentment at not being elected pope. It is at the heart of the contrast between contemporary Christian prelates and such exemplary past archbishops of Canterbury as Augustine (B only) and Thomas Becket (BC),

---

[38] Compare Pearsall's heading for Passus 17: "Liberum Arbitrium on Charity and the Church"; the subject is actually begun in Passus 16. Wendy Scase has recently provided an excellent discussion of the late fourteenth-century ecclesiastical controversies underlying Will's interactions with Anima/ Liberum Arbitrium. She focuses primarily on the political and institutional dimensions of Langland's anticlerical criticisms (leveled at ecclesiastics of all sorts – parish clergy, friars, bishops, popes, and others) rather than on the eschatological dimensions I am exploring here, but the complementary of our two approaches is suggested by the last section of her chapter on "Charity: The Ground of Anticlericalism," titled "The Last Days and the End of Glosing." See *"Piers Plowman" and the New Anticlericalism* (Cambridge: Cambridge University Press, 1989), 84–119, 112–19.

who, like their Master and his Apostles, were *metropolitani* willing to "soffr[e] deth also, / For to enferme þe fayth ful wyde-whare."[39] These bright and saintly mirrors of preaching and prelacy did not refuse the command "*Ite in vniversum mundum*," nor did they "huppe aboute [in Ingelond] and halewe men auters / And crepe in amonges curatours and confessen aȝeyn þe lawe," putting their sickles into other men's corn as do modern bishops *in partibus infidelium* (C.17.187–93a, 262–80a/B.15.443–51, 492–97a, 511–30a). Instead, they worked constantly to complete the evangelizing of all nations prophesied by Christ in Matt. 24:14 – "Et praedicabitur hoc Evangelium regni in universo orbe in testimonium omnibus gentibus: et tunc veniet consummatio" ["And this gospel of the kyngdom schal be prechid in al the world, in witnessyng to al folc; and thanne the ende schal come"]. Langland's point is not that all bishops should preach overseas, but that they should all imitate their saintly historical predecessors, bearing witness to the Gospel with their own lives *in their own provinces* (C.17.284), wherever those may be: at home, like Christ and Becket, or abroad, like the Apostles and Augustine of Canterbury.[40] In their criticism of contemporary bishops, both B and C bring back the episcopal titles *pastor* and *metropolitanus*, mentioned by Will to Anima/Liberum Arbitrium; C throws in a *presul* and another *pastor* to boot (B.15.497a, 516; C.17.193a, 267, 286, 293a). Will's opening *bourde* about Anima/Liberum Arbitrium's names, we discover, looks forward to the rhetorical climax of their respective discourses, where the highest-ranking leaders of the Church are called on to fulfill their apostolic duties, and the C text tightens that relationship by its additional repetitions of Will's initial jesting words.[41]

[39] The saints best known for preaching "In ynde, in alisaundre, in ermonye and spayne" (B.15.521/C.17.272) are the Apostles Thomas, Bartholomew, and James the Greater (India, Armenia, Spain) and the Evangelist Mark (Alexandria). The four places named are also fitting for their geographical range – covering the far-flung regions of the three known continents and thereby demonstrating just how "wyde-whare" the apostolic mission should extend.

[40] On the deeply historical basis of Anima's (and by extension, Liberum Arbitrium's) teachings here, see Simpson, *Piers Plowman: An Introduction*, 171, 177–78; as Simpson points out, the historicizing trajectory carries on in major ways through the Tree of Charity episode and Will's encounters with the typological personages Abraham/ Faith, Moses/Hope, and the Good Samaritan/Charity/Christ, moving from ecclesiastical history to salvation history (186–200).

[41] The question about Anima/Liberum Arbitrium's names has other important functions as well, including those pointed out by Middleton: "The topic of discussion . . . momentarily foregrounds the proprieties of naming, and sets up an occasion for Will to offer his own in return as a sign of his 'menyng,' just as his instructor has explained his capacities by glossing his name. Before introducing himself . . . , however, Will becomes diverted by the sheer rhetorical intricacy of Anima's gloss, eagerly seeking to know 'the cause of all hire names.' . . . Conceding to Anima [after being rebuked for prideful curiosity] that what he really seeks is not many things (the nice distinctions of the soul's many names) but only one, charity, Will's contrite return to a project of self-understanding marks the penultimate turning point in the poem. It initiates the long and sublime narrative sequence, the most sustained of the entire poem, that culminates in the narrator's vision of Christ's

Throughout Liberum Arbitrium's speech, as we have now seen in several instances, Langland's revisions have a holographic quality. The function of a given revision in C and its relation to material in B cannot be understood solely by a one-to-one comparison between the C material and the most nearly parallel B passage, though one should probably begin with such a comparison. Whatever local dissatisfactions contributed to Langland's desire to revise this section of the poem, the revision is ultimately global; even when he "patches" locally, the patches are cut from a single, tightly-woven fabric of global poetic purposes. He keeps Anima's whole discourse in mind as he works over its parts, transmuting them into Liberum Arbitrium's speech; in the revision process, he remains sharply aware of the complex connections between the elements of that discourse and strives to make those connections even stronger and fuller in C.[42]

The Church and Charity

Like all thinking Christians, Langland both fears and yearns after the Eschaton. His sensitivity to the wickedness, tribulations, and chaos leading up to the End can hardly be denied in the face of the last passus of *Piers Plowman*, or his several extended attacks on the degeneracy of contemporary institutions and individuals. Yet he also passionately desires the final community of the blessed shadowed forth, however imperfectly, in the various plantings, harvestings, manors, castles, families, and kingdoms throughout the poem. And the only way to reach that perdurable and peaceful commune is to undergo the

victory at the Crucifixion. . . . From [his anagrammatic self-introduction] forward to Will's Good Friday sleep lies an unbroken thematic path toward his one 'face to face' vision of charity, the thing itself, acting in human form 'in Piers armes.'" See "William Langland's 'Kynde Name,'" 44–47; also, Simpson, *Piers Plowman: An Introduction*, 183–84.

[42] I do not mean to imply that Langland's revisions in C.16–17 were necessarily complete (I suspect they were not) or fully successful, simply that they show a great deal of careful and often effective poetic decision-making, which deserves more attention than it has received in Langland criticism to date. A good deal of the poet's creative energy in the C revision went into what had been the fifth dream in B – Anima's discourse, the inner dream of the Tree of Charity, and the encounters with Faith, Hope, and the Good Samaritan. Indeed, after this segment of the poem, Langland's revisions are much less drastic (in B.18/C.20) or non-existent (in B.19–20/C.21–22). But the section of the poem from the end of the Haukyn/Activa Vita episode through the Good Samaritan's speech undergoes significant revisions at several points: the dream boundaries are altered, not altogether clearly; the passus boundaries shift, not necessarily for purely mechanical reasons; questions concerning the salvation of the heathen are answered from new vantage-points; large chunks of material (like the series of homely conceits for the conversion of the heathen) are dropped wholesale and other chunks added; Anima is identified specifically as Liberum Arbitrium; the Tree of Charity scene is re-worked in large and small; Abraham's speech is thoroughly revised; and so on and so on. Further work on these revisions and their relations to the rest of the C text remains a desideratum.

purgations of the Last Days, to strive to bring about the reform and conversion of the world's as-yet-unperfected institutions and individuals, in whatever way one can. For "prelates and prestes and princes of holy churche" (C.10.196), this responsibility manifests itself most fully in the cure of souls, and especially in the vocation of preaching: warning the wicked, encouraging the good, teaching and converting both Christians and non-Christians, even at the cost of one's life if need be.[43] For the religious orders, the essential responsibility is the life of prayer, poverty, and penance, which pleases God and teaches others by example; for those religious who are priests as well, the duties of preaching and confession also apply. And all men and women, clerical or lay, must do all that is in them to learn and carry on the central, all-encompassing craft of love, without which preaching, penance, and prayer are but "as sounding brass, or a tinkling cymbal."

Although the arboreal image of the Tree of the Church and C's language about the green leaves of grace do not return during the rest of Langland's attack on false preachers and prelates, one can clearly see how that attack develops from those images. Like Lyra's "doctor vel praedicator vanus & curiosus, quaerens auditorum applausum, & non fructum" (Glossa . . . et Postilla 5:349), Langland's hypocritical clergy preach and teach "fayre byfore folk" but do not have the fruit of works that is necessary for propagating faith, loving deeds, and peace among their listeners. Instead, they progagate werre, wrake, and wo through their avarice and ambition – the same faults that, in Langland's view, led the "gret clerk" and papàbile Mahomet into heresy and schism, the archetypal act of divisive hatred.[44] What the clergy should be spreading instead is the message of C.17.125–49, another passage added to the C text; answering Will's question, "What is holy churche, chere frende?" Liberum Arbitrium defines the Church as the unity of love itself:

> "Charite," he saide;
> "Lief and loue and leutee in o byleue and lawe,
> A loue-knotte of leutee and of lele byleue,
> Alle kyne cristene cleuynge on o will."   (C.17.125–28)

I have used the language of propagation here deliberately, to reflect Langland's arboreal imagery at the beginning of the discourse on charity and the Church. The general notion of spiritual propagation is of course an essential part of the arboreal metaphor for the Church, as it is for the biblical antecedents of that metaphor, the barren fig and the newly-sprouting fig. However, the particular words that Langland chooses to express the

---

[43] The line I quote here from C.10 occurs in another C-addition that highlights churchmen's duties to convert souls, travelling "as wyde as þe worlde were / To tulie þe erthe with tonge" (C.10.187–201). On these and related clerical responsibilities and the C text's increased emphasis on them, see also my article "*Piers Plowman* and the Liturgy of St. Lawrence: Composition and Revision in Langland's Poetry," *Studies in Philology* 84 (1987): 266–68 and 268 n. 35.

[44] Cf. Dante's treatment of the schismatics and makers of discord in *Inferno* 28.

propagation of goodness in the Church also have important connections with other spiritual propagations in *Piers Plowman*, and it is on those connections that I wish to close this essay. At the start of the Tree of the Church passage in B, Anima paraphrases pseudo-Chrysostom's words, telling Will that just as

> holynesse and honeste out of holy chirche spryngeþ
> Thoruȝ lele libbynge men þat goddes lawe techen,
> Right so out of holi chirche alle yueles spredeþ
> There inparfit preesthode is, prechours and techeris.
>
> (B.15.92–95)

In C, the poet reinforces the image of good deeds "springing" forth, like the leaves he is about to describe, by adding two more verbs of germination to describe the growth of holiness; he also points more explicitly to the priestly and prelatical calling of those who should be teaching God's law and to the perfection they should have:

> As holiness and honestee out of holy churche
> Spryngeth and *spredeth* and *enspireth* þe peple
> Thorw *parfit preesthoed and prelates* of holy churche,
> Riht so oute of holy churche al euel spredeth
> There inparfit preesthoed is, prechares and techares.
>
> (C.16.242–46; my emphasis)

For Langland, "enspiring" is not only the work of inspiration (based on the word *spiritus* "breath, spirit"), but also the work of sending forth spires, or leafy blades.[45] The double sense need not surprise us, given Chaucer's famous clause, "Whan Zephirus . . . / Inspired hath . . . / The tendre croppes" (*Canterbury Tales* I.5–7), which clearly envisions the west wind breathing into the young blades of spring and unfurling them from within. What is most interesting about the words "springen," "(en)spiren," and "spreden" is that they are all words that Langland applies to the action of the Holy Spirit, especially in his role as *inspirator* and medium of God's word in the world. In the C text, Faith says that "o speche and spirit springeth out of alle [persons of the Trinity]"; comparing the Trinity to Adam, Eve, and Abel, he tells Will that the Spirit proceeds from the Father and Son just as "Abel of Adam and of his wyf Eue / Sprang forth and spak, a spyer of hem tweyne" (C.18.189, 230–31).[46] In B, Wit describes speech as a "spire of grace" and "goddes gleman," suggesting the Spirit-inspired words that should be uttered with the gift of language (B.9.103–4). In both texts, Imaginatif tells Will that grace is a healing grass that grows through the

---

[45] R. A. Shoaf has conclusively demonstrated this double meaning for an earlier passage in the poem, in his "'Speche þat Spire Is of Grace': A Note on *Piers Plowman* B.9.104," *Yearbook of Langland Studies* 1 (1987): 128–33. See also Szittya, 253.

[46] On this passage in C.18, see my "Kindly Similitude: Langland's Matrimonial Trinity," *Modern Philology* 80 (1982): 117–28.

gift of the Holy Ghost, for the *Spiritus vbi vult spirat*;[47] moreover, he says that it is "a gifte of god and of greet loue spryngeþ" (B.12.68) or that God "sent forth the seynt espirit to do loue sprynge" (C.14.27). In both texts, we learn that the "*Spiritus paraclitus* ouerspradde" all the Apostles, teaching them "alle kynne langages" so that they could preach the Gospel (B.19.200–206/C.21.200–206). And there are other passages that employ the imagery of springing, though not the word itself, to describe the work of the Spirit – leaping from heaven into Mary's womb, or flaming forth when a torch catches fire.

The arboreal imagery in Liberum Arbitrium's speech thus superimposes the work of the Church and her priests with the work of the Holy Spirit – an appropriate conflation, since the Spirit pours forth his grace on the world most fully through the Church, and most especially through the sacraments and preaching performed by priests. For the clergy to be cold and loveless is for the primary medium of divine grace and love to be chilled; but once that clergy is purified so that its members seek after spiritual perfection instead of material gain, then grace and charity will be able to bring the unending heavenly summer to human hearts. What is charity? *Sub specie aeternitatis*, it is God's own *kynde*, the Holy Spirit, Grace, as the Dreamer will learn from the Good Samaritan. When it springs forth to earth, however, it manifests itself first in the Incarnate Word, conceived of the Virgin by the Spirit speaking through Gabriel; after Christ's Resurrection and Ascension, the Spirit springs forth again in tongues of fire, to animate the mystical body of Christ and to inspire its propagation through Piers's preacherly plowing. This indwelling of the Spirit in Holy Church happens not in the church as an imperfect and worldly institution, but rather in the Church as an organic, indivisible, spiritual community. In a very deep sense, Holy Church *is* charity, God's grace and *kynde* at work in the world: "a loue-knotte of leutee and of lele byleue," the mustard tree that "shooteth out great branches so that the birds of the air may dwell under the shadow thereof" (Mark 4:31–32; cf. Matt. 13:31–32, Luke 13:18). Once her barren roots and limbs are revivified from within or pruned away, she can complete the millenarian mission of converting all nations, bringing them to dwell in perpetual peace, "Lief and loue and leutee in o byleue and lawe, / . . . Alle kyne cristene cleuynge on o will."

Through its revised arboreal images and its definition of Holy Church as charity, Liberum Arbitrium's discourse prepares the way for the Tree of Charity even more fully than Anima had done, and with different emphases. Those images originate in Anima's description of the Tree of the Church, but the revisions in C intensify their eschatological overtones and increase their effectiveness in expressing both the ideal and the all-too-actual role of the

---

[47] The pun on *gras* and *grace* can be found elsewhere in the alliterative tradition, as Erik Kooper has shown; see '*Grace*: The Healing Herb in *William of Palerne*," *Leeds Studies in English* n.s. 15 (1984): 83–93; see also Susanna Greer Fein, "Why Did Absolon Put a 'Trewelove' Under His Tongue? Herb Paris as a Healing 'Grace' in Middle English Literature," *Chaucer Review* 25 (1990–91): 302–17.

Church hierarchy as a channel for grace and charity.[48] (For the laity's role in the propagation of charity, we can look forward to the Tree of Charity in the next passus.) In both B and C, the discourse also looks back to issues raised since Will set out in search of Dowel – the right use of clerical learning, the salvation of the heathen, religious poverty and hypocrisy; and it sets the stage for the exemplar *par excellence* of fruitful preaching and the loving fulfillment of prelatical duties, who will joust for man's soul even unto death. The heightenings of C's eschatological tone, created in part by the allusions to the Little Apocalypse and in part by the allusions to a universal peace and the tighter discussion of the conversion of Saracens and Jews, are admittedly a matter of degree rather than kind. However, when they are taken together with Liberum Arbitrium's increased emphasis on the Church herself as the manifestation of charity in the world, they draw our attention forward to the *aestas* promised by Christ himself, following and healing the winter-chill attacks of Antichrist:

> "Aftur sharpest shoures," quod Pees, "most shene is þe sonne;
> Is no wedore warmore then aftur watri cloudes,
> Ne no loue leuore, ne no leuore frendes,
> Then aftur werre and wrake when loue and pees ben maistres.
> Was neuere werre in this world ne wikkedere enuye
> That Loue, and hym luste, to louhynge it ne brouhte,
> And Pees thorw pacience alle perelles stopede."
>
> (C.20.455–61/B.18.409–15)

---

[48] As G. H. Russell has remarked, Anima's speech had already "draw[n] a picture, full of deliberately ordered apocalyptic significances" ("The Salvation of the Heathen," 109). What the C text does is to emphasize those significances through new images, allusions, and internal cross-linkages in Liberum Arbitrium's version of that speech.

The Triumph of Fiction
in the Nun's Priest's Tale

MONICA E. MCALPINE

The Nun's Priest's Tale triumphantly demonstrates the capacity of fiction to project a vision of human reality, however remote a fictional world may be in its literal particulars from human actuality. While clearly characterizing fiction as a mode of knowing typical of a fallen world, it nevertheless validates certain distinctive means and results of the art as compared with those of philosophy and theology, showing fiction to be independent of but not unrelated to those alternative modes of description. The triumph lies in the breadth and depth, paradox and poise of the vision the tale offers as well as in the way the tale transcends self-generated obstacles in order to achieve this victory.

The obstacles are well known. Some of the most brilliant criticism written about the *Canterbury Tales* has been devoted to detailing the mix of broad comedy and scalpel-like subtlety Chaucer deploys in mischievously setting up and then exploding the resources of fiction and the learned procedures of its interpretation. The dominant critical tradition, evolved over more than thirty years, sees the tale as a mock-epic treatment of language, rhetoric, and learning and of the human pretension that so often drives and directs their uses. Typically, the mockery is understood as not wholly negative in effect but as occasioning a release of energy in hilarity and delight, a release that has the power to cleanse our vanity-befogged vision. It is a requirement of this reading, though, that the poem have no meaning except its escape from meaning; this escape, involving a firm rejection of interpretative response, is thought to constitute the nature of Chaucer's tour de force in this text. As Derek Pearsall has succinctly put it, "the fact that the tale has no point is the point of the tale."[1]

Indeed, the possibilities for meaning have come to be arranged in a fairly rigid dichotomy. On the one side is what Pearsall calls "interpretative studies," embracing the efforts of allegorizers and moralizers, and on the other, "noninterpretative evaluation," focusing on the mock-epic satire, understood

[1] *The Nun's Priest's Tale*, ed. Derek Pearsall, vol. 2, pt. 9 of *A Variorum Edition of The Works of Geoffrey Chaucer* (Norman: University of Oklahoma Press, 1984), 12.

as destructive of any significance requiring or allowing interpretation (50, 65). Moreover, readers are often warned against "solemnity" (much as they used to be warned against "carnality" by Robertsonians) on the authority of a statement by Charles Muscatine which is interpreted over-precisely and taken out of context. Muscatine's view that the tale "tests truths and tries out solemnities" rather than asserting them would seem to leave room for a more exploratory approach than is now generally thought appropriate. Moreover, he went on to say that Chaucer's satire is less in need of demonstration than his "wise conservatism," in which the tale's solemn targets are not always funny and relativism is itself relative to the implied existence of absolute truth.[2]

Muscatine's reading has also been narrowed by conflation with E. T. Donaldson's argument that the point of the tale lies in "the enormous rhetorical elaboration of the telling." Donaldson established a more exclusive emphasis on rhetoric and, in contrast to Muscatine's belief in the orthodox piety of the tale, projected a suspiciously modernist "inscrutable reality" and "vast and alien universe" against which rhetoric is a "powerful weapon of survival" but ultimately an "inadequate defense."[3] The continuing tendency to see all the materials of the poem as manifestations of language (however broadly conceived) has restricted the poem's perceived import, weakening an appreciation of what Muscatine recognized as the work's almost encyclopedic range of references to human endeavors and concerns.[4]

Between the two antithetically defined camps of modern criticism of this text, there exists, at least theoretically, a great deal of room. This space has also been marked out in practice by readers, some of them cited in the course of my argument, who have explored the wisdom of the poem without imposing extrinsic allegorizations or resorting to flaccid moralizations. Is it possible that still other commentaries might have articulated the affirmations of this tale more fully if they were not constrained by the prevailing critical orthodoxy? The Nun's Priest's Tale is a masterful mock-epic work; it remains to ask whether, like the greatest comic fictions, it also turns laughter into vision. Perhaps this essay, whatever the fate of its specific arguments, may have some

[2] Muscatine's often quoted statement reads: "the *Nun's Priest's Tale* does not so much make true and solemn assertions about life as it tests truths and tries out solemnities. If you are not careful, it will try out your solemnity too." All the references to Muscatine in this paragraph are to *Chaucer and the French Tradition* (1957; Berkeley and Los Angeles: University of California Press, 1987), 242–43. Muscatine later restated his belief in the orthodox piety of the tale in *Poetry and Crisis in the Age of Chaucer* (Notre Dame: University of Notre Dame Press, 1972), 113, as noted by Pearsall (68).

[3] *Chaucer's Poetry: An Anthology for the Modern Reader*, ed. E. Talbot Donaldson (New York: Ronald Press, 1958), 941–2; and *Speaking of Chaucer* (London: Athlone, 1970), 149.

[4] At the same time, of course, such studies have made more sophisticated our understanding of Chaucer's materials and methods in this tale. See Ian Bishop, "The Nun's Priest's Tale and the Liberal Arts," *Review of English Studies* 30 (1979): 257–67; and Peter Travis, "The *Nun's Priest's Tale* as Grammar-School Primer," *Studies in the Age of Chaucer* 1 (1984): 81–91, and "Chaucer's trivial fox chase and the Peasants' Revolt of 1381," *Journal of Medieval and Renaissance Studies* 18 (1988): 195–220.

value as a call for a more open-ended exploration of the making of meaning in this text.

The reading of the poem as elevating only to subvert, as offering a mock-epic satire exposing only the limits of language and by implication of fiction, cannot account for the acknowledged brilliance of the poem's deployment of the resources of the art. The famed description of Chauntecleer's appearance may serve as an example (VII.2847-64).[5] As Muscatine says, it "expands, climbs, brightens, then bursts like a rocket into a shower of color."[6] Contrasting it with the preceding description of the widow, he comments on the description's shock effect and likens it to other examples of shifting perspectives, a major strategy of Chaucer's mock-heroics. An irreducible value in this poetry is not fully acknowledged, however, by citing local effects or mock-heroic strategy. Beyond offering a gratuitous display of Chaucer's facility, such passages constitute a fundamental declaration of *faith* in language – in its materials, methods, and power to signify. In the dominant reading, this power co-exists incoherently with the allegedly single-minded intent of the work to explode the potential-to-mean of rhetoric. I will argue that the tale has a broader agenda, one that ultimately affirms the value of the art whose limitations and misuses it so fully documents. As Morton Bloomfield said of this tale, the art that elevates in order to subvert also subverts in order to elevate.[7]

A key passage provides textual warrant for focusing on the authority of story – of language organized into narrative – and for considering that authority in a more dialectical way than the oppositional structure of the mock-heroic would ordinarily allow: "This storie is also trewe, I undertake, / As is the book of Launcelot de Lake, / That wommen holde in ful greet reverence" (VII.3211-13). The narrator affects to defend the significance of his fable, but the irony of his statement is transparent. He implies that his story is as meaningless, or at least that he intends to render it as meaningless, as certain romantic stories favored by women. The comparative structure, "also trewe . . . As," underpins this obvious irony, but Chaucer also uses this same structure to surface critical questions of his own. How true *is* the story of Lancelot? If it holds no truth, what makes it false? If it is true in some sense, what is the nature of that truth? The condescending reference to women functions both to explain the Nun's Priest's dismissive attitude toward the

---

5 All references to the texts of Chaucer's works are to *The Riverside Chaucer*, 3d ed., gen. ed. Larry D. Benson (Boston: Houghton Mifflin, 1987).

6 *Chaucer and the French Tradition*, 239.

7 Morton W. Bloomfield, "The Wisdom of the Nun's Priest's Tale," in Edward Vasta and Zacharias P. Thundy, eds., *Chaucerian Problems and Perspectives: Essays Presented to Paul E. Beichner, C. S. C.* (Notre Dame: University of Notre Dame, 1979), 70-82. On the limits of the mock-heroic aspect, see also Peter Elbow, *Oppositions in Chaucer* (Middletown, CT: Wesleyan University Press, 1975), 112: "The point that the poem makes most powerfully – and it must express one of Chaucer's deepest convictions – is . . . [that] to put events into words as full as possible of color, dignity, and extra meaning is as important an activity as humans can engage in."

story of Lancelot and to limit the authority of the Priest's view. Those who do not share his view of women are presumably also free to entertain other ideas about the story of Lancelot. Without repressing the hit at the absurdities of some romances, Chaucer reinstates the literal sense of the statement, implying that the story of a "fabulous" beast can be as meaning*ful* as the story of a non-existent knight. The linkage of stories that are *not verisimilar* with stories that are *not verifiable* suggests that fiction itself and its defense are a subject of these lines. Readers who are sure that this story of a cock and a fox must be without significance for humans because it is a story about animals are mistaken, even though the narrative repeatedly, hilariously invites them to take this position. They are mistaken because their position involves the risk of undermining the potential-to-mean of all fiction, a potential that Chauntecleer and Lancelot equally represent.[8]

A significant aspect of the Lancelot passage is the way in which a question about *interpreting* a story becomes a question about the value of story in general. The problem of perceiving meaning is linked to the possibility of generating meaning. Although I believe the argument for Chaucer's recuperation of the powers of art might be made in a number of ways, I am going to follow this thread from the interpretation of meaning to the making of meaning. Interpretation is both an activity dramatized in the tale and an issue thematized in certain ways not generally recognized. Interest has focused on the narrator's glossing of his beast fable and on the argument over dreams in the debate, but interpretation is also an issue in Chauntecleer's encounter with the fox and in the chase scene. These varied occasions for interpretation show that it is not an optional activity that always or only inflates significances to satisfy vanity or reduces significances to produce reassuring platitudes. Rather they show that interpretation is inescapable and applies to events as well as texts; that it is typically a complex, dialectical, and open-ended process; and that it can involve significant consequences. The sense that something is at stake in interpretation gives depth to the satire on language, rhetoric, and learning, and restores an essential link between fiction and experience. The nature of interpretation and the powers of fiction are clarified in tandem.

The human desire to interpret, its typical mixtures of motives, and its often misguided products are repeatedly skewered in the tale, but that desire and the necessities to which it responds are also validated by Chaucer and allusively placed in a theological perspective as part of a richly parodoxical treatment. The theological definition of the world as fallen shapes both the content of the

---

[8] The major study of the subject of fiction in the tale is Robert Burlin, *Chaucerian Fiction* (Princeton: Princeton University Press, 1977), 228–34. His conclusion is consistent with the dominant critical tradition: "The true 'moralitee' of the *Nun's Priest's Tale* extends the incidental abuses of language, 'jangling' and 'flaterye,' to puncture all the inflation of human discourse by means of rhetoric and fictions as, in essence, a striving after wind" (232). At the same time, he grants that "Chaucer's radical ambivalence toward the rationale of fiction . . . can only be properly expressed by the *experience* of fiction" (234). See also Saul Nathaniel Brody, "Truth and Fiction in the *Nun's Priest's Tale*," *Chaucer Review* 14 (1979–80): 33–47.

fiction and the project of testing and reaffirming the powers of fiction. Moreover, the refusal to interpret finds its representation in the tale, too, in the much-discussed behavior of the Nun's Priest; through him the dominant position of modern criticism is anticipated by Chaucer and shown to be only a partial and inadequate response to the problems of perceiving and creating meaning in a fallen world. We must achieve a more comprehensive understanding of interpretation than the one the narrator offers in order to perceive fiction in a Chaucerian perspective.

If the Priest's perspective were essentially Chaucer's, as many readers believe, the significance of the fable might well "[yield] to exposition only as a tone," as R. T. Lenaghan has suggested.[9] Because I believe the Priest and his attitudes are part of a larger pattern beyond his ken and orchestrated by Chaucer, I will attempt, while following A. Paul Shallers in rejecting morals and allegories,[10] to describe the implicit *vision* projected by the poem. That vision is distilled in the portion of the work already most familiar to Chaucer's audience, probably through visual representations – the chase scene.[11] If, as Kenneth Sisam suggested, the story constitutes a series of digressions delaying the moment of the famed chase,[12] that may be because the purpose of the story in one sense is to generate the significances that are then condensed in that glorious scene. As we have read the tale, so we will read the chase. Funny, disorderly, cathartic, even carnivalistic,[13] the chase scene is also comic in a visionary sense. There Chaucer climactically reclaims the authority of fiction tested in his tale as he projects a comprehensive vision of human life reminiscent of a story about Gawain, if not of Lancelot. For the chase scene provides a powerful counterpart to the *Gawain*-poet's cycles of history descending from Troy, in the other great work of the period devoted to the conundrums and urgencies, personal and social, of interpretation and choice.

The Nun's Priest's Tale is an elaborately patterned work that makes use of familiar Chaucerian devices: an early digression or amplification to channel the implications of the plot; complementarity of narrative and narratorial commentary; receding and projecting frames of reference; complication of traditional devices of closure. Chaucer alternates between concrete instances and generalization, and uses different kinds of generalizations to create a sense of deepening perspective from foreground to background. He builds an extraordinarily strong case for one position and yet insists on the validity of the opposite case as well. In thematizing interpretation as part of the project of

[9] R. T. Lenaghan, "The Nun's Priest's Fable," *PMLA* 78 (1963): 307.

[10] A. Paul Shallers, "The 'Nun's Priest's Tale': An Ironic Exemplum," *ELH* 42 (1975): 319–37.

[11] See Kenneth Varty, *Reynard the Fox: A Study of the Fox in Medieval English Art* (New York: Humanities Press, 1967).

[12] Kenneth Sisam, "Introduction," *Chaucer: The Nun's Priest's Tale* (Oxford: Clarendon Press, 1927).

[13] See Travis, "Chaucer's trivial fox chase," and John M. Ganim, *Chaucerian Theatricality* (Princeton: Princeton University Press, 1990), 98–106 and 113–17.

redeeming fiction, Chaucer employs these patterns and devices in a thoroughly dialectical way. He shows the unavoidable need for interpretation of both experience and texts and at the same time the fated fallibility of all interpreters and meaning-makers. He dramatizes the attempt to escape from this dilemma through the denial of meaning and the refusal to interpret, but shows that this stance is not sustainable. Eschewing morals and yet acknowledging the urgency of the human need for guidance, Chaucer demonstrates fiction's limited but crucial power – even when it does not provide verisimilar reflections of our actuality – to enlighten and sustain us through creating visions answerable to our reality.

The Fable

Fables in which a fox is a principal figure frequently involve a speech of persuasion or seduction on the fox's part and, sometimes less explicitly, an answering act of interpretation by the fox's auditor within the fable.[14] Readers or real-life auditors may be made aware of this act of interpretation by the intended victim's speech or reflections or only by his subsequent action or by the complementary and sometimes different interpretation that the fox's speech evokes from them. We see, for example, that Chauntecleer pays attention to some cues in Russell's speech and ignores others; we immediately understand that Russell's account of his relationship with Chauntecleer's father is open to a very different construction from the one the fox proposes. As readers we are thus conscious of the activity of interpretation, as are, typically, those animals in fable who escape a fox's machinations. Those who succumb, like Chauntecleer in that moment when he closes his eyes, stretches out his neck, and sings, may scarcely be conscious of interpreting at all, whether because they are blinded by vanity or for some other reason. One of the fable's implications, then, concerns the danger of obliviousness to the need for interpretation in experience – an observation that a single-minded emphasis on the follies of interpreting tends to occlude from view.

Indeed, one could say that the chief effect of the fox's seizure of Chauntecleer is to plunge the cock into urgent and hyper-conscious acts of retrospective interpretation. The experience of being seized and the instinct for survival purge Chauntecleer of the blinding effects of vanity. They reveal his earlier estimate of the fox's motives to have been mistaken, they reveal the fox's true motives, and they reveal the means – an appeal to vanity – by which the fox misled Chauntecleer; thereby they also suggest the means by which the cock may now turn the tables on the fox – by making a matching appeal to his vanity. All of this we infer from Chauntecleer's subsequent action in speaking

---

[14] Examples from *Caxton's Aesop*, ed. R. T. Lenaghan (Cambridge, Mass.: Harvard University Press, 1967), include: "Raven and the fox" (83–84), "Fox and the wolf" (108–9), "Wolf, the fox, and the mule" (137), "Fox and the goat" (167), and "Cock, the fox and the dogs" (223–25).

to the fox, for the cock's cogitations are represented in the text only by silence, a common though not uniform feature of Aesopic narrative. Part of the pleasure of reading those spare narratives lies in grasping and representing to ourselves – no doubt in different degrees of explicitness for different individuals – what it is that goes on in such silences. Within Chaucer's tale, the sharp contrast between Chauntecleer's silent calculations while in the jaws of the fox and his loquacious posturings while engaged in debate with Pertelote is instructive, amusing, and consoling – suggesting that even the most narcissistic of interpreters may be capable of clear thinking in a crisis, as he will need to be. Interpreting, as we will be reminded again later, can be a life-and-death matter.

The Debate

Although fables invite the kinds of interpretative responses just described, they do not problematize the activity of interpretation. Chaucer effects this further development through the debate on dreams between Chauntecleer and Pertelote. Inserting a debate after the chief character has been introduced but before the main action takes place, Chaucer prospectively shapes the meaning of that action,[15] placing squarely at the heart of the poem a question of exegesis, of interpretation.[16] Occasioned by Chauntecleer's dream, the debate is articulated as a consideration of the nature of dreams per se. But just as Chauntecleer's dream is an instance of all dreaming, so the nature of dreams is a puzzle representing other puzzles, whose exploration reveals as much about the nature of the knower as about the phenomenon itself.[17] What is most important about the debate is not how it relates to events that later befall Chauntecleer nor even the positions it articulates on dreams in general but what it reveals about how interpretative positions are chosen around any substantive issue. A discursive form, the debate voices what is unvoiced in the fable narrative – the intellectual, emotional, and temperamental factors involved in choosing interpretations.

Only Chauntecleer and Pertelote together can represent the Chaucerian paradigm of human knowing, and that is why it is crucial that readers not focus on deciding which of them is "right."[18] They approach the broad issue of dreams in two distinctive intellectual styles that are linked to gender but whose

---

[15] Burlin, 231, notes the close likeness to the structuring of the Merchant's Tale.

[16] Elbow, 95.

[17] Cf. *Boece* 5.pr 4.137–40: "for al that evere is iknowe, it is rather comprehendid and knowen, nat aftir his strengthe and his nature, but aftir the faculte (that is to seyn, the power and the nature) of hem that knowen."

[18] Sheila Delany makes a welcome protest against the denigration of Pertelote's perspective in "'Mulier est hominis confusio': Chaucer's anti-popular *Nun's Priest's Tale*," *Mosaic* 17 (1984): 1–8; reprinted in *Medieval Literary Politics: Shapes of Ideology* (Manchester: Manchester University Press, 1990), 141–50. I think that denigration is peculiar to modern criticism, however, and not integral to Chaucer's treatment of his fable.

significance is not exhausted by their associations with gender. In Elbow's terms (95–105), Chauntecleer's is the speculative intellect, focused on meaning, spirit, authority, and insight, while Pertelote's is the empirical intellect, focused on cause, body, experience, and action. Both are limited ways of knowing; neither is definitively superior to the other. Moreover, medieval authorities can be cited to support both the view that dreams are physiological events and the view that they are prophetic. Indeed, in order to support Chaucer's exploratory depiction of the ways of human knowing, the issue used had to be one for which there existed conflicting but equally authoritative positions. Each theory of dreams has, within the medieval context at least, truth value; and in human experience generally, each intellectual style has utility. Yet neither theory, it seems, can account for all dreams, nor can either type of intellect provide more than a partial understanding of any phenomenon.

Commentary on the debate usually emphasizes the ways in which vanity, concupiscence, and other weaknesses distort the rational workings of the mind. The relationship might also be expressed in reverse, however. The partiality and uncertainty of human knowledge open the gaps that are filled by desire. Mingling dream theory, exempla, and authorities with laxatives, beards, and treadings, Chaucer portrays this dialectical relationship, concretizing representative acts of human knowing in ways that invite readers to arrive inductively at the underlying insights. In the process, they recognize themselves, partly in spite of the fact that their representatives are chickens and partly because of the hilarious and sobering discovery that distinctively human traits can be communicated so clearly through subhuman figures. Using the distinctive means available in fiction, Chaucer defines, explains, and most of all, explores propositions about human beings which had already received alternative kinds of formulation, pre-eminently in the theology of the Fall.

The Adamic Motif

Any attempt to discuss this motif must overcome three objections arising from the tale's critical history.[19] First, some allegorical readings have depended wholly on external traditions of iconography without any literal warrant in the text. By contrast, the Adamic myth is anchored in the literal text: in the comparative reference to the seasons of Adam's fall and of Chauntecleer's adventure (VII.3187–97), in the Priest's proposed anti-feminist interpretation of the Fall (3257–59), and more allusively, in the fox's question to Chauntecleer, "konne ye youre fader countrefete?" (3321). These references are of different kinds and appear in different parts of the narrative; in proposing the Fall as a significant context, we are following Chaucer's lead. Second, readings of the tale as an *allegory* of the Fall have rightly been rejected as dead-end; they inhibit our interaction with the work because they assume that Chaucer regarded the doctrine of the Fall as a transparently intelligible

[19] Pearsall, *The Nun's Priest's Tale*, 50–64, 79–80.

teaching toward which he need only point his audience. On the contrary, the Priest's anti-feminist misinterpretation introduces the difficulty of properly understanding the biblical fable and tells us that its meaning is at stake as we interpret Chaucer's animal fable. Third and last, it has rightly been observed that Chauntecleer is obviously already fallen; therefore, his adventure cannot logically be read as a version of the original Fall. Indeed, the fox's question to Chauntecleer about imitating his father makes sense only if Chauntecleer's status is comparable not to Adam's but to fallen humanity's. Rather than invalidating attention to the biblical story, however, this fact helps us to align Chaucer's work more accurately with theological speculation on the Fall.

Theologians distinguished between the *peccatum originans*, the sin of Adam himself, the *peccatum originatum*, the inherited state of sinfulness of Adam's descendants, and personal sin, specific instances of wrongful action by individuals.[20] The second of these, the inherited state of sin, as the most distinctive part of the doctrine, attracted attention particularly in terms of specifying the exact nature of that inheritance. The identification in Genesis of certain consequences of Adam's sin – death, labor, pain in childbirth, and male domination – did not close the question but authorized attempts to define more inward effects. Aquinas analyzes four "wounds" to human nature: ignorance, weakness, concupiscence, and malice (*Summa Theologiae* 1a2ae.85.3). The motif of the wounds is traditional, reaching back to Augustine, who develops the motif not with scholastic abstractions but with homely details drawn from everyday life (*City of God*, 22.22). For example, he cites our difficulty in learning anything and our greater difficulty in remembering what we have learned as evidences of our inherited ignorance.

Chaucer's text does not present an allegory of the Fall, of the *peccatum originans*. Rather it constitutes a poetic equivalent of theological texts that seek to expound the *peccatum originatum*, the state of inherited sinfulness. The text is not a collection of symbols pointing to a doctrine whose meaning poses no challenge; it is rather a place where Chaucer deploys, in place of the theologian's logical analysis and scriptural exegesis, the resources of art to explore the implications of a major concept about the human condition. Further, while giving attention to the various wounds cited by Aquinas, Chaucer's fable is centrally concerned with the wound of ignorance, with all the factors and circumstances that disable human interpreters. While providing an occasion for the display of the vanity that will later prove almost fatal to Chauntecleer, the debate on dreams is also the principal vehicle for Chaucer's representation of the pre-existing, inherited state of ignorance, which in another sense explains Chauntecleer's succumbing to the fox. The allusions to the Adamic story deepen the receding perspectives of the narrative, exposing the theological underpinnings of the debate on dreams, which itself thematizes the activity of interpretation enacted in the fable.

---

[20] Henri Rondet, *Original Sin: The Patristic and Theological Background*, trans. Cajetan Finegan (Staten Island: Alba House, 1972), 7 and *passim*. Originally published as *Le péché originel dans la tradition patristique et théologique* (Paris: Librairie Fayard, 1967).

Finally, Chaucer is fully aware of the paradox of a fallible creature's struggle to understand rightly the doctrine of his own fallibility. In another typical Chaucerian strategy, the fox's question to Chauntecleer - "konne ye youre fader countrefete?" - cuts in several directions at once. Are you capable of singing as superbly as your father sang? Will you agree now to try to match his singing? Is it your fate to act as your father did, i.e., succumb to this fox? Is it your fate to act as your father did in general terms, though not necessarily in this specific instance? In this last sense, as applied to humans, the question is really the disguised statement of a truth; for every human being is constrained by the inherited state of sin to follow in Adam's footsteps in some manner. Distracted by the fox's appeals to his vanity, however, Chauntecleer misinterprets the history of his parents, just as the Nun's Priest misinterprets the biblical story of the Fall in anti-feminist terms and just as humans generally are likely to fail to grasp its meaning, whether theoretically, like the Priest, or practically, like Chauntecleer. Chaucer shows that the Adamic inheritance, as expressed in the wound of ignorance, interferes, paradoxically, with humans' right understanding of Genesis, although insight into Genesis is crucial to unraveling the perplexities of their present experience.

Narratorial Commentary

The narratorial commentary of the Nun's Priest constitutes, after the fable and the debate, the third, most overt aspect of Chaucer's thematizing of interpretation. The Priest is defined essentially by his activity of narration and the attitudes it implies,[21] and his narration is itself double-voiced, as has been well observed by Lenaghan.[22] One voice is that of "the naive, spouting *rethor*," and the other that of "the acute teller" of the tale, a sophisticated fabulist: "The *rethor* is an actor on the Nun's Priest's stage. The teller of the tale creates a caricature *rethor* by making his rhetoric ridiculous." The body of rhetorical assertions is explicit and voluminous, and yet as Elbow observes (110), commenting on a typical pattern in Chaucer, its invitation to say "yea" evokes only a "truncated" affirmation from readers, if any affirmation at all, the irony being so broad. By contrast, I would observe, the critical perspective on this rhetoric, the invitation to say "nay," is only

---

[21] By comparison, what H. Marshall Leicester, in *The Disenchanted Self: Representing the Subject in the "Canterbury Tales"* (Berkeley and Los Angeles: University of California Press, 1990), 12, calls "dramatization of the Canterbury sort" - e.g., the Priest's relationship to the Prioress as that may be reflected in the tale - is of relatively little importance. Ganim, 105-6, offers a tactful analysis, however, of how the Priest's presence in the Prologue to his tale anticipates his narrative stance. While I cannot detail here my reservations about Leicester's determination to attribute all effects produced by a text to its narrator, my reading does demonstrate what difference it may make to distinguish the Priest from Chaucer.

[22] "The Nun's Priest's Fable," 305.

implied, and yet it draws a resounding affirmation from readers. The dismissive perspective of the "acute teller" is commonly thought to be Chaucer's as well and essentially defines the dominant position of modern criticism, whose practitioners do not want to be caught in the Priest's "net," as Lenaghan terms it. With Elbow, however, I believe that the poem as a whole implies a third perspective. The Priest's narration, in both its voices, is part of a larger pattern concerning the making of meaning orchestrated by Chaucer.

The implication of the Priest in this pattern is most clearly suggested by a unique event in the course of his narration – his advance and withdrawal of the suggestion that Chauntecleer's adventure exemplifies once again the predictably disastrous results of feminine counsel first demonstrated in Adam's fall (VII.3257–66). The anti-feminist content, including the misrepresentation of the Fall, already indicates that the Priest is likely to be an object of the poem's scrutiny rather than its spokesman, but this narrative event is also significant as *gesture*, irrespective of its content. Here a narrator who has taken an implied stance against all interpretation projects and protects his own reading of the story and perhaps also of experience. The withdrawal of the reading, the unique element in this narrative event, covertly and not-so-covertly maintains the Priest's reading in two ways. First, since we know that he advances what he does not credit, we can assume that what he withdraws, he does credit. Secondly, the cancellation of the interpretation is a way of preserving it. By withdrawing this reading from the arena where it and other readings would be evaluated, the Priest can continue to enjoy the specious comfort of his own unexamined and uncontested act of interpretation. Through the Priest Chaucer dramatizes both the temptation to withdraw from interpretation, a complacent exemption of oneself from fallibility, and, ironically, the impossibility of completely suppressing either the urge to interpret or the desire to secure some of the satisfactions, however ill-founded, of interpreting.

It might be argued that the Priest's *lapse* into interpretation only constitutes more evidence that we should abstain from interpreting this cock-and-fox story. On the other hand, the fallibility of this narrator, as suggested clearly but not only by this unique narrative event, raises questions about the authority of his radically reductive position and about the appropriateness of identifying it in any simple way with Chaucer's. To do so is to run the risk of being caught in *Chaucer's* net, by associating ourselves with a position he has already co-opted in the service of a larger argument and vision. The pattern of the poem, as I have construed it in commenting on the fable, the dream, and the Adamic motif, already indicates that abstinence from interpretation is neither possible nor desirable in any world, Chauntecleer's or ours, that requires choices and assigns significant consequences to them, however bedeviled those choices may be by the limitations of human knowing and the vagaries of human passion. Chaucer brings this point home again in the crucial fourth site for the theme of interpretation, the famous chase scene.

The Chase Scene

Chaucer's hilarious sabotaging of the usual analogical relationship between humans and the animal figures of fable is generally thought to indicate that he meant to destroy this connection utterly within this text, as a principal strategy for rendering the story brilliantly pointless. This is not the only possible perspective, however. Alternatively, his playfulness may be seen as a way of unsettling his audience's traditional expectations as preparation for renewing the power of the connection in an original way. This he does, climactically, in the chase scene where the human and animal worlds of the widow's farm, subtly teased apart in the early lines of the poem, are suddenly, breathtakingly, reunited. The widow, stored in our memory like the Miller's carpenter in his hanging tub, bursts out of her cottage and out of the framing "real world" of this tale, passing over the dry ditch and the paling of sticks into Chauntecleer's world. And Chauntecleer, now so well known to us as the hero of his own story, becomes, for the duration of this scene as at no other moment in the poem, at once a "fabulous" beast and the widow's own rooster. At the same time the borders of the Priest's fictional world, too, are breached, opened to those of the actual world of the Priest and his pilgrim-audience, through his allusion to the Peasants' Revolt. Often thought to be only tangentially related to the scene and the story, the allusion is in fact intricately woven into both. The pursuit of the Flemings by Jack Straw and his "meynee" adds a second level of event, parallel to and mirroring the horizontal plane on which the primary series of chases – of humans and dogs, of cow, calf and hogs, of ducks, geese, and bees – is exploding by chain reaction. For the first time in the poem, in the comparison of the noises made by rebels and fox-chasers, human beings are members of both groups being compared; the distinction of species, animal and human, fades, and the distance between tenor and vehicle begins to collapse. Finally, the allusion itself involves a double synecdoche in which the attack on the Flemings stands for the Great Revolt in its entirety, and the Revolt, partly because of the context supplied by the Monk's Tale, acquires the status of a "Modern Instance," representing other events in secular history that demand and often defeat our understanding.[23]

These two features, the confounding of human and animal species and the merging of fictional and actual worlds, indicate first of all that Chaucer intends his animal fable to have implications for human experience and secondly that this scene is the place in the text where Chaucer addresses those implications most directly. We will find no Aesopic moral here, however, nor any explicit philosophical or theological formulation.[24] Instead, Chaucer gives us, in the

---

[23] The confusion of animal and human has been intricately analyzed by Travis, "Chaucer's trivial fox chase," 211–12. His discussion of the allusion to the Revolt (212–19) is also compatible in a number of ways with mine.

[24] In "The *Speculum Stultorum* and the *Nun's Priest's Tale*," *Chaucer Review* 9 (1974–75), Jill Mann writes well of "the basic intractability of human nature and human experience, its resistance to organisation in terms of intellectual and moral analysis" (277).

allusion to the Uprising, an alternative kind of application of fiction to actuality, a troubling *test case* whose significance it is wholly up to us to determine. The tale is not irrelevant to this interpretative task, however; rather it provides, in spite of its chickenyard setting, precisely what is lacking in the Monk's moralized tragedies, an *experience of fiction*, an imaginative engagement with a version of our reality that maps for us some of the essential coordinates of our earthly condition. Bringing the test case and the experience of fiction together, we confront the true nature of interpretation: invariably individual-istic, necessarily uncertain and fallible, and, often at least, highly consequential. Chaucer's procedure here seems an excellent example of what Donald Howard has described as the "birth of fiction" in the works of Boccaccio and Chaucer: the creation and deployment of hypothetical realities to be used by readers as tools for thinking about human experiences.[25]

Like so many Chaucerian devices of closure, then, the chase scene refers us back to the body of the tale. It also commands our special attention to itself, however, since among the several devices of closure Chaucer rapidly assembles here (including the resolution of the fable plot, the statement of the Aesopic morals, and the Priest's final address to the pilgrim-audience), the chase scene, as a distillation of the vision projected by this fiction, constitutes the tale's truest ending.

The broadly representative potential of a fox chase scene, comparable to that of pilgrimage, may have been suggested to Chaucer by what Travis has shown to be the prominent use of the proposition *homo currit* in texts on logic.[26] An important aspect of the scene in developing its emblematic significance is the structure of planes. The horizontal plane is dominant, as the fleeing fox draws behind him his determined pursuers, and as the participants set off chases-within-chases in a chain reaction. The actors are vehemently, single-mindedly intent on their own activities and purposes, enacting their freedom as they act on their interpretations. The actualities they represent are not limited to language and rhetoric but include as well communal life, society, history. The camera, so to speak, is drawn back just far enough to present the full scope of this action; at the same time, this very distance suggests the possibility of different perspectives not available to the actors themselves. As Donaldson and Burlin have remarked, we sense the poet's presence, and we can join him in contemplating his creatures with amusement, horror, affection, and self-recognition.[27] This sense of distanced perspective is also complemented, however, by the way the language of the passage creates a vertical axis intersecting the horizontal plane: there is a hell below (VII.3389), and there are heavens above (3401). The poet, his readers, his work of art, and by extension all fictions are implicated in the tale's central paradox of fallible interpreters attempting to grasp the meaning of a reality one of whose characteristics is

---

[25] Donald R. Howard, *Chaucer: His Life, His Works, His World* (New York: E. P. Dutton, 1987), 283–303.

[26] "Chaucer's trivial fox chase," 209–11.

[27] *Chaucer's Poetry*, 944; and Burlin, 227.

their own fallibility. Only the (implied) divine observer knows the full and true meaning of the chase.

Part of Chaucer's achievement here is to have created virtually single-handedly, though out of familiar materials, an emblematic image comparable to more conventional examples such as the dance of death. The comic poise implied by this image is peculiarly Chaucerian, and it is related to the absence of moralization. Chaucer's scene contains, I believe, no gloss upon itself. Aesopic narrative, overlaid with the Priest's ironical glosses, is replaced with a powerful kinetic image as free of gloss as Chaucer could make it, a distillate of the human reality he wishes us to contemplate. The pristine quality of the scene is suggested by the way the widow, her initial appearance controlled by the patrician condescension of the narrator,[28] now bursts from her cottage in her own autonomous being. Moreover, that hyper-conscious glossator, the Priest, now introduces his reference to the Great Uprising with an artless "a, benedicitee!" (3393). That is, he is, on this one occasion, affected by his own fiction and startled into introducing a spontaneous comparison.[29]

It is appropriate that the scene should be unglossed, for everything important has already been said. The morals that follow are mere detritus. Everything that *precedes* the chase scene is its gloss; as so often in Chaucer, the ending does not determine meaning but tests the meanings we have already found or takes their color. More importantly, the unglossed character of the scene is Chaucer's way of climactically demonstrating what fiction can do. Without any explicit moral or philosophical formulations, the scene embodies, the more richly because only implicitly, the experience and the vision of the tale as a whole. In one precisely detailed image of figures in motion across a landscape, Chaucer represents humanity entire and across time: its career full of delightful and dismaying significances, firmly conceived within a biblical perspective and yet resistant to confident, definitive interpretation. Partly to respect that richness of signification, which it is the triumph of fiction to have created, we should always project Chaucer's figures before our imagination in motion; their kinesis is part of their meaning.

In this delicate adjustment of horizontal and vertical planes, and in his placement of moving figures in relation to these intersecting planes, Chaucer sums up the vision and the poetic of the *Canterbury Tales*. By focusing on the temporal plane and by acknowledging, though not anticipating, the judgments of eternity, he represents the sublunar world accurately while simultaneously defining a sphere for the operation of fiction. In this way, too, and not only in brilliant rhetorical play or the comprehensive assemblage of Chaucerian subjects and strategies, the Nun's Priest's Tale represents the art of the *Tales* as a whole.

---

[28] Derek Pearsall, "Chaucer, *The Nun's Priest's Tale*, and the Modern Reader," *Dutch Quarterly Review* 10 (1980): 170–71.

[29] For a contrary view, that this allusion has the same characteristics as the Priest's other glosses to the fable, see Paul Strohm, *Social Chaucer* (Cambridge, Mass.: Harvard University Press, 1989), 165.

Seeing Things: Locational Memory in Chaucer's Knight's Tale

MARY CARRUTHERS

The modern idea of an author, it is said by those far wiser in this subject than I am, was born when Stephen Daedalus shakes the dull pavement of Dublin from his feet and vows to go into exile, there "to encounter . . . the reality of experience and to forge in the smithy of my soul the uncreated conscience of my race." In a similar moment of authorial pronouncement, Geoffrey Chaucer describes a different way of considering books, things, consciousness, reality, and the relationships among them:

> And with the shoutyng, whan the song was do
> That foules maden at here flyght awey,
> I wok, and othere bokes tok me to,
> To reede upon, and yit I rede alwey.
> I hope, ywis, to rede so som day
> That I shal mete som thyng for to fare
> The bet, and thus to rede I nyl nat spare.
> (*The Parliament of Fowls*, 693-99)[1]

This is a familiar moment to all readers of Chaucer, since ones like it occur also in the *Book of the Duchess*, *Troilus and Criseyde*, the Prologue to *The Legend of Good Women*, and *The House of Fame*. In bringing the reading of books and the experience of composition together in this way Chaucer was articulating in the

---

[1] All quotations from Chaucer are from *The Riverside Chaucer*, 3d ed., gen. ed. Larry D. Benson (Boston: Houghton Mifflin, 1987). In developing my ideas about memory in Chaucer's work, I would like to acknowledge in particular the following books: Robert O. Payne, *The Key of Remembrance* (New Haven: Yale University Press, 1963); Donald R. Howard, *The Idea of The Canterbury Tales* (Berkeley and Los Angeles: University of California Press, 1976); and V. A. Kolve, *Chaucer and the Imagery of Narrative* (Stanford: Stanford University Press, 1984). I first learned the art of reading non-representational poetry from Robert W. Frank, Jr. in "The Art of Reading Medieval Personification-Allegory," *ELH* 20 (1953): 237-50, and *"Piers Plowman" and the Scheme of Salvation* (New Haven: Yale University Press, 1957); it pleases me to be able finally to thank him.

vernacular commonplaces that had long flourished in the pedagogy of Latin grammar and rhetoric.

It is these that I want to focus on in this essay, in particular a concept that seems so straightforward in the passage I just quoted as to need no explaining. The concept is "thyng," the object of Chaucer's voluminous reading. This "thing" that he will find in his books will enable him "to fare the better" – both as a "maker" and (presumably) as a human being.

The word "thing" is used also by Chaucer in the Prologue to the *Legend* to describe the object of his pursuit; here, he says, he reads in order to find and have in mynd from old, proven stories, some "olde thinges" about holyness, victories, love, hate, and "other sondry thynges" – that word again! For if old books were gone, he continues (in a line made famous by Robert Payne) "Yloren were of remembraunce the keye." But what is this "thing" and what has memory got to do with it?

Let me begin first by defining some terms. *Memoria* is one of the five traditional divisions of rhetoric, usually called the "noblest" or the "fundamental" division to all the rest. Writers on the subject distinguish between "natural" memory, by which they mean each individual's native ability to record and recollect material and "artificial" memory or native ability enhanced by training, practice, and mnemonic discipline. In ordinary discourse, *memoria* includes trained memory, and I use it this way in this paper. In memory training, an additional distinction was made between "memoria verborum" or word-for-word memorizing (also called memorizing "verbaliter") and "memoria ad res," memory "according to the thing" or memorizing "sententialiter." This translates in practice to remembering the chief words and ideas of a text, its "gist" in our terms. Either method was considered to be legitimate *memoria*, leaving the choice (after elementary schooling in the subject) up to each individual's discretion, ability, and needs. But for an orator, all the ancient authors agree, *memoria ad res* is the most useful kind of remembering.[2]

Memory was analyzed as the end-product of sensory perception and was thus assumed to be physiologically produced. It is an *affectus* or emotional change in the body. What is produced is an image that can be seen and read by the eye of the mind. However information is initially received, it is transformed by the "inward sense" into a seeable image and recorded in memory in that fashion. The distinction we now make between "verbal" and "visual" memory is not made by the writers on memory; *memoria* is always a matter of images, both pictorial and graphic. These images are most like letters on a written surface, etched into physical loci or "places" in the brain. Our memories are most like a book, which, in recollecting, we read. Each bit of information, encoded as a visual image, occupies a particular place; it can

---

[2] I have described in detail the ancient and medieval sources of mnemonic technique and its basic role in medieval pedagogy in *The Book of Memory* (Cambridge: Cambridge University Press, 1990). *Memoria ad res* and the nature of "division" and "composition" in mnemonic training are defined there most fully in pp. 80–107.

therefore be uniquely addressed and so recalled. The various mnemonic or "artificial memory" systems are basically addressing and filing schemes that enable textual information to be recalled in a manner that frees one from mere "rote" reiteration and allows one both to recall particular information instantly, and to manipulate, shuffle, collate, and concord it freely. They provide one with a random-access memory.

The length of a particular memorized "bit" is set by the limits of the human short-term reiterative ability, which seems to be "seven plus-or-minus two" items. In memorizing a long text, one was taught to divide it into segments short enough to be easily recalled as a single unit and then to lay each segment away together with its address in the order of the whole text. Any readily-reconstructable order will do, but the most common are numbers and alphabets. The address provides the mnemonic hook which draws in the particular words of the segment. Because human long-term memory is virtually limitless in its capacities, an enormous amount of information can be stored in this fashion – indeed one's entire education can be laid away, readily inventoried in the storehouse of *memoria*.

In a preface written for novices beginning their study of Latin, Hugh of St. Victor describes in detail just how this task was to be done.[3] It is the best description we have from the Middle Ages, but the method itself is also described by Quintilian and was fundamental in Hellenistic elementary pedagogy. Hugh says that to memorize the Psalms, one first sketches out a "linea" or diagram in one's mind, of 150 consecutively numbered *sedes*, "seats" or "locations," one for each psalm. Into each one, one places the first few words of the text. So, in the first compartment one would put "Beatus vir qui non abiit in consilio impiorum": perhaps a few less words, perhaps a few more but no more than one can encompass in "one glance" of one's mental eye – the unit of what we call "short-term memory." In the second bin, one puts "Quare fremuerant gentes" and so on. For the rest of each psalm, you should construct subsections, also numbered in order, as many as are needed for the divisions you make of the long text. And what you end up with is a grid structure, each cell of which is addressed uniquely in the same system (chapter and verse) that the Bible still has. And why do we do this, asks Hugh rhetorically? So that we can immediately and directly find whatever piece of text we want, in whatever order we need it, and so that we can collate (that is, bring together) a number of texts to support whatever theme we may choose. For, he says, do you think that scholars wanting a particular Psalm text turn through the pages in a book? "Too great would be the labor in such an activity." With texts written upon one's heart, one has a fully accessible library of one's own, the ever-present "liber copiae" or "copy-book" (*copia*-book) that prudence and eloquence require.

Reading and composition both were taught from antiquity on as complementary activities and defined as activities that both served and depended on memory. In his treatise on reading, *Didascalicon* (3.9), Hugh of St. Victor

---

[3] A translation of this text is given in Appendix A of *The Book of Memory*.

says that "reading proceeds by dividing" – "modus legendi in dividendo constat."[4] These chunks, these "things," laid away in memory then must provide the building-blocks of all new work. As division is the mode of reading, so composition – the "placing together" of bits laid away by division – is the mode of text-making, what we call "writing." The memory bits culled from works read and digested are ruminated into a composition – that is basically what an "author" does with "authorities."

Ancient pedagogy and psychology treated composition – invention and its related aspects of "ordering" and "style" – as essentially a recollective activity. This analysis is profoundly different from modern ideas of "composition," and this difference has been a major source of misunderstanding as moderns attempt to discuss medieval views of "invention." In pre-modern usage, both concepts, composition and invention, employed a locational model of memory and intellection. The storing of memory-sized "bits," *ad verba* or *ad res*, in addressed "seats" or "backgrounds" makes up an "inventory." From this, one first "invents" by finding matters previously put away and then placing them together (*con-positio*) in a new "place."

This new "place" or related set of places is a wholly new structure, a mental diagram or "picture" of the new work. Notice that, although the notion of places is fundamental, their ordering or arrangement is what crucially fashions a "composition." Thus a composition can be thought of as a "common structure" (*communis locus*) fashioned by the inventor into which are newly gathered up materials from one's memory (*res memorabiles*, material both worthy-of and able-to-be remembered/recollected, because it has been properly digested and inventoried – "divided," the mode of reading). The notion of inventory, matters in a structure, is as fundamental to *composition* as it is to reading. We can see this most readily in two favorite metaphors from antiquity, those of the bee and of the builder.

The bee trope came most familiarly to the Middle Ages in the form given to it by Seneca, whose letters were a standard item in the later medieval curriculum *ars dictaminis*. "We should follow, men say, the example of the bees, who flit about and cull the flowers that are suitable for producing honey, and then arrange and assort in their cells all that they have brought in" (*Moral Epistles* 84.3).[5] Composition begins in reading, culled, gathered, and laid away distinctively in separate places, "for such things are better preserved if they are kept separate"; then, using our own talent and faculties, we blend their variety into one savour which, even if it is still apparent whence it was derived, will yet be something different from its source.

In this trope composition, like reading, is assumed to depend on a memory properly stored with discrete, immediately recoverable "places" into which

---

[4] Hugh of St. Victor, *Didascalicon (De Studio Legendi): A Critical Text*, ed. Charles H. Buttimer, Studies in Medieval and Renaissance Latin Language and Literature 10 (Washington: Catholic University Press, 1939), 58.

[5] Seneca, *Epistulae morales*, trans. R. M. Gummere. Loeb Classical Library, 3 vols. (London: Heinemann, 1953–1962), 2: 276–77.

material is "collected." One can see readily the analogy between this and storing a bee hive: consider also the mnemonic grid of cells filled with Psalm text. For Seneca, *memoria* is not an alternative to creativity but the route to it.

Ancient and medieval pedagogy commonly distinguished three stages in the process of composing. First came invention, taught as a wholly mental process of searching one's memorial inventory. It is done with postures (such as reclining with eyes shut) and in settings that are also the signals of meditation; indeed, it is best to think of invention as a meditational and hence recollective activity. It results in a product called the *res*, and in this context the word has the same sort of meaning that it does in the pedagogy of memory training. *Res* is the "gist" of one's composition; more complete than what modern students think of as an outline, it should, according to Quintilian, be formed fully enough to be readily finished by touches of ornamentation and rhythm. In other words, the *res* is like an early draft, still requiring shaping and adjustment. But it differs crucially from our notion of a draft in that it is a *mental* product.

The post-invention stage is, properly, composition itself, the bringing of matters (*res*) into the compositional locus. Its products are called *dictamen*; it might but need not involve writing instruments. The *dictamen* is most like what we now call a "draft"; a number of versions, each unfinished, could be involved. When the *dictamen* was shaped satisfactorily, the composition was fully written out on a permanent surface like parchment in a scribal hand; this final product was the exemplar submitted to the public. The word "writing" properly refers to this last inscribing process, which the author might do himself but usually did not.

At the beginning of his *Poetria nova*, Geoffrey of Vinsauf discusses invention in terms of making a diagram, a plan, for a building. This architectural metaphor became a common late medieval trope; many will remember it from the end of Book 1 of Chaucer's *Troilus and Criseyde*, where Pandarus composes his design for bringing the two principals together in one room. He composes mentally, "thenkyng on this matere" (matter is an English word for the compositional *res*):

> For everi wight that hath an hous to founde
> Ne renneth naught the werk for to bygynne
> With rakel hond, but he wol bide a stounde,
> And sende his hertes line out fro withinne
> Aldirfirst his purpos for to wynne.
> Al this Pandare in his herte thoughte,
> And caste his werk ful wisely or he wroughte.
>
> (*Troilus and Criseyde*, 1.1065–71)

Chaucer's method in these lines of remembering Geoffrey of Vinsauf is an example of *memoria ad res*, the "thyng" or the idea and main words "clothed" newly but recognizably in his own composition.

The builder trope sees the process of composing as the laying-out of the *res* in a spatial design that has distinct locations related in an ordered series.

Once the res is/are placed (and remember that res are both the "'things" found in one's memorial store or "inventory" and the "thing" that results from the orderly "arrangement" of them in one's own composition), they are "clothed" with language suitable for the occasion. These are the first three traditional "stages" or "parts" of rhetorical composition: invention, arrangement, style. In Geoffrey of Vinsauf's description, as also in ancient rhetoric, the language of mnemonic technique permeates what he says about composing.

> Si quis habet fundare domum, non currit ad actum
> Impetuosa manus: intrinseca linea cordis
> Praemetitur opus, seriemque sub ordine certo
> Interior praescribit homo, totamque figurat
> Ante manus cordis quam corporis; et status ejus
> Est prius archetypus quam sensilis. Ipsa poesis
> Spectet in hoc speculo quae lex sit danda poetis.
> Non manus ad calamum praeceps, non lingua sit ardens
> Ad verbum: neutram manibus committe regendam
> Fortunae; sed mens discreta praeambula facti,
> Ut melius fortunet opus, suspendat earum
> Officium, tractetque diu de themate secum.
> Circinus interior mentis praecircinet omne
> Materiae spatium. Certus praelimitet ordo
> Unde praearripiat cursum stylus, aut ubi Gades
> Figat. Opus totum prudens in pectoris arcem
> Contrahe, sitque prius in pectore quam sit in ore.
> Mentis in arcano cum rem digesserit ordo,
> Materiam verbis veniat vestire poesis.   (*Poetria nova*, 43–61)

[If one should lay the foundation of a house, his rash hand does not leap into action; an internal string of one's heart pre-measures the work, and the inner person will pre-write the series in a particular order, and the hand of the heart rather than of the body figures the whole thing; and it is a mental rather than a physical thing. In this model poetic craft itself may observe what law should be given for poets. The hand should not be swift to the pen, nor the tongue be burning for a word; commit neither one to be ruled at the hands of Fortune; but, that your work may have a better fortune, as a first-walk-about [*praeambula*] of the matter, your discriminating mind suspends the offices [of pen and tongue] and for a long time should mull over the theme within itself. The interior compasses of the mind should pre-measure the whole area of the matter. A sure order should predetermine from what point the pen will take its course, and where it fixes its limit (Cadiz). Prudently draw up your whole work into the citadel of your breast, and let it be first in your breast before it is in your mouth. When in the secret recess of the mind order has distributed the *res*, poetry may come to clothe the matter with words.][6]

First, invention takes place in the mind, "mentis in arcano" (60), "in pectoris arcem" (58), with the "manus cordis" (47) rather than that of the body and by means of "intrinseca linea cordis" (44) – an image I will return to. The use of *cor, cordis* (and its synonym, *pector*) specifies the seat of this activity as the memory and the activity itself as one of recollecting. From the time of Varro, Latin *recordari*, "to remember," was considered to derive from *cor, cordis*, "heart"; Jerome says, in his gloss on Ezekiel 40:4, that the word "cor" is a synonym of "memoria" (and the English idiom "to learn by heart" is a translation of the Latin one).

In the memory, things are enclosed, as in a recess (60) or a citadel (58) or a box (the words *arx, arcis, arcana,* and *arca, arce* are all commonly used for the idea of memory as a "storage chest" in which memorial things are placed and contained). Composition begins with the laying out of a mental diagram or "picture": "intrinseca linea cordis" ("his hertes line [sent] out fro withinne"). *Linea* is often used in memory advice for the mnemonic scheme which one uses to store material, whether initially or for one's own composition. Here, I think, Geoffrey is envisioning the mental action of constructing or building a mnemonic plan or schema.[7] This interior string (the basic meaning of "linea"), of the sort a master-builder would use in laying out the plan of a building, first measures out the poetic work. And with it one draws an interior diagram (a secondary meaning of "linea" for many writers, including Hugh of St. Victor). The diagram must have a fixed order (45) which the "hand of the heart" (47) has "pre-written" (*praescribit*) and "figured as a whole" (46). Notice the emphasis on visualization in the choice of the verbs "praescribo" (for writing is visual) and "figuro": Hugh of St. Victor, describing his technique for making a compositional plan, uses the verb "pingo," "I paint." This procedure results in an "archetypus" measured out in memory, the first stage in creating a compositional *res*.

The sketched-out *archetypus* is the set of backgrounds into which the main points, the matter, of the composition will be placed. This "diagram" can take a number of forms, but a building is a favorite one – the architectural mnemonic described in antiquity may lie distantly behind this. But there is important biblical precedent as well, such as the measuring out of the Temple in Ezekiel, the divine city of Revelation, the instructions for making the Ark of the Covenant, and those for Noah's ark (which Hugh of St. Victor elaborated).

---

[6] Geoffrey of Vinsauf, *Poetria nova* in Edmond Faral, *Les arts poétiques du XIIe et du XIIIe siècle* (1924; reprint, Paris: Champion, 1953); my translation is based on that of Margaret F. Nims, *Poetria nova of Geoffrey of Vinsauf* (Toronto: Pontifical Institute of Mediaeval Studies, 1967).

[7] Later in the *Poetria nova* (2013–15), discussing mnemotechnique, Geoffrey comments on the usefulness of *formae* or diagrams in both storage and recollection: "loca, tempora, formae / Aut aliquae similes notulae mihi sunt via certa/ Quae me ducit ad haec."

There are other mnemonic figures which act as compositional backgrounds: a ladder or a cross (perhaps the most common), the six-winged seraph (which provided the structure for Alan of Lille's much-admired sermon). A bit later in this passage, Geoffrey of Vinsauf intimates that he has a circular structure in mind, another common shape, often subclassified as a "rose" or a *rota*, "wheel," or (most likely here, given the reference to "Gades") a *mappa mundi*. All of these are called, in the common language of the twelfth-century schoolroom, *formae*, a technical word used like the technical meaning of modern English "form," "a mold" (such as a dressmaker's or carpenter's form).[8]

Geoffrey describes a sort of interior walk-about, a pre-visualizing, inspectional amble through one's matter (*factum*, literally "that which is given to one," distinguished in this context from the compositional *res* or finished draft that precedes the *dictamen*; cf. lines 60–61). This is also done before any words are articulated or written out. In lines 49–54, Geoffrey describes the interior inspection of material stored in memory places in the characteristic manner of memory arts. One does not compose either "orally" or "literately" – notice – but *before* any external articulation occurs, one forms everything mentally, using one's mnemonic forms. "Mens discreta," "a discriminating mind" (referring not to its moral superiority so much as to the activity of separating, culling, and organizing that it is undertaking),[9] as "praeambula facti," literally as "a first-walk-about of the matter,"[10] suspends all outward activities, and for a long time "secum," "within itself," "tractet," "should-compose-by-drawing-matters-together," concerning its yet-unformed topic. Here again, the early commentary on the *Poetria nova* is helpful in

---

[8] Geoffrey of Vinsauf writes of the mnemonic value of *formae* in line 2013 of the *Poetria nova*; Thierry of Chartres is even clearer, unsurprisingly, on what such mnemonic *formae* are. In his commentary on the memory section of the *Rhetorica ad Herennium*, he glosses the use of *forma* in Book 3.19.31, "id est compositione ... *Forma* tamen refertur ad manu compositos locos," that is, the "artificial" or imaginary backgrounds whose fashioning and use are discussed in that section of the *Rhetorica ad Herennium*; see *The Latin Rhetorical Commentaries by Thierry of Chartres*, ed. Karin M. Fredborg (Toronto: Pontifical Institute of Mediaeval Studies, 1988), 305.

[9] This notoriously difficult passage is perhaps best clarified by an early school commentary on the *Poetria nova*, which glosses the phrase "mens discreta <praeambula>" (line 52) as "that is, organizing your work with discrimination beforehand"; see Marjorie C. Woods, ed. and trans., *An Early Commentary on the "Poetria nova" of Geoffrey of Vinsauf* (New York: Garland, 1985), 16–17.

[10] *Praeambula* is, of course, English *preamble*, but that translation would obscure what I think is a literally-intended, if wholly mental, "walk" taken through the divided-up "bits" or "cells" of one's initial structure as one proceeds to "gather" into them the matter of one's composition. The meaning of *factum*, I think, should be understood in the context of the title of Valerius Maximus' florilegial collection, *Dicta et facta memorabilia*, where *facta* are the stories and other "facts" that made up matter suitable for further composition. Thus a medieval *factum* brings with itself more built-in structure and decorum than our "facts" do now. See Albert Blaise, *Lexicon Latinitatis Medii Aevi*, Corpus Christianorum, Continuatio Mediaevalis (Turnhout: Brepols, 1975), s. v. *praeambulus* and the related forms *praeambulo* and *praeambulator/perambulator*; and also s. v. *factum*.

understanding exactly what stage of composition *thema* represents: it is "informis materia," matter without the *forma* which the "intrinseca linea cordis" will supply.[11]

Traho is the word used most commonly for the act of composition in late medieval Latin. As I have argued at length elsewhere,[12] in the context of literary composition its meaning is predicated on the notion that one has a store from which one "draws" out matter ("things") previously "drawn" into memory storage copiously from one's reading. So "tractet secum de themate" means that one should draw out of one's inventory the ex-tracted "things" laid within one's memory that concern the theme of one's own composition. These extracts are drawn into the orderly places measured out in a series that one already has visualized or "figured" to oneself.

Then, "Circinus interior mentis praecircinet omne / Materiae spatium" (55–56): like a mapmaker, one "pre-circles" with one's inner compasses (remember the "linea" of line 44) the whole "space" of the matter. Notice again the emphasis on space and on pre-visualization – the entire composition of matters in their ordered places is prefabricated and prelimited, "drawn-together" ("Contrahe," 59) "in pectoris arcem," the citadel of memory. And only then does poetry come to clothe the matter with words (61), and the work proceeds from the stage of *res* to that of *dictamen*. So composition is depicted as an activity of recollecting material previously gathered-in from reading. It is wholly mental in all but its final stages (and may be to the very moment of its dictation to a scribe), an activity of concentrated previsualization, in which the notion of place, *locus*, plays a critical role. "Location" – places in an order – is basic to all ancient and medieval memory technique. We are somewhat used to thinking of the technique in the task of storage, the laying-away of the mental inventory, but are perhaps less accustomed to think of mnemonic places with images drawn into them as a compositional tool. Douglas Kelly and others have developed the concept of "topical invention" as a powerful composing tool in medieval literature; relating this notion of "topic" to a mnemotechnical context serves to ground "topical invention" in a commonly known, elementary pedagogy, for as early as the time of Aristotle, the usefulness of "topics" for the invention of argument was related to their use in "artificial memory."[13]

---

[11] See Woods, 18–19.

[12] *The Book of Memory*, 202–3.

[13] See Douglas Kelly, "Topical Invention in Medieval French Literature," in James J. Murphy, ed. *Medieval Eloquence: Studies in the Theory and Practice of Medieval Rhetoric* (Berkeley and Los Angeles: University of California Press, 1978), 231–251; and "Obscurity and Memory: Sources for Invention in Medieval French Literature," in Lois Ebin, ed., *Vernacular Poetics in the Middle Ages* (Kalamazoo: Medieval Institute Publications, 1984), 33–56: what Kelly identifies as "obscurity" in vernacular French poetry is similar to mnemonic *brevitas*, the *summae* in which "matter" is stored by the technique of *memoria sententialiter*, inviting expansion and adaptation during recollection. Aristotle likens the use of "topics" in argument to the use of "locations" in artificial memory in *Topica* 8.13. On the matter of "topics" in

In light of this assumption that locational memory – images in backgrounds – serves composition as well as memory storage, I would now like briefly to look at some structures in Chaucer's Knight's Tale. Recall that after the tale, the other pilgrims (especially "the gentils") all agree that it is "worthy for *to drawen* to memorie" (*trahere* again). I want to concern myself in these remarks not with the question of whether or not, in some real way, the Knight's Tale is *worthy* to remember – that is, not with its philosophy – but, accepting the pilgrims' judgment that it is worthy, how might the tale itself help them to "draw it to memory"?

Clearly most readers wouldn't attempt to remember it *verbaliter*, for the poem is well over 2000 lines. But there is much "matter," many "things," in it that can be drawn and (re-)collected *sententialiter*. How do you, as its reader, remember the Knight's Tale? I remember it as a series of locations, many of them architectural, but all, even those outdoors, of moderate extent and well-lighted (two universal features of successful mnemonic backgrounds) into which "images" have been distinctively "placed."[14] I begin with the highway into Athens just beside the temple of the goddess Clementia, lined by the company of Theban ladies clad in black; then the prison tower and its garden, into which V. A. Kolve, among others, has gathered much matter; Theseus' "place" in his hall, with Palamon and Emily to either side of him. And especially I return to the grove, which is used as a *locus* three times in the tale: first, as the "background" for Palamon and Arcite's bloody duel on May 3; then, as the place on which the amphitheater containing the lists for the joust is erected; thirdly, as the place of Arcite's funeral procession and pyre. I see the action of each of these scenes clearly painted in its location. Each has a distinguishing sound or melody (or hushed silence) associated with it that summons up a primary emotion (woe, lust, anger, courage, awe), and each serves the nexus of the tale's matters; recalled in order, they summarize the things in the Knight's Tale that are worth remembering. In other words, these are structures that serve both the composer's and audience's needs, that help to make it possible "to drawen to memorie" the "thynges" that we can *use* to "fare the bet" by placing them in our own inventory.

Locational mnemonics help to account for the "episodic" quality of romance narrative, for like beads on a string or like rooms in a house plan, the story moves from one "place" to the next, each location "gathering in" images charged with emotional content which serve to focus the matter. The structure of *Sir Gawain and the Green Knight* is another good example of such user

medieval logic and mnemonic technique, see Eleonore Stump, *Boethius's De topicis differentiis* (Ithaca: Cornell University Press, 1978), esp. 18–26; and G. R. Evans, "Two Aspects of *Memoria* in Eleventh and Twelfth Century Writings," *Mediaevalia* 32 (1980): 263–78.

[14] The basic features of memory places are enumerated by all ancient and medieval authorities. They include moderate extent; moderate lighting, neither dim or glaring; simplicity without crowding; clear distinction from one another. Within these locations, the images are placed. See, for example, the advice of Thomas Bradwardine in Appendix C of *The Book of Memory*.

friendliness. Its narrative is "fixed" in a short set of distinct locations: Arthur's court, Bercilak's court, the Green Chapel. These serve as heuristic "hooks" for the matter of the story; a further aid is the juxtaposition of the bedroom/hunt locations, a sort a subset of ordered "backgrounds," each pair of which is clearly "marked" by an animal: deer, boar, fox. Gawain's rides from one location to the next are like the lines linking the places in a diagram. The "matter" is discovered and remembered in the story's locations. *Sir Gawain and the Green Knight* is an exceptionally memory-friendly poem for its readers, and if you get its locations firmly within your mental compass, the whole *res* of the poem is easily retained (a useful feature when lecturing).

The Knight's Tale is equally memory-friendly. "Order" has been its philosophical benchmark for virtually every one of its readers, but a surprising number have also complained about its *lack* of "organic" structure, its discursiveness, and its love of lists, sometimes even seeing these qualities as an expression of satire at the Knight's expense.[15] I would like to concentrate on one set of these apparent "blemishes," the inordinately (for modern students) long and endlessly detailed descriptions of the oratories of the pagan gods in Part III. They are given 200 lines, nearly a tenth of whole poem, yet these structures serve no commensurate narrative purpose; and the philosophical one they have been said to serve (how disorder can be contained by art) seems a dubious moral, undercut at once by what happens in the story. Yet they are among the tale's most memorable "things" – which is, of course, their point.

These "places" operate as powerful summary inventories of the tale's themes of love and battle, disorder and order, human woe and divine omnipotence; coming at the center of the tale, they serve as effective mnemonics for both reader and composer. The language of *memoria* is striking in these descriptions. Chaucer himself gives the clue, when he says that the westward temple is made (notice the verb of fashioning) "in memorie / Of Mars" (1906–7). Each construction follows exactly the same master plan, as though they had been plotted on the same diagram (which, I think, they were). Into this *archetypus* is drawn matter organized around the central image, whether of Venus, Mars, or Diana. Let's start, as the Knight's Tale itself does, with Venus (1918–66).

First come wall paintings of the characteristics of love, "Wroght on the wal, ful pitous to biholde" (1919): these are "broken slepes, and the sikes colde / . . . That loves servantz in this lyf enduren." Then come personified qualities of love: "Plesaunce and Hope, Desir, Foolhardynesse"; "Jalousye" with her marigolds and a cuckoo, "and alle the circumstances / Of love, which that I rekned and rekne shal, / By ordre weren peynted on the wal" (1932–34). The narrator can *reckon* ("recall") this material because he can *reckon* ("count") it "by ordre," "in order." Notice that we aren't told *what* order: the important thing is that they are "in order," for it is that quality that makes it possible for them to be "reckoned."

---

[15] A few of the earlier critics to so complain are mentioned in the note on critical commentary on The Knight's Tale by Vincent DiMarco in *The Riverside Chaucer*, 828–29.

After these various qualities of love's servants are reckoned up some memorable facts and stories about Venus – for example, her "principal dwellynge" on the mount of "Citheroun," together with her garden. "Nat was foryeten," "not forgotten," is Idleness, her porter; nor the tales of Hercules, Medea, Circe, Solomon, Turnus, and so on, all of which bring to mind the general idea (res) that "as hir list the world than may she gye" (1950). Then, in lines 1955–66 the statue of Venus is described, with images associated with her: her citol, her rose garland, her doves, her blind son.

I would like to suggest that this "portreiture" serves as a memory image, a picture-inventory of "things": qualities, stories, and themes, "the matter of Venus," as it were. Venus is being "remembered" ad res. The language of memory (often presented, occupatio-style, as "not-forgetting" – see 2021) is even more evident in the description of Mars's building. The wall here is also all painted in an order – notice that we are carefully told what comes "first" (1975, 1995) and next, in sequence. Notice the emphasis on what the narrator sees, "first" and then "next" and "next" and "then." Notice that the barber, the butcher, and the smith are "of Martes divisioun" (2024), glossed commonly as "influence," but referring here, I think, to "Mars" as a compositional "division," a section or "heading" under which a number of "things" can be brought – "the matter of Mars," as it were.

Notice also that everything is "painted." Mnemonic images are by definition pictures, even if what is painted are the graphic representations of words. But the word "pictura" is commonly used by such writers as Hugh of St. Victor for the compositional diagram or set of "places" into which "things" are set in order. I've already mentioned that such picturae can take shapes that we no longer associate with diagrams – roses, for example, or six-winged seraphs. The most elaborate compositional pictura that has survived from the Middle Ages is Hugh of St. Victor's ark diagram, now called "De arca Noe mystica" but called in several manuscript colophons "De pictura arche."[16] And I have shown similar language in Geoffrey of Vinsauf's advice concerning invention, conceived to be the making and gathering of a compositional inventory by recollection. The three "oratories" of the gods in the Knight's Tale are such memorial picturae.

The descriptions of the temples of Venus and Mars are translated ad res by Chaucer from Boccaccio's Teseida. Their memory function in that poem is made clear by Boccaccio's gloss on each. The "pictures" come, in Boccaccio, when the prayers of Palemone and Arcita rise, and it is the prayers which are described as "seeing" the portraiture. This metaphoric trope realizes a long-standing notion, aphoristically expressed by Isidore of Seville, that "letters are markers for things, signs of words, whose power is such that without a voice they speak to us the spoken words of those who are not present."[17] Taking the form of the speaker who is no longer present,[18] the words of each prayer "look

---

[16] See The Book of Memory, 231–32.
[17] Isidore of Seville, Etymologiae, 1.3.1–3.
[18] I have discussed some other examples of this trope in The Book of Memory, 18, 225.

over" the inventory of "things" set in order, and – as an example to his readers – Boccaccio added a meditation as his gloss to each description in his poem.

There is some doubt whether Chaucer knew the final autograph of the *Teseida*, the manuscript in which Boccaccio added his gloss on these images.[19] But Chaucer understood their function in the story perfectly well anyway, as memorial inventories that can serve as the *archetypus* for a readerly composition, the gathering-in of "things" to meditate on. I say this confidently because he paints a "picture" of Diana in exactly the same way, though he did not find this in Boccaccio. And Chaucer's picture of Diana is specifically the place of a memorative inventory – it is painted in order, like the other two, with a library full of "things" gathered from reading, more than the narrator wants on this occasion to "draw to his memory," he says (an invitation to the audience to draw both into and from their own memories in order to add to his list): "Ther saugh I many another wonder storie, / The which me list nat drawen to memorie" (2073–74).

The three painted temples, the "portreiture" of the gods, are set physically within a building that itself serves to "draw in" much of the matter of the Knight's Tale. The circular "theater" which Theseus constructs, a mile in circumference, is pierced by two gates, to the east and west, above each of which is placed one of the oratories, with that to Diana positioned exactly to the north "in a touret on the wal" (1909), decorated, Tuscan fashion, with white and red striations. To the south is the great public gate through which the procession of Theseus rides. The architecture is positioned so precisely, "by ordre," because the structure serves as a kind of "memory theater," a location not only for a third of the physical action of the tale but for much of its "matter" as well.

In Boccaccio's version of the story, the temples of the gods are not found in the wall of the amphitheater which Theseus builds: rather, the three principals pray at temples throughout the city. The amphitheater is described only at the end of Book VII, and, although it is described carefully, Boccaccio does not make of it what Chaucer does. In the Knight's Tale, Theseus' architectural hand is emphasized – he devises the structure in all its detail, including the equidistant compass points of the three oratories and the great south gate. Moreover, the amphitheater is situated precisely in the grove where Palamon and Arcite fought first without judge or officer: "The lystes shal I maken in this place" (1862), says Theseus, using the language of locational memory. As builder (and poet, for he could say with Geoffrey of Vinsauf, "Ipsa poesis / Spectet in hoc speculo quae lex sit danda poetis") Theseus uses the

---

[19] The arguments for Chaucer's knowledge of the various manuscript redactions of Boccaccio's poem are summarized by R. A. Pratt in his introduction to the sources of The Knight's Tale in W. F. Bryan and Germaine Dempster, *Sources and Analogues of Chaucer's Canterbury Tales* (1941; reprint, New York: Humanities Press, 1958). More recently, the evidence was summarized by Piero Boitani, *Chaucer and Boccaccio* (Oxford: Medium Ævum Monographs, 1977). There remains no firm evidence that the version of the *Teseida* known to Chaucer contained the author's glosses.

"background" of the grove as a *locus* for both of his compositions – the amphitheater and the funeral pyre for Arcite (2858–60). And for readers of the tale its "dicta et facta memorabilia" are more readily recalled when this structural fact is used as a means for recollection.

There is thus a more self-consciously "built" quality to the Knight's Tale than there is to Boccaccio's *Teseida*, in keeping, I believe, with its announced desire to be memorable, to be a "noble storie" not only *worthy* to draw to memory but literally "memory-able," user-friendly for human memories. Readers have long noted the Knight's concern for them and his firm, self-conscious control of his material evident in such "micro-rhetorical" tropes as *occupatio* and other forms of summary and digestion. At the "macro-rhetorical" level, too, the tale aids its readers, chiefly in the way it is structured by images-within-backgrounds.

Some years ago I published a short essay on Chaucer's interest in the classical architectural mnemonic, as evidenced by some of the structures in *The House of Fame*.[20] I suggested there that this mnemonic, at the time Chaucer was composing, was strongly associated with things Italian and with early humanism. In the *archetypus* of a round theater here in the Knight's Tale, with its Italianate architecture, its sources in Boccaccio, and its *titulus* from Statius, Chaucer seems to me again to be deliberately invoking his Italian connection. But the general method is not new; its roots are in the traditions of Hellenistic education that also shaped monastic pedagogy, especially that of meditational composition. The use of location and *picturae* to organize the whole extent of a composition in order to "draw in" worthy "thynges ... to memorye" is a technique that serves both composer and the readers who go on to make their own meditational compositions from the matter of the Knight's story.

[20] Mary J. Carruthers, "Italy, *Ars memorativa*, and Fame's House," *Studies in the Age of Chaucer* 2 (1987): 179–85.

Partitioned Fictions: The Meaning and Importance of Walls in Chaucer's Poetry

KATHRYN L. LYNCH

> Thus have I, Wall, my part discharged so;
> And, being done, thus Wall away doth go.
>
> (William Shakespeare, *Midsummer Night's Dream*)

Chaucer's earliest fictions, the dream visions, are both literally and figuratively partitioned or walled fictions. In the first two of these, the narrator's dream begins with walls decorated by literary examples – in the *Book of the Duchess* depicting both text and gloss of the *Romance of the Rose* and in the *House of Fame* the Ovidian and Virgilian background to the story of Troy. In the *Parliament of Fowls* the dream action takes place in a park "walled with grene ston" (122) and defined by a literary gate, and the dream section of the Prologue to the *Legend of Good Women* occurs again in a "lytel herber . . . / Ybenched newe with turves fresshe ygrave" (G 97–98; see F 203–204).[1] Enclosed space appears naturally within the dream visions, since the form itself, as many have pointed out, involves the enclosure of one narrative sequence within another.[2] The dream vision is thus a walled or partitioned form, a feature that lends it a good part of its interest and strength, since parallel sections of the poem can be set off against each other like rooms; Chaucer's dream visions regularly include such partitioned off sections – for example, the stories of Ceyx and Alcyone in the *Book of the Duchess* or of Scipio Africanus in the *Parliament of Fowls*, each of which has a shape suggestive of the narrative subsequently dreamed.

Although Chaucer eventually stopped writing in the dream vision form, he never left behind his taste for enclosed fictions: *Troilus and Criseyde* also includes separated narrative structures, with the narrator negotiating the distance between the authoritative tale as told by "Lollius" and the events that Pandarus

---

[1] All quotations of Chaucer's works are taken from *The Riverside Chaucer*, 3d ed., gen. ed. Larry D. Benson (Boston: Houghton Mifflin, 1987).

[2] See, for example, Judith M. Davidoff, *Beginning Well: Framing Fictions in Late Middle English Poetry* (Rutherford, N. J.: Fairleigh Dickinson University Press, 1988); and J. Stephen Russell, *The English Dream Vision: Anatomy of a Form* (Columbus: Ohio State University Press, 1988), 115–37.

attempts to author, which recede beyond his grasp; and, of course, the storytelling contest of the *Canterbury Tales* offers another way to enclose one fiction within another. Moreover, even as Chaucer never lost his taste for enclosed fictions, so also he never lost interest in enclosed spaces. The new, more novelistic and open literary forms that he chose in his later career complicated the relationship between real and metaphorical space – literal walls no longer coincide exactly with moments of narrative transition or enclosure – but, as we shall see, the walls, both literal and figurative, of Chaucer's early poetry continue to structure and define the role of fiction in his later works as well. In *Troilus and Criseyde* and the *Canterbury Tales*, the literal walling off of interior spaces leaves figurative space outside for comment and self-reflection, just as did the multiple narratives of the dream visions.

The wall was the bearer of a primary cultural charge that Chaucer would explore ever more insistently in his later poetry.[3] By protecting their indwellers from attack and plunder, walls were the very condition of civilized life.[4] But the wall also traditionally signalled the contaminations and failures of

---

[3] Almost nothing in scholarship on Chaucer addresses the significant role played by walls in his writings, and very little the fascinating more general question of the use of space, and this only in selected poems where space seems deliberately thematized, like the Reeve's Tale. See, for example, Robert W. Frank, Jr., "The *Reeve's Tale* and the Comedy of Limitation," in *Directions in Literary Criticism: Contemporary Approaches to Literature*, ed. Stanley Weintraub and Philip Young (University Park: Penn State Press, 1973), 63–64. Gerhard Joseph, in "Chaucerian 'Game' – 'Earnest' and the 'Argument of Herbergage' in *The Canterbury Tales*," *Chaucer Review* 5 (1970–71): 83–96, traces the opposition between enclosed and enlarged spaces in Fragment I and relates these to the opposition between game and earnest. Another handful of studies, like Laura Kendrick's "Chaucer's *House of Fame* and the French Palais de Justice," *Studies in the Age of Chaucer* 6 (1984): 121–33, traces parallels between specific buildings in Chaucer's poetry and the actual architecture of his time. See also the more general discussion of contemporary architecture in H. M. Smyser, "The Domestic Background of *Troilus and Criseyde*," *Speculum* 31 (1956): 297–315. Most reference to architecture in Chaucer is of the sort popularized by Robert M. Jordan in his 1967 book *Chaucer and the Shape of Creation* (Cambridge, Mass.: Harvard University Press, 1967); that is, related to the aesthetics that underlie poetry and the visual or architectural arts and not really about space as it is literally represented in poetry; see also Elizabeth D. Lloyd-Kimbrel, "Architectonic Allusions: Gothic Perspectives and Perimeters as an Approach to Chaucer," *Mediaevistik* 1 (1988): 115–24. More recent interest in the topic of privacy in the Middle Ages promises further attention to space that unites both literal and thematic interests; see, for example, Sarah Stanbury, "The Voyeur and the Private Life in *Troilus and Criseyde*," *Studies in the Age of Chaucer* 13 (1991): 141–58.

[4] This image is pervasive in medieval writing from romances and chronicles in which ruined or broken walls emblematize the decay of civilized life to a fifteenth-century Italian philosophical dialogue, Leon Battista Alberti's *Della tranquillità dell'animo*, which has recently been shown to have at its heart an architectural allegory that opposes interior and exterior space as images, in Christine Smith's words, of "spiritual tranquillity and the variability of fortune" (107); see "*Della tranquillità dell'animo*: Architectural Allegories of Virtue in a Dialogue by Leon Battista Alberti," *Journal of Medieval and Renaissance Studies* 19 (1989): 103–22.

civilization. As classical writers were fond of pointing out, in the Golden Age no walls were necessary.[5] No one would have been more dramatically aware of both kinds of walls than the poet who as Clerk of the King's Works from 1389–91 supervised numerous building and repair projects and who had earlier lived in an apartment within the walls around London, over the city gate at Aldgate, for eleven years, during which time the peasants stormed the city walls in the uprising of 1381. This experience would have vividly illustrated the fine line between culture and anarchy. Not only life, but art too underscored the primacy of walls – around Troy, Thebes, Babylon – which delimit and circumscribe meaningful action throughout the classical texts that Chaucer spent his life translating and interpreting. Cities *were* their walls, as suggested by the Latin word *moenia*, meaning both the walls and the city enclosed within them. Indeed, because of its cultural associations as an image,[6] the wall offered an important way for Chaucer to talk about the strengths and weaknesses of imaginative art itself. As the decorated walls of the dream visions indicate, the wall could itself be historiated, thus standing for the page of a text. Like the dream visions, then, Chaucer's later walled narratives also "consistently explore the fundamental terms of literary representation."[7]

Theseus' Wall: The Beginning of Pilgrimage

Chaucer's Knight's Tale offers an excellent gloss on the dubious benefits of a walled civilization in a hostile and malevolent universe and of both the futility and dignity of the artfulness that attempts to carve meaning out of chaos; here the wall emblematically both imposes human order and reflects the forces that will defeat it. As many critics have pointed out, the Knight's Tale seems to take

---

[5] See, for example, Virgil, *Eclogues, Georgics, Aeneid I–VI*, trans. H. Rushton Fairclough, rev. ed., Loeb Classical Library (Cambridge, Mass.: Harvard University Press, 1938): *Georgics* 2.155–57; *Eclogues* 4.31–33. See also Ovid, *Metamorphoses*, trans. Frank Justus Miller, Loeb Classical Library, 2 vols. (Cambridge, Mass.: Harvard University Press, 1977), 1.97. I am grateful to Kenneth Rothwell for helping me find these references.

[6] Geoffrey of Vinsauf's discussion of invention in the *Poetria nova* opens with an image of the poet as architect planning a house in advance of building it; *Poetria nova*, trans. Margaret F. Nims (Toronto: Pontifical Institute of Mediaeval Studies, 1967), 16–17. And as Frances Yates has pointed out, the classical and medieval arts of memory, which recommended the placement of unusual images in halls or rooms in the memory, influenced the formal use of imagery in medieval art and poetry and associated poetic images with architectural ones; Frances Yates, *The Art of Memory* (Chicago: University of Chicago Press, 1966). See Mary Carruthers' essay on "Seeing Things: Locational Memory in Chaucer's Knight's Tale" in this volume and Beryl Rowland's discussions of the influence of the tradition on Chaucer: "The Art of Memory and the Art of Poetry in the *House of Fame*," *Revue de l'Université d'Ottawa* 51 (1981): 162–71; and "Bishop Bradwardine, the Artificial Memory, and the *House of Fame*" in *Chaucer at Albany*, ed. Rossell Hope Robbins (New York: Burt Franklin, 1975), 41–62.

[7] Robert R. Edwards, *The Dream of Chaucer: Representation and Reflection in the Early Narratives* (Durham: Duke University Press, 1989), xvi.

as its main subject "the struggle between noble designs and chaos."[8] That struggle is frequently dramatized in the tale in terms of construction and dismantling, in terms of walls made and broken. Moreover, Theseus also illustrates the specific dilemma of the artist or poet struggling with the difficulty, even intractability, of his material. The tale's narrator, the Knight, in his frequent and sometimes clumsy use of the trope *occupatio* also points up the difficulty of adapting poetic material, faced as well by the poet who abridged Boccaccio's *Teseida*.

Within the Knight's Tale, Theseus is the master builder, though each of his constructions is, in some sense, doomed, and he must repeatedly "his firste purpos modifye" (2542). Each effort to impose a final structure on experience is succeeded straightway by a reconfiguration of the field and a new need. No sooner is "al the regne of Femenye" (866) brought under control than civilized customs of burial must be restored to Thebes, paradoxically by destroying the city ("And rente adoun bothe wall and sparre and rafter" [990]); the walling up of Palamon and Arcite is undermined by love and friendship, as is Arcite's ensuing exile when he discovers the enabling power of bars or walls: "hadde I dwelled with Theseus, / Yfetered in his prisoun everemo. / Thanne hadde I been in blisse and nat in wo" (1228–30). Eventually destiny becomes the enemy of Theseus' plans (1663), reuniting Palamon and Arcite in the grove outside of Athens and leading Theseus to them.

This grove becomes very important, marking as it does a space outside Athens' walls where Theseus fashions his two most impressive artifacts: the "noble theatre" (1885) of the tournament, pre-existent in Boccaccio, and Arcite's funeral pyre. The first is the one of the few places in the tale where Chaucer abandons his usual method of abridgement and expands on Boccaccio. So much does Chaucer wish to stress the effort to subdue the wildness of this grove that, impossibly, both theater and pyre occupy the same space, with hardly any time intervening before building the second to dismantle the first (cf. 1862 and 2860–64). Both the lystes and the funeral pyre represent significant attempts on Theseus' part to bring the ordering force of civilization to dangerous and uncivilized space, where violent and libidinal energies might thrive. As V. A. Kolve says, "The wild wood is transformed – by art and ceremony and rule of law – as Theseus seeks to translate human

---

[8] The phrase occurs in Charles Muscatine, "Form, Texture, and Meaning in Chaucer's *Knight's Tale*," *PMLA* 65 (1950): 929; also, *Chaucer and the French Tradition* (Berkeley and Los Angeles: University of California Press, 1957), 190; it is taken up again by Robert W. Hanning in his "'The Struggle between Noble Designs and Chaos': The Literary Tradition of Chaucer's Knight's Tale," *The Literary Review* 23 (1980): 519–41. Much recent criticism has focused on the degree to which the poet means to stress the Knight's and Theseus' impositions of order or the corresponding disruptions and disorder, on whether an optimistic or pessimistic interpretation is justified by the text. See the summary of recent criticism in Lois Roney, *Chaucer's "Knight's Tale" and Theories of Scholastic Psychology* (Tampa: University of South Florida Press, 1990), 4–8, and in Lee Patterson, *Chaucer and the Subject of History* (Madison: University of Wisconsin Press, 1991), 165–69.

aggression, sexuality, and (finally) sorrow into forms that will allow civilized life to continue."[9] But how successful are these attempts? And how civilized this civilization? Although Theseus' ritualistic clearing of space is the basic event of human culture, it also is a curtailment of culture to its barest minimum. In Winthrop Wetherbee's words, "Civilization itself is reduced to the primordial clearing of the forest, and the trappings of courtly life become mere talismans, an offering to the dark powers."[10] And as Lee Patterson has argued, Theseus' attempts to "chasten [Thebes] into civilization" are doomed to fail, since Thebes is the primal site of fratricide, self-destructive appetite, and "endless repetition."[11] The act of building thus becomes a synecdoche for the whole equivocal enterprise of civilization.

Nowhere is ambivalence about civilization more clearly represented than in the walls of the amphitheater. The beautiful, even luxurious, walls of the three temples to the gods depict an underlying violence and sexuality that could menace the very foundation of society: "the derke ymaginyng / Of Felonye" (1995-96), "Woodnesse, laughynge in his rage" (2011), "the firy strokes" of love's desire (1922), the pains of childbirth extended by long labor (2084). Simply by representing these threats in images, the murals bring them under some limited control. But, like all solutions offered in this tale, the control is only temporary; the fact that narratives from classical poetry also appear on these walls underscores the double-edged quality of a human culture that simultaneously suppresses and indulges its most dangerous impulses. Palamon and Arcite go back to Thebes "with his olde walles wyde" (1880), locus of the original violations of law, to mount small armies of knights to battle over Emelye, a battle that will itself be indecisive, as the gods overturn Arcite's victory in his seemingly random and senseless death. Even Theseus' famed First Mover Speech (2987-3040) is less than fully satisfactory, stressing as it does the wastage of civilization – "the grete tounes se we wane and wende" (3025) – and counseling nothing more profound or uplifting than making the best of what cannot be changed (3041-44). All seems designed to call into question the "o parfit joye, lastynge everemo" (3072) that Theseus predicts for Palamon's and Emelye's marriage of expedience. The fairy tale ending rings less than true to the rest of the tale.

Nonetheless, the tale does dramatize and do honor to the efforts of the noble leader. Most readers of the Knight's Tale are struck by the poignance of Theseus' continual attempts, however limited and ineffectual, to arrange and

---

[9] V. A. Kolve, *Chaucer and the Imagery of Narrative: The First Five Canterbury Tales* (Stanford: Stanford University Press, 1984), 131. See also Derek Pearsall, *The Canterbury Tales* (London: George Allen and Unwin, 1985), 131.

[10] Winthrop Wetherbee, *The Canterbury Tales* (Cambridge: Cambridge University Press, 1989), 44.

[11] Patterson, 200; also 76-77 and *passim*. I had Patterson's excellent *Chaucer and the Subject of History* only when making final revisions of this essay. His analysis of the contradictions of history coincides at many points with my own reading of Chaucer's ambivalence about civilization, though mine is cast in primarily spatial terms.

articulate his world.[12] As Joseph Westlund puts it, the "balance is precisely right in a tale presented at the beginning of a spiritual quest. . . . The poem creates both a sense that man's state is tragic, and that there is some kind of order in the universe."[13] A similar argument is cast in interesting spatial terms by Gerhard Joseph, who notes how the tale dignifies civilization by continually redefining its location:

> . . . the enclosures of the Tale get progressively larger: we move from the cramped "tour, that was so thikke and stroong," to a grove in which Palamon and Arcite can maneuver in single combat, to the three temples of the amphitheatre, and finally to the "noble theatre" itself of which "the circuit a myle was aboute, / Walled of stoon, and dyched al withoute" (1887–88). The point of such gradual widening is clear: the larger the arena in which violent passions can play themselves out, the less destructive and the more susceptible to ritual they become.[14]

The Knight's Tale thus uses its walls – the walls of temple, amphitheater, city – to give us a keen sense of what is at stake in Theseus' attempts to domesticate wild space. The misfiring of these attempts does not wipe out their nobility, despite the ragged humor of Theseus' soldierly sensibility. Indeed, the very repetition of attempts, even where marked by illogic, becomes a kind of ritual or ceremony of man's arrangement of nature. Set in pagan times, the Knight's Tale thus provides an entirely appropriate image for the beginning of the Canterbury pilgrimage: lacking a window on the divine, man as the artisan of his own rough-hewn destiny, maker of walls, continually reinventing and reinterpreting the space of the journey.

Amphion's Wall: The End of Pilgrimage

Thebes, site of primal violation, building and rebuilding, provides the reigning spirit for both the first and last Canterbury Tales. Its ambivalent civilization dominates the Knight's Tale probably more than that of Athens, and, as we shall see, the darker powers invoked by the Theban perspective also come to dominate the last of the Canterbury Tales in verse.[15] Significantly, the founder and early ruler of Thebes, Amphion, also offered to medieval writers an especially powerful figure of art as domesticator and

---

[12] The notable exception, of course, is Terry Jones in *Chaucer's Knight: The Portrait of a Medieval Mercenary* (Baton Rouge: Louisiana State University Press, 1980). For further references, see Patterson, 167.

[13] Joseph Westlund, "The *Knight's Tale* as an Impetus for Pilgrimage," *Philological Quarterly* 43 (1964): 537.

[14] Joseph, 84.

[15] Most early manuscripts place the Manciple's Tale directly before and connect it to the Parson's Tale, and it is generally accepted as the penultimate tale and the last fictional tale in verse. For further discussion and debate, see the explanatory notes to Fragments IX and X in *The Riverside Chaucer*, 951, 954–55.

one that explicitly connected artistic prowess with the building of urban culture out of walls. Chaucer refers to Amphion three times – first as one of the two significant founders of Thebes in the Knight's Tale (I.1546), second in the description of January and May's wedding in the Merchant's Tale (IV.1716), where Amphion appears in his artistic identity as the peer of Orpheus (whose formative art also went beyond idle entertainment), and third at the opening of the Manciple's Tale, where these two images come together as Chaucer compares Phoebus Apollo's song to Amphion's: "Certes the kyng of Thebes, Amphioun, / That with his syngyng walled that citee, / Koude nevere syngen half so wel as hee" (IX.116–18). This last reference introduces themes that will become central to the Manciple's view of art and speech.

The Manciple's Tale begins with an alignment of Apollo, protagonist of the tale, and Amphion, as they were both conventionally known, for their building of walls (Apollo and Neptune took human form to build the walls of Troy) and for their lyre playing. It immediately strengthens the parallel by praising both specifically for singing, roughly equating their art in the tale with the voiced art of the crow; when Phebus breaks "his mynstralcie" (267), that action becomes analogous to the moment when the crow is bereft of "al his song" (305). The wall image appears again late in the tale in what seems initially to be an entirely distinct context, when the Manciple recalls his mother's words of advice: "My sone, God of his endelees goodnesse / Walled a tonge with teeth and lippes eke, / For man sholde hym avyse what he speeke" (322–24).

Robert Jordan remarks on the "comic excess" of this metaphor.[16] The force of this wall of lips and teeth, this grinning wall of silence, however, seems to me more sinister than comic. The wall here inverts Amphion's powerful expressive wall of song, framing the tale with two walls, one that builds a positive sense of art's possibilities and one a negative. In the Manciple's Tale, voices are choked into silence; and walls, rather than organizing and enabling culture, finally only divide a man's private truth from any possibility of public action. This progressive closing down gives the Manciple's Tale a shape exactly opposite to that of the Knight's Tale, which we saw gradually enlarged or widened the arena of its action, thus dignifying the uneven advances of civilization. In the Manciple's Tale, the walled city of Thebes is quickly replaced by Phebus' house; the house, itself the wife's figurative cage, by the bird's literal cage; the cage by teeth, an image of the body itself as a prison. The focus is ever more private as these various substitutions demonstrate the closing down of possibilities for art and social action. As the Knight's Tale makes a good beginning to the earthly pilgrimage, the Manciple's Tale is the inevitable ending of that pilgrimage. As Shakespeare says in his farewell to poetry, in "despair / Unless I be relieved by prayer."

[16] Robert M. Jordan, *Chaucer's Poetics and the Modern Reader* (Berkeley and Los Angeles: University of California Press, 1987), 158.

Chaucer may have gleaned this awareness of the two sides of the wall from Horace's *Ars poetica*, where he would have found the following highly suggestive passage:

> Silvestris homines sacer interpresque deorum
> caedibus et victu foedo deterruit Orpheus,
> dictus ob hoc lenire tigris rabidosque leones.
> dictus et Amphion, Thebanae conditor urbis,
> saxa movere sono testudinis et prece blanda
> ducere quo vellet. fuit haec sapientia quondam
> publica privatis secernere, sacra profanis,
> concubitu prohibere vago, dare iura maritis,
> oppida moliri, leges incidere ligno.
> sic honor et nomen divinis vatibus atque
> carminibus venit.

> [While men still roamed the woods, Orpheus, the holy prophet of the gods, made them shrink from bloodshed and brutal living; hence the fable that he tamed tigers and ravening lions; hence too the fable that Amphion, builder of Thebes's citadel, moved stones by the sound of his lyre, and led them whither he would by his supplicating spell. In days of yore, this was wisdom, to draw a line between public and private rights, between things sacred and things common, to check vagrant union, to give rules for wedded life, to build towns, and grave laws on tables of wood; and so honour and fame fell to bards and their songs, as divine.][17]

The emphasis in these lines is on how the poet, "prophet" and "builder," might play a role in ordering and civilizing his society. But, as in the Knight's Tale, scarcely concealed in the accomplishments of civilization are the forces of disorder that constantly threaten to overwhelm the artist's "supplicating spell." Art here is intimately related to the "vagrant union," the transgression, it barely manages to regulate.

If the Knight's Tale, however, is the fable of subjugating disorder, the Manciple's Tale again provides an apt contrast, since the walling in of crow and wife – the paradoxical "fostering" in a "cage" – fails to control or to elevate the bestial and transgressive sexual appetites of bird and woman. The "vagrant" forces are not here vanquished. Likewise, the "word" – Phebus', the crow's, the Manciple's, even Chaucer's – "cozens" the "werkyng" (210), blurring the very distinctions "between public and private, between things sacred and things common" that verbal art originally meant to establish:

---

[17] Horace, *Satires, Epistles and Ars Poetica*, trans. H. Rushton Fairclough, Loeb Classical Library (Cambridge, Mass.: Harvard University Press, 1929), 482, 483.

> Ther nys no difference, trewely,
> Bitwixe a wyf that is of heigh degree,
> If of hir body dishonest she bee,
> And of a povre wenche. . . .   (212–15)

Though elsewhere, as we shall see, Chaucer clearly endorses such a critique of overly subtle language, here his characterization of the Manciple's rudeness focuses attention on how gross transgressions of the law, of the "rules," say, "for wedded life," dismantle all other categories and distinctions upon which a civilized life depends. Where humans spawn and kill like beasts, there is no room for language or art; the dividing and distinguishing walls of articulated speech are obliterated by silence.[18]

Interestingly, just before the lines quoted above, Horace had warned against the dangers of verbal commitment; though he refers to the danger of embarrassment from mediocre rather than false art, his words resonate for the Manciple's Tale, which displays a world where transgression and punishment overcome words of truth: "What you have not published," writes Horace, "you can destroy; the word once sent forth can never come back" ("delere licebit / quod non edideris; nescit vox missa reverti" [389–90]). Because of its relation to the story of Amphion, I suggest that this passage rather than the rhetorically similar caution in Horace's *Epistolae* 1.18.71, provides the true source of the Manciple's mother's caution:[19]

> My sone, if thou no wikked word hast seyd,
> Thee thar nat drede for to be biwreyd;
> But he that hath mysseyd, I dar wel sayn,
> He may by no wey clepe his word agayn.
> Thyng that is seyd is seyd, and forth it gooth,
> Though hym repente, or be hym nevere so looth.   (351–56)

Whether or not the Manciple's Tale was written early or late in Chaucer's career, it seems significant that the poet closes the last verse fiction of the *Canterbury Tales* with this ventriloquized warning against speech: Amphion's wall has become a muffling wall of teeth; though hortatory, the last words are walled off themselves; they are indirect discourse enclosed by a framed narrative, enacting as well as counseling silence: "Kepe wel thy tonge and thenk upon the crowe" (362).

---

18 Many recent interpretations of the Manciple's Tale have focused on its commentary on language, especially seeing it in relationship to the renunciation of poetic language in the Parson's Tale; see the summary of criticism provided by Donald C. Baker, *The Manciple's Tale*, vol. 2, pt. 10 of *A Variorum Edition of The Works of Geoffrey Chaucer* (Norman: University of Oklahoma Press, 1984), 32–37.

19 Compare the note to lines 355–56 in *The Riverside Chaucer* and Baker's Variorum Edition. The attribution to the *Epistolae* is ubiquitous.

Thisbe's Wall: The Dangers of Passage

In both the Manciple's Tale and the Knight's Tale, Chaucer draws on an inherent ambiguity in his subject. Walls are the ultimate liminal or threshold object, literally occupying the space between inside and outside. Walls divide, they also join. They separate, they connect. In being between, they are of no space and of two spaces. The ambiguities involved are summed up in the several and opposing meanings of the verb "cleave," which even in Chaucer's time could mean "to stick together, cohere" (*MED*) as well as "to split; cut open or apart" (*MED*). *Pearl* alludes to both meanings in the line "I knew me keste þer klyfez cleuen" (66),[20] where the gulf both enables vision and disrupts it. In a significant extension of its root meaning, "cleave" might also signify inherence as "a natural or essential part or aspect . . . [one's] allotted share or possession" or persistence, endurance, lastingness (*MED*). Simultaneously, to cleave might mean to crumble, to break up. Walls similarly point to the divisions and organizations of space required for civilized concourse and also to the very act of civilizing, no sooner undertaken than doomed by the ingredients of its mutability: lime, mortar, dust.

It is not uncommon for Chaucerian narratives to require the ambiguity of walls to motivate their action. In the Knight's Tale the tower in which Palamon and Arcite are imprisoned is "evene joynant to the gardyn wal" (1060), a proximity that occasions the love between the two young knights and Emelye. Similarly, in the Legend of Ariadne, the princess and her sister overhear Theseus complaining because his cell is "joynynge in the wal" to a privy over which they have their rooms (1962). Patterson calls the second "a mocking prefiguration, or echo" of the first,[21] and indeed the shift in register from garden to privy calls attention to an ambiguity about romantic love itself. Moreover, in both cases, the wall both enables and impedes the action, simultaneously creating and preventing opportunity.

The Legend of Thisbe, also from the *Legend of Good Women*, epitomizes this sort of double movement, sounding the changes on the words "clifte" and "cleve." We are told at first that the wall that separates the lovers "was clove a-two, ryght from the cop adoun, / Of olde tyme of his fundacioun," suggesting a substantial rift. "But yit this clyfte was so narw and lyte / It nas nat sene, deere ynogh a myte" (738–41). The space is barely sufficient for their whispers to pass through (745–46); thus Pyramus and Thisbe wish that the wall would "cleve or fallen al a-two" (758), to make room for their kisses – and yet they *do* kiss the stone and the hole *is* adequate to convey their plans back and forth and to set their meeting – foreshadowing the wound Thisbe will later make "large ynogh, I gesse" to cause her death (893). As Sheila Delany has observed, these

---

[20] *The Poems of the Pearl Manuscript*, ed. Malcolm Andrew and Ronald Waldron (Berkeley and Los Angeles: University of California Press, 1979).
[21] *Chaucer and the Subject of History*, 240.

clefts may carry sexual overtones;[22] such meanings, however, augment rather than contradict my argument. The body has its own architecture – clefts, walls, membranes, limbs, stones – and Thisbe's sexuality correspondingly offers Pyramus both a challenge and a threat, while also undercutting the high romance of the lovers' situation. On a primal level, sexual union disintegrates and reconstitutes both individual and family identity, and this paradox is quite likely to be one referent of the wall imagery in the poem.

Within the city, the wall sustains a balance, strong enough to prevent the lovers' consummation, strong enough to enforce parental taboos, but weak enough to permit the gradual growth of love. Like the walls that separate Theseus and Ariadne or Palamon, Arcite, and Emelye, this wall is the enabler or condition of that very love: an impediment to transgression but also an invitation. It is when the two lovers venture outside the walls of the city – "the whyche toun the queen Semyramus / Let dychen al aboute and walles make" (707–8) – that the primitive forces of bloody nature and misunderstanding destroy them. It is thus no accident that the legend opens with lines that yoke Semiramis – figure not only of barbarous, uncontrolled lust, but also of the dangerous multiplications of language[23] – with the civilizing force of the ditches and walls she constructs around Babylon.

Indeed, compared to Ovid, Chaucer's version of the story works to highlight the dubious power of walls.[24] Ovid begins with Pyramus and Thisbe and their nascent love – "he, the most beautiful youth, and she, loveliest maid of all the East" – Chaucer with the impediments to that love, first the city surrounded by ditch and walls, then the two fathers who have erected, "as ofte in grete tounes is the wone," a stone wall between their dwellings. It is not until twenty lines into Chaucer's story that the reader even discovers the names of the lovers. Moreover, Chaucer seems to have been attracted to the parts of Ovid's story that blame and praise the wall for dividing and connecting Pyramus and Thisbe, stressing the "lym and stone" of which the wall is composed (765), highlighting the cleft to which he refers four times against Ovid's single "fissus," and doubling the length of Ovid's apostrophe to the

---

[22] Sheila Delany, "The Naked Text: Chaucer's 'Thisbe,' the *Ovide Moralisé*, and the Problem of *Translatio Studii* in the *Legend of Good Women*," *Mediaevalia* 13 (1987): 275–94.

[23] In *Inferno* 5.54, Dante calls her "empress of many tongues" ("imperadrice di molte favelle"); ed. and trans. Charles S. Singleton (Princeton: Princeton University Press, 1970), 50, 51.

[24] It is generally agreed that Ovid's *Metamorphoses* provided the chief source for Chaucer's version of the tale; the edition used here is the Loeb Classical Library, trans. Miller, 1: 182–91. That does not, however, close the matter. In the essay cited above, Sheila Delany has recently argued that Chaucer was also working from the *lai* of Thisbe in the *Ovide moralisé*. Some details, in fact, are more similar to the *Ovide moralisé* than to Ovid – for instance, Thisbe's intent to enlarge her wound or the opening with the place name, Babylon. Whether or not Chaucer was working from the *lai*, however, his decision to follow one or another version in each case retains significance.

wall (from five lines to eleven). Chaucer seems especially interested in the way that walls are required to thwart the destructive powers of love and desire but are also naturally self-undermining, needing only time and the corrosive effects of the human will to give way altogether.

Even more to the point perhaps, the walls of the Thisbe legend seem specifically connected to language; in both Ovid and Chaucer, it is more than mere love that the "ston-wal" conveys, but the "swote soun" (752) of love's words: the apostrophic lament to the wall itself; the lovers' plighted troth (777); their plans "to stele awey" (779). Ovid calls the wall, with its little chink, "vocis iter," the path of words. Chaucer further highlights the mediating role language plays within the walls when he attributes some of the lovers' interest in one another to the gossip of "women that were neighebores aboute" (719–20; also 726–27). Once beyond the city walls, however, stable and determinate meaning "preserved," as Robert Edwards has put it, "by the ditch, walls, and hard tiles of Babylon gives way to the signs that Piramus misreads."[25] Rather than the love fulfilled that we hope to find beyond the boundaries and repressions of city culture and authoritative truth reported by Ovid (725), there is the dim light of the moon, the rapacious lion with mouth already bloodied presumably from an earlier kill, the renting of clothing and bodies, the pouring forth of blood, and an avalanche of words. Though cut free of the stichomythic divisions of dialogue, these words, heavily apostrophic, are recognizably those of the lovers before their extramural tryst, but now their latent disruptiveness is fully realized, dramatizing the dangers of love talk, and the dangers, by implication, of all reading, interpreting, and speaking beyond the walls.

In many ways this legend is itself hard to read. Its experience of love and lovers threatens the totalizing schema of the legendary, since Pyramus does not support the thesis about the wickedness of men that the poet has been commanded to pursue. But Chaucer's concern with walls, with how confinement dramatizes the contrast between order and chaos, may partly explain his inclusion of the Thisbe story.[26] If an interest in the partitionings of nature and culture, of invention and authority, can be expressed through the imagery of architectural barriers, we can, I think, see Chaucer here exploring the uneasy balance between tradition and experience. Pyramus and Thisbe are safe inside the city, like a poet within a static, monologic tradition; outside lie opportunities for novelty, dissent, invention, temptations to self-annihilation and anarchy. To some extent, the *Legend of Good*

---

[25] Robert Edwards, letter to the author, 15 September 1990. Palamon and Arcite experience similar confusions about the relation between signifier and signified: Is Emelye woman or goddess? Is prison a literal or metaphorical construct? What are the meanings of the gods' responses to their prayers? This confusion, however, does not seem linked to their position within or outside of walls.

[26] Other stories in the *Legend of Good Women* that may also pursue this theme include the Legend of Dido, with its cave and decorated wall; the Legend of Hypermnestra, which ends with an image of confinement; and the Legend of Ariadne, which stages two falling-in-love scenes upon walls.

Women is surely about the balance between these extremes, even if it is an equipoise that poem never itself achieves.

Breaching the Walls of Troy

The dangers of passage are explored even more fully in Chaucer's full-length romance of siege and traffic inside and outside walls, *Troilus and Criseyde*, of all Chaucer's poems the one that makes the most complex and thoroughgoing contrast of space walled in and space walled out. Indeed, we shall see that walls are prominent throughout *Troilus and Criseyde*, a poem that is in its own way also about being within and beyond the pale. One might even say that Trojan dependence upon walls prefigures Trojan decline, especially given the violations involved in Calchas's, Criseyde's, and Antenor's passages of the city walls and the council's refusal to depend on Hector's – their wall's (2.154) – advice. Early in Book 4 (124–25), Calchas indicates that one reason for Troy's fall is the refusal of King Laomedon to pay the gods for its walls.

Troilus and Criseyde brings together many of the concerns we have seen elsewhere in Chaucer's *oeuvre*: the ambiguity of walls, which both impede and enable; the connection of walls with poetry and especially with the problematic referentiality of fictional language when used to give public expression to essentially private desire; and, for the first time, the uneasy continuum between the space outside and that inside, when the discourse of one blends into the other. In Eugene Vance's words: "we of the audience are always capable of seeing beyond the told violence of erotic passion, of the 'hertes werre,' to that larger *untold*, and seemingly forgotten violence of the martial realm unfolding outside the city's walls. In Chaucer's *Troilus* walls prove to be only false boundaries, since they do not, in the final analysis, protect the knights and ladies of Troy from answering to the harsh claims of history."[27] There are two sieges here – the siege of Troy, of course, public and political in character; and the private "love-siege" of Criseyde – both successful. But, as this comparison makes clear, the besieged walls are more than Vance's "false boundaries"; they are the *sine qua non* of siege, the resistance that makes love and war possible, enabling as well as preventing intercourse. And they are specifically walls of words as well as stone, making explicit the equation between city walls, the walls of palaces and houses, and the walls of poetry.

---

[27] Eugene Vance, *Mervelous Signals: Poetics and Sign Theory in the Middle Ages* (Lincoln: University of Nebraska Press, 1986), 265. In recent years many readings of the poem have, like Vance's, stressed its self-referentiality and its commentary on language and especially on competing literary traditions. Two of the most comprehensive and distinguished are Winthrop Wetherbee, *Chaucer and the Poets: An Essay on "Troilus and Criseyde"* (Ithaca: Cornell University Press, 1984), and John V. Fleming, *Classical Imitation and Interpretation in Chaucer's "Troilus"* (Lincoln: University of Nebraska Press, 1990); Wetherbee and Fleming share the belief that Chaucer's reading of classical and contemporary literature was searching and informed.

In Book 1, the poem names Pandarus's love-plot a house in a variation on the passage I noted earlier from Geoffrey of Vinsauf's *Poetria nova*: "For everi wight that hath an hous to founde / Ne renneth naught the werk for to bygynne" (1.1065-66; see note 6 above). The action, once it does begin to take place, occurs inevitably in Pandarus's house, as Troilus confronts his lady, herself distracted by the plots of the false Poliphete, and later as the two, having negotiated the fiction of Horaste, first make love. It is also interesting to note how frequently the escalating pace of action is measured in increasingly interior spaces, as characters mew themselves up in closets and "stuwes," and how frequently this mewing up also involves reading or listening; the "paved parlour" where Pandarus finds Criseyde and her companions reading about the siege of Thebes (2.82) becomes the enclosed garden where she hears Antigone sing of love (2.812-910) and the chamber she retreats to "ful pryvely . . . for to rede" Troilus' declaration of love (2.1173-79). In each case, the closeting involves both a major step forward in the narrative and also an attempt to interpret or fix the meaning of the action, of course finally unsuccessful.

In Book 4, after Pandarus' control of the story has been definitively contested, the scene shifts to Criseyde's house, signifying that at this point hers will be the words and plots that count. Criseyde's shift out of Troy is echoed by Troilus and Pandarus, who, discontent in their own houses, go to visit Sarpedon; her absence is then confronted directly by Troilus on his return, when Criseyde's empty house figures it to him absolutely and without remedy:[28] "whan he . . . gan biholde / How shet was every wyndow of the place, / As frost, hym thoughte, his herte gan to colde" (5.533-35). His visual and verbal rehearsal of the places of their love becomes a revisiting of all the places of the poem – "lo, yonder saugh ich last my lady daunce" and so on:

> Thanne thoughte he thus: "O blisful lord Cupide,
> Whan I the proces have in my memorie
> How thow me hast wereyed on every syde,
> Men myght a book make of it, lik a storie."   (5.582-85)

Pandarus is (relatively) silent, his house of words now vacant; Criseyde's palace is also uninhabited; Troy literally emptied out, its possibilities exhausted. Troilus, whose name gives him a special connection to the place of his birth,[29] has nothing more to do than wait on the walls of the city, looking toward the tents of the Greek camp, which he views now with the same nostalgia that had colored his vision of Criseyde's house:

> Upon the walles faste ek wolde he walke,
> And on the Grekis oost he wolde se;
> And to hymself right thus he wolde talke:

---

[28] The critical history of this passage, with special attention to its word play as well as its rhetorical form, is reviewed by Fleming, 1-44.
[29] See Patterson, 111.

> "Lo, yonder is myn owene lady free,
> Or ellis yonder, ther tho tentes be."   (5.666–70)

Criseyde herself has the complementary experience. Exiled to the tents of the Greek camp,

> Ful rewfully she loked upon Troie,
> Biheld the toures heigh and ek the halles;
> "Allas," quod she, "the plesance and the joie,
> The which that now al torned into galle is,
> Have ich had ofte withinne yonder walles!"   (5.729–33)

But the contrast is instructive, since the walls of tents are not to be equated with the walls of palaces and cities; they are the temporary walls of war, portable and insubstantial. Just as the space outside Semiramis' Babylon or Theseus' Athens was wild and ungoverned, so the Greek camp is beyond the walls of Troy and so beyond their civilizing influence. Although of course chiefly a function of the fighting that occurs outside the city walls, this wildness is more importantly characterized as a matter of language. The courtly language at which Pandarus is adept itself "writes" the story of Troilus and Criseyde up to a point; past that point, it is an inadequate language – it increasingly leaves out too much, and what it does encompass is more and more clearly false. Pandarus' representation to Criseyde of how he first witnessed Troilus's love sickness "In-with the paleis gardyn" (2.508) might be true, as might his tale of Poliphete – though here he is at the least unkindly exploiting Criseyde's fears; the story of Horaste, however, is patently false.

Book 3, ironically presided over by Calliope, muse of heroic poetry, is characterized not only by the consummation of love but also by the most blatant and explicitly pointed misuse of language yet in the poem, culminating in a set of exchanges on the topic of reference in language. Pandarus' acknowledgment that he has become for Troilus "Bitwixen game and ernest, swich a meene / As maken wommen unto men to comen" (3.254–55) is soon undercut by Troilus' attempt to blur reality with an oversubtle emphasis on motive, "for wyde-wher is wist / How that ther is diversite requered / Bytwixen thynges like" (3.404–6). Similarly, Criseyde's denunciation of those who excuse jealousy by giving it the false name of love (3.1023–29) is followed immediately by what amounts to a retraction, allowing some license with the term: "But certeyn is, som manere jalousie / Is excusable more than som, iwys" (3.1030–31). Underlying all is a confusion of substance and accident – "so like a sooth at prime face" (3.919) – in language. The "accident" referred to here is Pandarus' story requiring Criseyde to provide solace posthaste to the unfortunate Troilus. Though necessary to advance a love that all desire and that is at least partly grounded in real and profound emotion, that story is untrue. It is feigning "for the nones" or "for the lasse harm," but feigning nonetheless.

The poem partly aims to show how easily such feigning loses its good name and becomes mere self-indulgence, with no possible moral veneer. In Book 4,

Troilus again opposes substance and accident in mourning his unwillingness to ravish Criseyde; it turns out, however, that the substance to which he refers is first the "sikernesse" of love and then, more vulgarly, "substaunce / Of tresour," the wealth that could support the lovers in their exile (4.1505–16). Troilus loses his one real opportunity to speak up for straight referential language, when he fails to second Hector's famous "Syres, she nys no prisonere . . . / We usen here no wommen for to selle" (4.179, 182). Indeed, this failing is common to the Trojan people as a whole, since Paris's unlawful abduction of Helen lies at the root of the war. Trojan disregard for the distinction between Antenor and Criseyde finally leads to the fatal breaching of the walls, when the first is admitted and the second expelled. The language of courtly love, with its glosses, evasions, and overly subtle distinctions, does not hold up under pressure of history or under scrutiny of the public eye. It can hold off or obscure history temporarily, but it cannot halt the inexorable progress of the real threat outside the walls. The lovers' arrogation of religious and martial language in the early books had pointed as much to a lack in the discourse of courtly love as to its power. As Vance puts it, "In spatial terms . . . we have a dramatic setting in which any occurrence in the speech of lovers of the conventional oxymorons of violence (flames, wounds, dying, etc.) cannot fail to point outward to an extramural violence that is *not* figurative but 'real'" (283). Conversely, the real violence outside the walls merely echoes the figurative violence that has already been done to language inside; only when this linguistic degradation is complete does the scene of action shift to the space outside, as a signal of emptiness within the walls. Diomede's "tonge large" (5.804), his utter disregard for language ("I shal namore lesen but my speche" [5.798]), and the "straunge" wording of Criseyde's letters or speech to Diomede are but mirrors of what discourse has already become within Troy. Ironically, linguistic performance inside the walls becomes in the end at least as delusional as that outside; rather than Calchas, who like Cassandra at least speaks the truth, the real masters of "ambages" – words with two faces (5.897–99) – are Pandarus and Troilus, who square off in opposition to the forces of history. In ever more inventive attempts to deny the truth of Criseyde's betrayal, Troilus and Pandarus walk and "play" on the walls of Troy and visit its gates; but the reality of Trojan falsehood in its various forms finally enters in. Outside and inside mingle in blood, and Troilus' famed "trouthe" comes too late to save his city.

Lucrece's Inviolable Walls

The dynamics of this mingling are thrown into relief when *Troilus and Criseyde* is contrasted to the Legend of Lucrece, the tale in Chaucer's legendary of female saints that most closely mimics and revises the structure of the earlier poem. Lucrece tells the story, far briefer, of another siege, where the language of one place invades and disrupts another. This time, however, the structure of invasion is simpler and starker. The offending words are spoken solely by men and are the direct result of the moral wildness involved in the soldier's life outside the walls:

> Whan Ardea beseged was aboute
> With Romeyns, that ful sterne were and stoute,
> Ful longe lay the sege and lytel wroughten,
> So that they were half idel, as hem thoughten;
> And in his pley Tarquinius the yonge
> Gan for to jape, for he was lyght of tonge,
> And seyde that it was an ydel lyf;
> No man dide there no more than his wif.
> "And lat us speke of wyves, that is best;
> Preyse every man his owene as hym lest,
> And with oure speche lat us ese oure herte." (1694–1704)

This game causes Tarquinius and Colatyn to invade the space of Rome, closely identified here with Lucrece, as they negotiate the "estris," the private quarters of her house. Much is made of this invasion and Lucrece's vulnerability: "And prively into the hous they gon, / Nor at the yate porter nas there non, / And at the chambre-dore they abyde" (1716–18), eavesdropping on speech that serves as a model in this tale for accurate and referential language – "Hyre contenaunce is to hire herte dygne, / For they acorde bothe in dede and sygne" (1738–39). It turns out that the seemingly idle wife is busier, at spinning, and more constant than the men. Thus, as the God of Love required, sin is attached to men, virtue to women; and the poetic sin of the *Troilus* is overturned. Retrospectively, however, Lucrece's pious wish for her husband's safety in the siege – "God wolde the walles were falle adoun!" (1726) – is given sinister and ironic meaning when her own walls fail to protect her. The private space marked off by the walls of her house, then the walls that are her body, become an opportunity for Tarquinius, who now knows his way around Lucrece and who, once more outside the walls of Ardea, is busily rehearsing her charms, making them a kind of romance just as Troilus had romanticized Criseyde: "Thus lay hire her, and thus fresh was hyre hewe; / Thus sat, thus spak, thus span; this was hire chere / Thus fayr she was, and this was hire manere" (1761–63). He has constructed of her body and her house a collection of memory *loci* that guide him back to her and give him a kind of warrant to gain a rough and degenerate access. Even his language moves down a notch, reflecting the degradation of his sensibility, which is now all directed toward the self and the satisfaction of private desire: " 'For, maugre hyre, she shal my leman be! / Hap helpeth hardy man alday,' quod he" (1772–73).

His fantasy realized upon Lucrece has the piteous and disastrous results that everyone knows; despite her guilelessness and guiltlessness, no number of "ensamples" can prevent her from doing away with herself – "I wol not have noo forgyft for nothing" (1853) – and to some extent rightly so. The structure of the poem demands it: the penetration of the world within the walls by the world outside involves a loss of innocence that can never be repaired. Lucrece's silence, immobility, and concern for her name – as Tarquinius "that art a kynges eyr" is unconcerned for his – is in some ways the only possible response to the ambiguities of language that his sin introduces into Rome, for life after the rape would require a reconfiguration of language to account for motive and intention, similar to that engaged in by Troilus, Pandarus, and Criseyde.[30] And yet the extremity of Lucrece's response – embodied in the care she takes while dying "Lest that hir fet or suche thyng lay bare" (1859) – gives pause. There is much that is problematic here and that thus calls into question the project and status of the legendary. Some moral casuistry would certainly be appropriate for Lucrece. As her friends tells her, the rape "was no gilt; it lay not in hir myght" (1849). Surely these friends are right, and guilt has something to do with intention and is not simply the inner reflection of act. Indeed, this is the substance of Augustine's "gret compassioun" for Lucrece to which Chaucer makes oblique and ironic reference (1690–91): though not guilty of adultery, Lucrece, in Augustine's view, *is* guilty of the greater sin of homicide when she punishes her innocent self by taking her own life.[31] The legend of Lucrece is thus also partly the story of a too literal observance of the distinctions or "rules" – as Horace said – "for wedded life," a too willing and unshrinking obeisance to the walls.

To sum up, the wall was an ideal image for the civilizing power of art since in classical and medieval times the wall was in fact the condition of stable culture, and a primary function of walls in many of Chaucer's fictions (for example, *Troilus and Criseyde* and the Knight's Tale) is political defense. Moreover, walls were specifically connected to the lyric and poetic arts through mythographic characters, like Amphion and Apollo, who were known as both poets and wall-builders. But walls have two sides, and every immurement also suggests a loss: first a loss of freedom and possibility but even more fundamentally the inevitable wastage that time brings to every structure. *The Canterbury Tales*, indeed, are defined by opposing possibilities for the verbal arts as represented in the wall image. If the Knight's Tale, on the one hand, celebrates the repeated taming of the wild space beyond the walls, the Manciple's Tale explores the powerful and violent forces of disorder that the walls of language may fail to contain.

Indeed, this double-sidedness is a central effect of the wall in a number of Chaucerian narratives, where the wall as a threshold object simultaneously invites and discourages connection. In both the legend of Thisbe and in *Troilus and Criseyde* a contrast is drawn between the determinate and fixed meaning within the walls and the dangerous and disruptive forces that lie beyond them. *Troilus and Criseyde*, however, goes even further, in dramatizing how behavior within the walls – overzealous storytelling and oversubtle, evasive, and self-

---

[30] One might say, to use the terms of Carolyn Dinshaw's analysis, that the effect of Tarquinius's rape would be to cause Lucrece to "read like a woman," a possibility that the project of the *Legend of Good Women* excludes; see *Chaucer's Sexual Poetics* (Madison: University of Wisconsin Press, 1989), 84–87.

[31] See Saint Augustine, *The City of God* [1.19], trans. George E. McCracken, Loeb Classical Library, 7 vols. (Cambridge, Mass.: Harvard University Press, 1957).

delusional manipulation of distinctions – occludes real reference and blunts the civilizing force of language. As a narrative of siege and invasion, then, *Troilus and Criseyde* prefigures the later legend of Lucrece, another story in which the moral and lexical wilderness outside breaks in upon the inside and perpetrates the ultimate violation of boundaries, the rape. In this tale, Chaucer also moralizes Lucrece's purity as one sort of art, upright and perfectly referential, and Tarquinius' as another, idle, oblique, overimaginative, and self-referential. But Chaucer's ambiguous irony also calls Lucrece's punctiliousness into question. In going too far, this parable of moral purity becomes also an affirmation of the Troiluses, Pandaruses, and Criseydes of the world, who, like Chaucer, are capable of "ambages," of testing the limits of language, in effect, of "playing" on the walls.

Chaucer's Discourse of Mariology: Gaining the Right to Speak

CAROLYN P. COLLETTE

When the Wife of Bath announces that "Experience thogh noon auctoritee" is sufficient warrant for her to speak about the woe in marriage, she appropriates for herself the right to speak publicly about topics – women, sex, marriage, and the learned tradition of anti-feminism – that were the province of men, part of the male domain of language and of the written text. Even today the Wife of Bath seems bold as she opposes herself, her life, her experience, and her own unique pattern of language to the male-centered cultural tradition of the Middle Ages. For Chaucer's audience she must have seemed admirable or foolish as she affirmed her right, however briefly, to control the stories of her culture, to pass them on, in effect, to "peynte the leon" by herself. By and large at the end of the fourteenth century and for the next two hundred years, women who wrote in English did not claim the authority of their own personal experience to command attention but framed their right to speak within the authority of religious tradition.[1] In this paper I want to consider how two of the more conservative narrators among Chaucer's Canterbury pilgrims – the Prioress and the Second Nun – establish their claim to be heard. The Wife of Bath claims experience as the authority for her voice. What, we may ask, do these religious women claim as the authority for their voices in a culture that valued female silence and distrusted female speech?

By way of sketching a preliminary answer to this question this paper will read their Prologues against the most obvious source of authority they claim as the foundation for their right to be heard – their invocations to the Virgin Mary. Doing this means following an approach long available to Chaucer scholars but, except for the work of Sister Madeleva, one relatively unexplored; it means considering how the themes and language of their Prologues – their discourse – draw upon the traditions, the motifs, and the

---

[1] The topic of how women writers of the English Renaissance claim the authority of the virtuous woman by drawing on a discourse of religion is discussed by Elaine Beilin in *Redeeming Eve: Women Writers of the English Renaissance* (Princeton: Princeton University Press, 1987).

127

symbolism of Marian veneration that characterized late medieval Catholicism in England.[2] Such a reading of the Prologues as both drawing on and contributing to the sacred and secular poetry composed to honor the Virgin during the late fourteenth and early fifteenth centuries reveals that the two Prologues are more similar than they appear and that the tales that follow them share a common subtext focused on the power of the Virgin to sustain the speech of those who venerate her.

Writing about the Virgin Mary is always difficult because she is a liminal figure who unites heaven and earth, the human and the divine. As such she functions as the central figure of a myth in the sense that in the idea of "the Virgin Mary" medieval culture located a dynamic equilibrium of tensions both exalting the female and stressing her humility. During the late Middle Ages the Virgin wore many faces; she was the handmaid of the Lord, the *mater dolorosa*, the virgin mother, the Queen of Heaven. In focusing on the Virgin's power as it is invoked in these Prologues, this paper does not seek to deny the multiplicity of her roles nor to minimize her humility. Rather, it offers a complementary perspective, arguing that the explicit and implicit allusions the Prioress and her Nun make to the liturgy of the Virgin and the traditions of her life constitute a specific, well-formulated pattern of references to the Virgin as a female exemplar of wisdom and purity, a guide to heaven, a protectress of devout women, a figure who in every way justifies their right to speak – to contribute to the tale-telling of the pilgrimage.

What constellation of ideas, stories, and myths did the phrase "the Virgin Mary" conjure for late medieval English people? Where did they encounter the texts and images that comprised that body of meaning? To answer these questions it is not necessary to review what is already well-established about the earlier medieval dissemination of the cult of the Virgin or the wide circulation of stories about the miracles attributed to her.[3] What bears more directly on the argument of this paper is the fact that the Virgin and a series of services in her honor were a common part of daily religious life during the later Middle Ages, for laypeople as well as clergy. By the second half of the fourteenth century church records in England show that there the "daily recital

---

[2] For previous discussions of the cultural centrality of the Virgin and of Chaucer's references to well-known religious liturgies celebrating her, see Hardy Long Frank, "Chaucer's Prioress and the Blessed Virgin," *Chaucer Review* 13 (1978–79): 346–62; and Sister M. Madeleva, *A Lost Language and Other Essays on Chaucer* (New York: Sheed and Ward, 1951), 52–55.

[3] On the ancient English tradition of devotion to the Virgin, see Rosemary Woolf, *The English Religious Lyric in the Middle Ages* (Oxford: Clarendon Press, 1968), 116ff.; and Beverly Boyd, *The Middle English Miracles of the Virgin* (San Marino, Ca.: The Huntington Library, 1964), 3ff. On the Miracles of the Virgin and the Prioress' Tale, see Robert W. Frank, Jr., "Miracles of the Virgin, Medieval Anti-Semitism, and the *Prioress's Tale*," in *The Wisdom of Poetry: Essays in Early English Literature in Honor of Morton W. Bloomfield*, ed. Larry D. Benson and Siegfried Wenzel (Kalamazoo: Medieval Institute Publications, 1982), 177–88, 290–97.

of the offices of the Blessed Virgin and of the dead was now obligatory on all, and that by virtue of the general custom of all nations."[4] During the late Middle Ages this daily veneration was supported by the fact that the Hours of the Virgin occupied a central position in the *prymer*, those books, frequently in the possession of laypeople, of collected prayers and devotions that formed the equivalent of universal prayerbooks. While there were some variations in order and inclusiveness, virtually all *prymers* still in existence agree in a common core of devotions: the Hours of the Blessed Virgin, the Seven Penitential Psalms, the Fifteen Gradual Psalms, the Litany, the Office for the Dead, the Commendations (Littlehales, xxxix). The popularity of these books is attested by the frequent reference to *prymers* in wills as well as in literature; the Prioress's own tale describes the little boy studying from his *prymer*. Apparently these texts formed a basic part of the religious culture of the period. An Italian visitor to England in the late fifteenth century reported that English people "all attend mass every day, and say many Paternosters in public, the women carrying long rosaries in their hands, and those who can read carry with them the office of Our Lady, and say it in Church in a low voice with some companion, verse and verse after the manner of the churchmen" (Littlehales, xxxvii–xxxviii).

The veneration of Mary demonstrated in the recitation of these hours, known as the Little Office of the Virgin, was complemented by a series of feasts established to mark the major events of her life. December 8 was the Feast of Mary's Conception, February 2 the Feast of the Purification, March 25 the Feast of the Annunciation, August 15 the Feast of the Assumption, September 8 the Feast of her Nativity; she was particularly celebrated in the Christmas liturgy, and by the late Middle Ages, Saturdays were set aside as special days of devotion to the Virgin. Devotion to Mary was enjoined by the Lateran Council of 1215 which added the Ave Maria to the Pater Noster and the Creed as prayers to be recited by all. Theologically, the reasons for this increasing level of devotion were centered in the exaltation of her unique relationship to Christ, so that she "should have a share in the praise which the religious orders constantly offered to God" (Woolf, 118). Sarah Weber, writing about the theology underlying the religious lyrics of the period, says, "Her place closest to Christ, and her life in the most perfect image of His, is praised, meditated on and invoked. Her life is celebrated through the course of the year in the seasonal cycles, and the hours of each day are consecrated to her in the *Horae*, in which the life of Christ" is seen through the present joy of Mary, who by the Assumption is the promise of man's final joy.[5]

Stories of Mary, her girlhood, her devotion, her family, and especially her relationship with her mother, St. Anne (who also received increasing veneration during this period), were commonplace parts of late medieval

---

[4] Henry Littlehales, ed., *The Prymer or Lay Folks' Prayer Book*, EETS OS 105, 109 (London: Kegan Paul, Trench, Trübner & Co., 1895), xxxv ff.

[5] Sarah Appleton Weber, *Theology and Poetry in the Middle English Lyric: A Study of Sacred History and Aesthetic Form* (Columbus: Ohio State University Press, 1969), 15.

religious and folk lore, spread in large part by the diffusion of various books of the Apocrypha, especially the eastern Gospel of Thomas and the Book of James, known in Western culture as the Pseudo Matthew.[6] In these stories the Virgin's life, about which nothing is known from the canonical Gospels, is described in detail; the special circumstances of her conception and birth, her natural devotion to God, her virginal fostering in the Temple where she was attended by her handmaids, her proof of her faithfulness to her virgin vows after she was discovered to be pregnant, the independent testimony of the midwife that after the birth of Christ Mary remained *virgo intacta*, all were common stories during the period, stemming from the Apocrypha.[7] In the context of this paper it is notable, too, that in the apocryphal stories of Mary's life, she is a strong central figure who preaches enlightenment to the Apostles just before her death.[8] Marina Warner argues, "The walls and retables, the manuscripts and liturgical objects, the embroidery on medieval vestments, the misericords of choir stalls and even the bosses in chapel vaults are incomprehensible without a knowledge of these myths woven around the central protagonists of the central Christian mystery of God's Incarnation" (29).

In addition to the various forms of ecclesiastical veneration of the Virgin – the services, the images, the popular stories of her life – throughout the fourteenth and fifteenth centuries English poetry celebrated the events of her life and the spiritual temperament that underlay the divine miracle centered in her body. Anonymous lyrics and the works of major poets like Chaucer and Lydgate attest to the hold Mary, her life and her body, exercised over the popular imagination. The lyrics, the poetry, and the Hours of the Virgin are united in emphasizing the centrality and apparently the cultural popularity of a core of interpretants and referents associated with the idea of "the Virgin" during this time. Mary was omnipresent in the liturgy, in the fabric of ecclesiastical life, in story, and in literature; she was a unique figure whose power bridged this world and the next, life and death, sinner and salvation. She redeemed Eve's loss and all women's shame by her virtue, her inner spiritual radiance, and her outer physical beauty. She was Christ's devoted mother, a channel to Him for the Apostles in the apocryphal tradition and a channel to Him for medieval Christians who bid her pray for them, to use her power of speech and language to win mercy and ultimately salvation.

Even more directly relevant to this paper, though, is the fact that the Virgin was conceived of as especially aware of devout women. In Matins she is addressed as "Seynt marie, mekest of alle meke wymmen . . . holieste of alle

---

[6] Marina Warner, *Alone of All Her Sex: The Myth and the Cult of the Virgin Mary* (New York: Random House, 1983), 30.

[7] These stories were collected and retold in a variety of fashions. One form, the life of the Virgin, is represented in this paper by Lydgate's *Life of Our Lady*, a compendious account of the stories and myths that surrounded the medieval idea of "the Virgin."

[8] See Montague Rhodes James, trans., *The Apocryphal New Testament* (Oxford: Clarendon Press, 1924), for the Gospel of Bartholomew.

holi wymmen,"[9] and she is petitioned in Matins and in Evensong to "Preie for þe puple; bide for þe clergie; biseche for deuoute wommans kynde. . . ." Such references validate their relationship to the Virgin who intercedes for all the faithful who pray to her but who is apparently particularly mindful of devout women. While neither "holi" nor "devout" is a term restricted to cloistered women, both are presumably terms that apply to the Prioress and her Nun who, in the discourse of their Prologues, align themselves with Mary both as petitioners and as probationers in the art of using language adequately and appropriately. In including the discourse of Marian veneration in her opening, each narrator has defined herself as Mary's handmaid and wrapped herself in the Virgin's mantle. As the two tales unfold, we see that they are both *exempla* illustrating how emulating Mary's virtues can help the faithful overcome the limitations of material life and preserve the power of speech.

The Prioress's tale is clearly the more obviously rooted in the Marian tradition, for it is a miracle of the Virgin, one of the stories told to magnify and to glorify the Virgin's power in suspending the laws of nature on earth for those who venerate her. The tale, together with the Prologue, forms a united whole centered in the themes of a mother's love for her child, praise and celebration of the Virgin, and her power over the ordinary forces of the natural world. In light of the extensive, if ambiguous, description of the person and the spirituality of the Prioress in the General Prologue, Chaucer criticism has focused on the diminutive, the child-like in both her tale and its prologue.[10] It is generally assumed that in the Prologue the Prioress's spirituality is of a simple sort and that she aptly likens herself to a nursing infant unable to speak, but, as we shall see, a great deal more is happening in the Prologue than

---

[9] All citations of the Hours of the Virgin (services for Matins, Lauds, Prime, Tierce, None, Evensong, and Compline) are from the Middle English version of the *Prymer* edited by Littlehales. The Middle English version is used here because its language, dating from the early fifteenth century (Cambridge MS. Dd. 11, 82), reflects the vernacular phrasing and conceptualization of Mariology. Since Chaucer's female narrators speak in the vernacular, it's reasonable to look for approximately contemporary language to compare to theirs.

[10] While a great deal has been written about the Prioress's tale and a fair amount about the Second Nun's, what has been written tends to cluster around several well-explored topics. In the Prioress's case the nature of her spirituality and the anti-semitism of her tale have attracted most attention; among the works that explore the tale in directions similar to the one this paper adopts, see Robert Worth Frank, Jr., and Hardy Long Frank (above, notes 2 and 3); and Alfred David, "An ABC to the Style of the Prioress" in *Acts of Interpretation: The Text in its Context 700–1600: Essays on Medieval and Renaissance Literature in Honor of E. Talbot Donaldson*, ed. Mary J. Carruthers and Elizabeth D. Kirk (Norman, Okla.: Pilgrim Books, 1982), 147–57. On critical responses to the tale and its anti-semitic dimension, see Louise O. Fradenburg, "Criticism, Anti-Semitism, and the Prioress's Tale," *Exemplaria* 1 (1989): 69–115. In the case of the Second Nun's Tale, the topic of Marian devotion has not really been explored yet. For a review of the criticism of each tale up to the year 1989, see Carolyn P. Collette, "Critical Approaches to the Prioress' Tale and the Second Nun's Tale," in *Chaucer's Religious Tales*, ed. C. David Benson and Elizabeth Robertson (Cambridge: D. S. Brewer, 1990), 95–110.

modern readers see at first. For a medieval audience the stanzas of the Prologue would echo with the language and the themes of the Hours of the Virgin. Certainly the idea of child-like innocent faith is conceptually central to the Prologue, for it appears at the end of the initial stanza – "by the mouth of children thy bountee / Parfourned is, for on the brest soukynge / Somtyme shewen they thyn heriynge" (VII.457–59) – and at the end of the last stanza of the Prologue – "But as a child of twelf month oold, or lesse, / That kan unnethes any word expresse, / Right so fare I, and therfore I yow preye, / Gydeth my song that I shal of yow seye" (VII.484–87) – framing, as it were, the Prioress's introduction to her tale.[11] These allusions to the nursing infant have traditionally been understood within the context of Psalm 8, which is part of the Matins liturgy of the Hours of the Virgin. In a recent article, "*Loves Hete* in the Prioress's Prologue and Tale," Marie Borroff explicates part of the complex web of signification attendant on these images:

> Alluding to the "infants and sucklings" of Psalm 8, out of whose mouths God has perfected his praise, the Prioress implicitly distinguishes this miraculous activity (an infant [Latin *infans*] being literally "one incapable of speech") from that of the adult "men of dignitee" who are most fully qualified, by authority and learning, to "perform" God's praise in the natural order of things. She herself, a woman and therefore presumably lacking the qualifications of these male divines, resembles rather the inarticulate infants. . . . She thus becomes one of the infants of the Psalm, and the Virgin, by implication, becomes the mother suckling the infant upon her breast. Insofar as her "declaring" of her story, despite this virtually inarticulate state, is made possible by the help and guidance of the divine mother, it is itself a miracle of the Virgin, spreading her praise through her own intercession. . . .[12]

Within the context of this tale about voicing praise of the Virgin the interpretation offered above is central to understanding how and in what way meaning is created in the language the Prioress uses. But to stop here is to neglect the rest of the verse from which the lines "But by the mouth of children thy bountee / Parfourned is, for on the brest soukynge / Somtyme shewen they

---

11 *The Riverside Chaucer*, 3d ed., gen. ed. Larry D. Benson (Boston: Houghton Mifflin, 1987). All subsequent quotations from Chaucer's works are taken from this edition.

12 Marie Borroff, "*Loves Hete* in the Prioress's Prologue and Tale," in *The Olde Daunce: Love, Friendship, Sex and Marriage in the Medieval World*, ed. Robert R. Edwards and Stephen Spector (Albany: State University of New York Press, 1991), 230–31. Elizabeth Robertson, "Aspects of Female Piety in the Prioress's Tale," in *Chaucer's Religious Tales*, ed. C. David Benson and Elizabeth Robertson (Cambridge: D. S. Brewer, 1990), 145–160, makes a similar point that the image "suggests the idea that the child's dependence on the female breast will lead to words of wisdom" (153). She also refers to Caroline Bynum's exploration of this theme in *Holy Feast and Holy Fast: The Religious Significance of Food to Medieval Women* (Berkeley and Los Angeles: University of California Press, 1987). On the idea of nurturing central to the Christian story, see Bynum's *Jesus as Mother: Studies in the Spirituality of the High Middle Ages* (Berkeley and Los Angeles: University of California Press, 1982).

thyn heriynge" are taken. In the Middle English *Prymer* the complete second
verse of Psalm 8 reads: "Of þe mouþ of ȝonge children not spekinge &
soukynge mylk, þou madist perfitli heriyng for þin enemyes; þat þou distrie þe
enemye & avengere." The Eighth Psalm, part of Matins, is a song in praise of
the Lord's strength, his domination, and his creating man "a litil lasse þan
aungelis . . . ordeyned . . . aboue þe werkis of þin hondis." Rather than focus
on the child here, the psalm focuses on the power of the Lord to raise even
children to be his saints and prophets, to defeat his enemies. Verse 7 of Psalm
19 (also part of Matins) makes the same point in the same discourse, that the
power of the Lord is so great it can strengthen and enlighten even little
children: "The lawe of þe lord is wiþ-out wem, & conuertiþ soulis; þe
witnessyng of þe lord is feiþful, & ȝyueþ wisdom to litle children."

But more is happening in the Prioress's allusion than this elevation of
children. The reference to the nursing infant draws on a complex, interwoven
set of themes and metaphors centered in the Virgin's milk, which literally
sustained Christ's life, but metaphorically came to represent the grace,
wisdom, and strength he offered by being born through her. The Prioress's
image of the infant sucking at the breast and her later identification of herself
with that infant can be understood within the context of intense symbolism
centering in the milk as a powerful religious image. Marina Warner makes the
point this way:

> The milk of the Mother of God became even more highly charged with
> the symbolism of life, for the life of life's own source depended on it.
> When the medieval mystic meditated on the Incarnation, he saw not only
> a mother nursing her baby – an event in historical time – but an eternal
> mystery whereby the Christian soul is perpetually nourished and
> sustained by grace, of which Mary's milk is a sublime epiphany. Thus the
> Church, too, *Ecclesia*, associated with Mary, is depicted as a mother, as in
> Isaiah's passage on Jerusalem, which is now read in the mass of the Feast
> of Our Lady of Lourdes: "Behold, I will extend peace to her like a river,
> and the glory of the Gentiles like a flowing stream: then shall ye suck, ye
> shall be borne upon her sides, and be dandled upon her knees" (Isaiah
> 66:12). (194)

The Middle English Hours of the Virgin mention this theme at least twice,
linking the act of suckling with grace and wisdom. In the service for Lauds,
this prayer, where the Virgin's milk is linked to salvation for Christians, is
addressed to her: "O þou ioieful womman, hiȝe aboue þe sterris, him þat made
þee of nouȝt, wiseliche þou ȝaf souke wiþ þin hooli tete. That sorie eue dide
awey, þou ȝeldist wiþ hooli fruyt. Þou art maad wyndowe of heuene, þat
soreuful men entre as sterris. . . ." The anthem for Lauds stresses that Mary
suckled Christ not as an infant but as the King of Heaven: ". . . and þou,
maiden, alone to ȝyue souke to þe king of aungelis!" Later in the day, in the
service for Compline the topic comes up in Psalm 131 (Vulgate 130) as a trope
for proper orientation of the soul: "As a child wened on his modir, so ȝelding
be in my soule!" (3). Lydgate's *Life of Our Lady* emphasizes the same points –

the abounding grace of Mary's milk; its river-like abundance; its symbolizing the bond between Christ and his Mother, between human and divine; and its metaphoric, spiritual sustaining virtue for Christians, for whom it is a symbol of protection against sin and death:

Ther was his [Christ's] foode and his norchyng pure,
Sothefaste seler of his sustynaunce;
The tune of lyfe that euere dyd endure,
Ilyche fresshe vnto his pleasaunce,
Withe sacrede lycoure of holy habundaunce,
That noon but he may touche nor aproche,
For it for hym was only set abroche.

For in that licour was full remedye,
Holy refute, and pleynly medycyne
Ayayne the venyme brought in by envye,
Thorugh fals engyne and malyce serpentyne,
Whan the snake made Adam to dyne
Of the Appull that was intoxicate,
Falsely with god to make hym at debate.

But nowe the mylke of thy pappes tweyne,
Benygne lady, is to vs tryacle, –
Whiche in thy brest sprenketh fro a vayne, –
Ayenst dethe to be to vs obstacle.
O how it is a passyng high myracle,
Thorugh goddys myght and by nought elles,
Oute of a breste to see two small wellys

Of mayden mylke spryng as a Ryuer,
To yefe hym drynke that is kyng of alle.
O goode lady, o hevenly boteler,
When we in myscheve to the clepe and calle,
Some drope of grace lat vpon vs falle;
And to that seler make a Redy waye,
Wher thou alone of mercy beryste the keye.

And of grace lat be no scarste,
Gode lady that arte of grace well. . . . (3.1688–1717)[13]

The medieval celebration of Mary never forgot that she sustained Christ's life, both by virtue of her physical body and by virtue of her goodness. Metaphorically her milk, in sustaining Christ's life, sustains all humankind;

[13] *A Critical Edition of John Lydgate's Life of Our Lady*, gen. ed. Joseph A. Lauritis (Pittsburgh, Pa.: Duquesne University Press, 1961), 549–51. All subsequent quotations from Lydgate's *Life of Our Lady* are taken from this edition. Although it postdates Chaucer's work by approximately fifty years, Lydgate's poem is useful in that it builds on the popular traditions, stories, and myths associated with the Virgin during this period. In so doing, it becomes a representative of late medieval popular piety centered in the Virgin.

literally it is grace abounding. To refer to her milk in the image of a nursing infant is thus both to acknowledge Mary's power and to position oneself as a child in relation to her, in order to gain wisdom, strength, and grace to live in the world. In light of this tradition the Prioress's apparent focus on her child-like state may be less an acknowledgement of her own ineptitude than her recognition that she, like all humans, is dependent on Mary and her son for enlightenment and grace, qualities the Prioress needs to tell her tale in a manner worthy of its subject. To focus too narrowly on the Prioress's child-likeness may be to read the metaphor literally and to miss its full meaning. In picturing herself as a nursing infant the Prioress aligns herself here with a widespread, popular spiritual trope of enablement.

The Prioress similarly underscores the Virgin's power and strength in alluding to her role in the conception of Christ when in the third stanza of the Prologue she introduces the paradox of Mary's virgin motherhood by the metaphor of the burning bush: "O mooder Mayde, O mayde Mooder free! / O bussh unbrent, brennynge in Moyses sighte" (467–8). A popular image in medieval devotion, the Prioress's chiasmus is echoed in the Anthem for the service of Sext that links the paradox with a petition to the Virgin to exert the power that she possesses by virtue of this manifestation of her sublime spirituality, to pray for the faithful: "Bi þe buysch þat moises siȝ vnbrent, we knowen þat þi preisable maidenhede is kept. modir of god, preie for us!"

The Prologue moves from the paradox of the Virgin's motherhood to a complex theological point, one well understood in the Middle Ages. The Prioress's lines, "That ravyshedest doun fro the Deitee, / Thurgh thyn humblesse, the Goost that in th'alighte, / Of whos vertu, whan he thyn herte lighte, / Conceyved was the Fadres sapience . . ." (469–72), attest to the Virgin's active participation in the Incarnation by virtue of her spiritual purity, and her intellectual wisdom rooted in her humility.[14] Her excellent goodness manifest in the popular tradition of her piety and devotion to God mean that, as Roman Catholic tradition puts it, "She conceived her Son in her soul before she conceived him in the flesh, as the Fathers of the Church vie with one another in declaring. She gave birth to him through complete docility to the Holy Spirit who came to overshadow her."[15] "The Church sees her as standing to attest her consent to Christ's sacrifice; that her will is in the most perfect accord with that of her Son who is offering himself freely to the Father . . ." (Suenens, 63). Her "yes" in the *ecce ancilla domine* allows her to participate as co-redemptrix in human salvation. Here again the liturgy of the Virgin and the elevated courtly discourse at times used in poetry to address and describe her beauty enter into understanding the full medieval signification of this line. The Virgin's beauty

---

[14] Sumner Ferris makes this point succinctly in his article, "The Mariology of the *Prioress's Tale*," *American Benedictine Review* 32 (1981): 232–54, when he says, "Four compendious lines thus establish clearly, and with the closest approach to theological language in the *Tale*, the Blessed Virgin's active role in the Incarnation" (239).

[15] L. J. Suenens, *Mary the Mother of God*, vol. 44 of *The Twentieth Century Encyclopedia of Catholicism* (New York: Hawthorn Books, 1959), 52.

was conceived and communicated in terms of the Song of Songs 4.7 ("Tota pulchra es, amica mea, et macula non est in te") as well as within the context of Psalm 44 (Vulgate): "Et concupiscet rex decorum tuum" (44:12).[16] The Virgin is both the humble handmaid of the Lord and the radiant, immaculate, beautiful epitome of humankind whose goodness attracts God's favor. She was worthy in every respect to conceive the essence of the Godhead as the infant Christ. Much of the popular apocryphal literature describing her girlhood as a life lived in holy innocence, within the sheltering walls of the temple, can be read as an attempt to explain how and why she was so "attractive" to God.

Central to the idea of her power to attract God was the tradition of the Virgin's own fitness to enclose within her body the wisdom of God. The conception of Christ is the conception of the "Fadres sapience" (472) – that is, wisdom, the Logos.[17] Mary was the appropriate mother for God because she had from her birth trained her spirit and her mind to do God's will in all humility. Again Lydgate offers an illuminating parallel in the first book of his *Life of Our Lady* where he likens the Virgin to Minerva:

> And as Mynerua, the mothir of prudence
> Is holde a mayde, Right so this hevynly quene
> Bare in hir wombe, the fadirs sapience
> And mothir was and a mayden clene
> Of god provydede playnely for to been
> Socour to man, and helpe in all our nede
> Whanne she was borne, this floure of womanhede. . . .
>
> (1.176–82)

In the stanza we have been discussing, Chaucer's Prioress recognizes and emphasizes the connection between wisdom and humility in the Virgin:

> O mooder Mayde, O mayde Mooder free!
> O bussh unbrent, brennynge in Moyses sighte,
> That ravyshedest doun fro the Deitee,
> Thurgh thyn humblesse, the Goost that in th'alighte,
> Of whos vertu, whan he thyn herte lighte,
> Conceyved was the Fadres sapience,
> Help me to telle it in thy reverence!   (467–73)

Here the dynamics of the stanza combine to produce some ambiguity in identifying the antecedent of the pronoun in the phrase "Of whos vertu." A

---

[16] Woolf (124 f.) discusses the combination of theology and the discourse of French love poetry that supports this theme of the Virgin's physical beauty. The Latin phrases quoted here are to be found in her text (125).

[17] It's interesting to note that Chaucer seems to oppose *sapience* here to *science* ("Ther may no tonge expresse in no science," 476) in a passage intimating the inability of human language adequately to praise the Virgin. In the Second Nun's tale Cecile is described as an image of "the cleernesse hool of sapience" (111). Sapience seems to denote the wisdom of grace as opposed to the possession of mere knowledge.

good case can be made, however, that because the subject of the stanza is Mary, it is her "vertu," which is the strength of her humility, through which "Conceyved was the Fadres sapience." Such a reading is reinforced by the Second Nun's Prologue – "Thow Mayde and Mooder, doghter of thy Sone, / Thow welle of mercy, synful soules cure, / In whom that God for bountee chees to wone" (36–38) – where the same idea that the Virgin's goodness attracted the divinity is expressed as well as in this anthem for Compline: "Wiþ gladnesse, halewe we þe mynde of blessid marie, þat sche preie for us to oure lord ihesu crist."

The next stanza of the Prologue introduces the theme of the Virgin's guidance and the light she sheds to open the way to God, her ability to anticipate human needs as well as to respond to human prayer:

> For somtyme, Lady, er men praye to thee,
> Thou goost biforn of thy benyngnytee,
> And getest us the lyght, of thy preyere,
> To gyden us unto thy Sone so deere.   (477–80)

The Hours of Evensong and Compline both contain this prayer bidding the Virgin to make clear the way to Christ, to guide the souls of the faithful: "Maide, þou art aloon deboner among alle! make us unbounde of synnes, & be chast and deboner. ȝyue us clene liyf. make redi a siker weie, so þat we, seynge god, be glade euere more." Matins combines this theme of the Virgin's making ready the way to heaven with the theme of her great worthiness to conceive the Son of God:

> Holi modir of god, þat worþili disseruedist to conseyue him þat al þe world miȝte not holde! wiþ þi meke biseching wasche awe oure giltis, þat we þat ben aȝenbouȝt moun stie up to þe seete of endeles blis, þere þou dwellist wiþ þi sone wiþ-outen tyme.

Reading the Prologue against the Hours of the Virgin and the popular tradition represented by Lydgate's *Life of Our Lady* reveals that every reference to the Virgin in this Prologue is a reference to her as a powerful figure, a *vates*, a maternal source of strength and of wisdom, a human woman in whom, because of her great faith and because of her mental and spiritual preparation, the laws of nature are overcome.[18] Because of who and what she is, her words have enough power to open the gates of salvation. It is a unique female power, as we have seen, centered in her motherhood, her conception, birth, and nourishing of Christ. To invoke the Virgin is to mantle oneself with this power, to align oneself, insofar as humanly possible, with it.

While the Prioress's Prologue from beginning to end draws meaning from a discourse rooted in veneration of the Virgin as powerful mother and guide,

---

[18] Lydgate devotes considerable attention to this theme in Book 3, where Nature "dyd obeye / To a mayde, and gafe vp hol her right, / Wysely aduertyng she was to feble of myght / In this matier to holde champartye" (3.978–81).

the Prologue to the Second Nun's Tale introduces yet other dimensions of the Virgin's power. Although the Second Nun and her tale have received less critical attention than the Prioress's Tale, the Second Nun's Tale, taken with its Prologue, is a more complex and challenging unit, because of the tension and hints of suffering it intimates. Where the Prioress celebrates Mary's triumphant motherhood of God and validates the fact of universal human childlikeness in the presence of Jesus, Mary, and their wisdom, the Second Nun invokes a darker side of the soul's relation to Mary's power – her strength against the devil, a strength rooted in her bodily purity and her ability to shed light on the dark and twisted path of the sinner who seeks salvation. At times, as in the actual invocation to Mary, for example, the echoes of Marian discourse are clear. At other times, as in the passages on idleness, the connections are not so apparent. The Second Nun weaves Marian themes into a much more personal and agonized statement than the Prioress does. She begins the Prologue to her tale with a warning against "Ydelnesse" and its author, Satan, stressing the fiend's "thousand cordes slye / [with which he] Continuelly us waiteth to biclappe, / Whan he may man in ydelnesse espye" (VIII.8–10). While Mary has not yet been invoked, the medieval audience would likely have associated her with this theme, because in the literature of her miracles and in popular tradition at this time, the Virgin was regarded as Satan's arch-enemy. Rosemary Woolf says:

> The two situations for which the Virgin's help was especially invoked in the Middle Ages were the day of death and the Last Judgement. . . . Accounts of the Virgin putting devils to flight occur in the miracle stories of the Virgin, such as the one in which a dying monk sees this drama taking place in his room. . . . [T]he theme of the devils lying in wait for the soul at death is extended by that of the Devil ever ready to trap the sinner during his lifetime, and of the Virgin's championship of the sinner in this battle. In this very common subject there are signs of a popular mythology. . . . [T]he learned tradition of the Virgin as the pre-eminent enemy of the Devil gave the opportunity for a more striking though fantastic manner of representing her power. Her dominion over the Devil, based upon the traditional exegetic application to the Virgin of Genesis iii.15, *ipsa tibi conteret caput tuum*, became constantly exemplified in miracle stories in which the Virgin physically intervened in the unending warfare, and by skill or cunning overcame man's enemy. (121–23)

Theologically her strength against the devil comes from the fact of her innate purity. Suenens puts it this way: "Mary is the only creature in whom Satan's power was completely overcome and over whose soul and body he has never any hold" (92). This purity, the root of her ability to "ravish doun fro the deity" the Holy Ghost, is manifest in the Apocryphal tradition of her unending busyness and her constant avoidance of idleness. Here is Lydgate on the Virgin's life in the Temple:

For all her life, there to slepe and wake
Hym forto serue, with perfite humblesse
That all maydenes, may ensample take
Of hir alone, to leve in clennesse
And specially, of hir deuote mekenesse
Benyng, port, contenaunce, and chier
If that hem list of hir thay might ler

Full of vertu, devoyde of all outerage
Hir hert was, that god to dwelle in chees
And day by day, Right as she wex in age
Right so in vertu, gan she to encrese
And nyght ne day wolde she neuer sees
To exclude slouthe, and vices to werrey
With handeȝ to werke, or with mought to pray

For but in god, hir hert nought delitede
So vpon hym, entierly was hir thought
And frome above, by grace he hir visited
That euery thyng, but hym, she sett at nought
Of worldly luste, she hath so litille rought
That oute of mynde, she lete it ouere slyde
That nought but god, may with hir abyde

. . .

And of hir Rull, this was hir vsaunce
Fro day to day, this holy mayde enter
Fro prime at morowe, by continuance
To thre at bell to be in hir prayer
And till the sonne was at mydday spere
On golde and silke and on wolleȝ softe
With hir handys, she wolde wyrke ofte

And even at none to brynge hir her fode
Fro god above, ther was an Angell sent
Whiche that she tooke, as for hir lyfelode
Thankyng hym aye, with hir hole entente
And aftir mete, a noon this mayde is went
Agayne to praye, tyll phebus went to west
And Evyn at eve, with hym she tooke hir Rest.

(1.218–38, 246–59)

. . .

To pray and Rede, that was euere hir lyve
Off hert wakir, by deuocion
To god all way with thought contemplatyf
Full fervent euere in hir intencion
And Idyll, neuere from occupacion
And specially vnto almes dede
Hir honde was euere redy at þe nede.

(1.414–420)

139

In fact Mary leads precisely the kind of life the Second Nun advocates as a bulwark against the temptations of the devil.

Just as the Virgin occupies her time in weaving and in praying, to avoid the traps of idleness, so will the Second Nun turn her attention to prayer and praise, by creating a translation, praise rendered as an appropriate act of *bisynesse*. The aim of this translation will be to tell the life of St. Cecile, whom the Second Nun links to Mary by calling her "thy mayden" (33). For both Mary and the Second Nun the use of language as an expression of correct spiritual orientation underlies prayer and translation. As we have seen above, the Virgin's ability to intercede, to speak effectively, comes directly from her unique spirituality. Unique though it is, her life is the pattern for all Christians, particularly for devout women. The message is clear: effective female speech comes from spiritual purity and busyness.

The Second Nun's actual invocation to Mary begins, "And thow that flour of virgines art alle, / Of whom that Bernard list so wel to write" (29–30). The lines echo an anthem in the Concluding Devotions to the Hours: "O marie, flour of virgines, as þe rose or þe lilie." The Second Nun moves on to address Mary as "Thou confort of us wrecches," echoing for the medieval audience the recurrent burden of prayers to the Virgin in the Hours for help against the fiend:

> To thee at my bigynnyng first I calle;
> Thou confort of us wrecches, do me endite
> Thy maydens deeth, that wan thurgh hire merite
> The eterneel lyf and of the feend victorie,
> As man may after reden in hire storie. (31–35)

In the cycle of devotion in the Hours, the celebration of the Virgin's motherhood of Christ alternates continuously with prayers for her intercession and help for wretches, for those suffering pain or sorrow, as in this prayer at Tierce: ". . . & þorouȝ þo biseching of þe glorious euerlastinge maide marie, we moun be deliuerid of þis sorewe þat we han now. . . ." In the *Stella Maris (Ave Maris Stella Dei Mater)* of Evensong the faithful pray to Mary to "make us vnbounde of synnes." In the Hours, salvation is linked to purity of life, just as is the power of Mary's intercession. Thus, although she will return to the theme of Mary's intercessory powers, the Second Nun, like the Prioress, celebrates the paradoxes of virgin motherhood and her humble splendor, both sources of her power in heaven:

> Thow Mayde and Mooder, doghter of thy Sone,
> Thow welle of mercy, synful soules cure,
> In whom that God for bountee chees to wone,
> Thow humble, and heigh over every creature,
> Thow nobledest so forforth oure nature,
> That no desdeyn the Makere hadde of kynde
> His Sone in blood and flessh to clothe and wynde.

Withinne the cloistre blisful of thy sydis
Took mannes shap the eterneel love and pees,
That of the tryne compas lord and gyde is,
Whom erthe and see and hevene out of relees
Ay heryen; and thou, Virgine wemmelees,
Baar of thy body – and dweltest mayden pure –
The Creatour of every creature.

Assembled is in thee magnificence
With mercy, goodnesse, and with swich pitee
That thou, that art the sonne of excellence
Nat oonly helpest hem that preyen thee,
But often tyme of thy benygnytee
Ful frely, er that men thyn help biseche,
Thou goost biforn and art hir lyves leche.   (36–56)

This passage that begins with the English echo of Dante's description of the
Virgin in *Paradiso* 33,[19] draws upon Dante's language as well as a host of
popular religious ideas similarly explored in late medieval English devotional
poetry. To trace the lines of influence to Dante is to see only half of the picture.
The poetry of the "cloistre blissful of thy sydis," as has been noted, is taken
from the *Quem Terra* of Matins. The Middle English *Prymer*'s rendering shows
how close the Second Nun's passage is to the discourse of the English version
of the Hours, how rooted in popular Christianity:

> The cloistre of marie beriþ him whom þe erþe, watris &
>   heuenes worschipen, louten & prechen, þe which gouerneþ
>   þe þre maner schap of the world.
> The wombe of þe maide beriþ him whom sunne, & moone, &
>   alle þinges seruen bi tymes; fulfillid of grace of heuenes.

The passage affirms human nature and human flesh, particularly the female
flesh of the Virgin, locating the center of affirmation within the oxymoron of
the incarnation of the creator of all life. The second stanza of this passage
echoes the *Leccio* I of Matins, as well as the literary source more usually cited,
drawing attention to the private, enclosed, cloistered nature of the Incarnation
of Jesus: "Holi maidenhede, & wiþ-outen wem, y noot what preisynge y mai
seie to þee, for him þat heuenes myȝte not take, þou bare in þi wombe."
  Thematically the Prologue moves next to the trope of light as enlightenment, a metaphor which will also underlie the structure of the tale's attention
to sight and insight. Repeating the Prioress's link between Mary's showing the
way to salvation and shedding light on that way, the Second Nun continues to
associate the Virgin with light throughout the rest of the Invocation to her,

---

[19] The footnotes in the *Riverside Chaucer* still refer the reader to the literary tradition of
Dante's influence on Chaucer. While such influence is undoubtedly important in
reading these lines, it is only one line of influence; in fact, it is conceivable that both
Dante and Chaucer had a common source in the language of Marian devotion.

praying to be released from "thennes that most derk is" (66), asking of the
Virgin "light" to guide her soul. Once more the language of these prayers is the
language of the Hours, where the Virgin is described in a prayer for Lauds as
"wiket of þe hiȝ king, & þe greet ȝate of liȝt þat schyneþ briȝt. folkis
raunsoned, reioice ȝe [of] þe liyf ȝouun bi a maide!" and in the *Stella Maris* for
Evensong, the Virgin is bid to "Louse þe bondis of gilti men! profere liȝt to
blynde men." Once again Lydgate's *Life of Our Lady* offers a poetic version of
this theme, as he refers to the Virgin in similar terms:

> Right so this mayde, at hir natyuytee
> The nyght of dethe devoidede hath awaye
> And bright kalendes, most lusty for to se
> Of phebus vprist, withoutyn more deley
> For she is Aurora, sothely this is noo nay
> Oute of which, as propheteȝ can devise
> The sonne of lyfe, to vs gan first aryse.   (1.162–68)

Perhaps most prominent in the Prologue, however, is the adversarial nature
of the world the Second Nun conceives. The story she will tell, introduced by a
disquisition on how the devil waits to trap the unwary, is the story of how St.
Cecile "wan thurgh hire merite / The eterneel lyf and of the feend victorie"
(33–34). Similarly, in the liturgy of the Hours, the theme that the faithful
Christian is surrounded by temptation and enemies recurs in virtually every
service. This sense of the enemy lying in wait heightens the Christian's
dependence on Mary and introduces a note of perpetual anxiety. In fact the
Second Nun's Prologue resonates with just that kind of anxiety, darkly hinting
that the Second Nun has been estranged from Mary:

> Now help, thow meeke and blisful faire mayde,
> Me, flemed wrecche, in this desert of galle;
> Thynk on the womman Cananee, that sayde
> That whelpes eten somme of the crommes alle
> That from hir lordes table been yfalle;
> And though that I, unworthy sone of Eve,
> Be synful, yet accepte my bileve.   (57–63)

In this passage, often a center of discussion because of the male pronominal
reference the Second Nun uses, the medieval audience would have heard
echoes of the *Salve Regina* from Compline: "Hail, quene, modir of merci, oure
liyf, oure swetnesse & oure hope, hail! to þee we crien, exiled sones of eue; to
þee we siȝen, gronynge in þis valey of teeris; þer-for turne to vsward þi
merciful iȝen, & schewe to us ihesu. . . ." Once more the discourse the Second
Nun uses comes from the liturgy of the Virgin. Once more the Virgin is
addressed as able to reclaim and re-direct the sinner. Describing herself as like
the Canaanite woman, outside the pale, living in sin yet believing, the Second
Nun goes on to bewail her sin and her bondage in it:

And of thy light my soule in prison lighte,
That troubled is by the contagioun
Of my body, and also by the wighte
Of erthely lust and fals affeccioun;
O havene of refut, O salvacioun
Of hem that been in sorwe and in distresse.... (71–76)

Mary shines resplendent as the way out of this conflict. She is, after her son, the way and the light of faithful Christians, all the more necessary because they live in a world that threatens constantly to attack and to undermine their hope of salvation and their resolutions of good living. This, too, is a recurrent theme in the prayers of the Hours of the Virgin in which repeated petitions ask for help against the enemy, and in which several separate offices incorporate Psalms focused on this theme.[20] In this nexus of prayer and petition and veneration, the Virgin emerges as a tower of strength, literally a haven of refuge, a shield against sin. William of Shoreham's fourteenth-century lyric, "Marye, mayde mylde and fre," describes her as the fulfillment of numerous Old Testament types, foreshadowings of the redemption she would bear: she is the "þe slinge, þy sone þe ston, / þat dauy slange golye op-on"; "þe temple salomon"; Judith, Hester, Rachel, "Fayrest of alle wymman"; "Þat vnicorn þat was so wyld / Aleyd hys of a cheaste: / Þou hast y-tamed and i-styld / Wyþ melke of þy breste."[21] Such a conception of the Virgin leaves her suffering aside in order to celebrate her triumphs. She is capable, she enables, and most of all, in this tradition of her strength, she speaks. The Hours are a cycle of petition imploring her to embody her strength in words:

Graunte us, þi seruauntis, lord god, we preien þee, þat we moun be ioieful euere more in heelþe of soule & of bodi; & þorouȝ þe biseching of þe glorious euerlastinge maide marie, we moun be delyuerid of þis sorewe þat we han now, & vse fulliche þe ioie wiþ-outen ende, bi oure lord ihesu crist, þi sone, þat lyueþ & regneþ wiþ þee in oonhed of god þe holigost, bi alle worldis of worldis. amen![22]

Her intercession on behalf of the faithful and the sinner alike is predicated on the power of her language to alter the reception or denial of salvation. The Middle English translation of the *Stella Maris*, part of Evensong, stresses that the Virgin has power over language as well as over the reality that language represents:

---

[20] One can read this theme throughout the Hours. See, for example, Prime, Psalm 53:5, 7 (Vulgate); Tierce, Psalm 119 (Vulgate); Sext, Psalm 122 (Vulgate); None, Psalm 125 (Vulgate).

[21] Carleton Brown, ed., *Religious Lyrics of the XIVth Century*, 2d ed. (Oxford: Clarendon Press, 1952), 46–49.

[22] This prayer appears in the Hours of Lauds, Prime, Tierce, Sext, None, and Evensong.

Hail, sterre of þe see, holi modir of god! and þou, euer maide, holi ȝate of heuene, Takyng þat word "hail" of gabrielis mouþ, sette us alle in pees! chaungynge þe name of eue, Louse þe bondis of gilti men!

Looked at in light of these themes in the Hours of the Virgin, the two tales told by the nuns resonate with significant language and significant themes. The entire structure of the Prioress's Tale is infused with the expectation that enemies abound; indeed the little boy's oft-remarked "martyr complex" seems to spring from an expectation of universal, dangerous opposition to the worship of Christ and the honor of Mary. A certain ominous note is present from the beginning of the tale where we learn that the Jewry is sustained by the Christian lord of that country for his own ends and profit: "Ther was in Asye, in a greet citee, / Amonges Cristene folk a Jewerye, / Sustened by a lord of that contree / For foule usure and lucre of vileynye" (488–91). The "world" of the tale like the "world" of the Hours is a dangerous place. The narrative of the little boy's experience of the song and of the religious ecstasy of venerating Mary is focused on the purity of his senses, a theme repeated over and over in medieval Mariology, in the Hours as well as in poetry and lyrics we have seen. A song about the Virgin's strength and power, *Alma Redemptoris Mater*, attracts the little boy to learn and to sing it because its beauty appeals to his innocence (537–39). His devotion, manifest in his singing the words of the song, inspires not the Jews but Satan, Mary's archenemy, in turn to incite the Jews to violence:

> Oure firste foo, the serpent Sathanas,
> That hath in Jues herte his waspes nest,
> Up swal, and seide, "O Hebrayk peple, allas!
> Is this to yow a thyng that is honest,
> That swich a boy shal walken as hym lest
> In your despit, and synge of swich sentence,
> Which is agayn youre lawes reverence?" (558–64)

Satan actually incites the men who will arrange the murder in two ways: he draws attention to the words which oppose Hebrew "lawes reverence," and he links the power of offensive speech to the power of movement, the ability to go into and move through the Jewry. Speech is tied to the power to assert one's presence in the world; it is a dangerous thing, as the murders make clear in their resolve "This innocent out of this world to chace" (566).

The actual murder focuses on everything most foully opposite to the Virgin's cleanness and purity. The child's body, pure by virtue of his childlike innocence, is dumped into a "pit" (571), a point the Prioress emphasizes by specifying that the pit is actually a "wardrobe / . . . Where as thise Jewes purgen hire entraille" (572–73). The little boy is defouled yet instantly redeemed and purified in the next stanza:

> O martir, sowded to virginitee,
> Now maystow syngen, folwynge evere in oon
> The white Lamb celestial – quod she –

> Of which the grete evaungelist, Seint John,
> In Pathmos wroot, which seith that they that goon
> Biforn this Lamb and synge a song al newe,
> That nevere, flesshly, wommen they ne knewe.   (579-85)

It's clear that the little boy is given an eternal right to speak because of his action. But while he is subsumed into the framework of eternity, the story proceeds on earth with the mother's heart-rending search for her son, a search that is ended only by the little boy's body still singing the words of *Alma Redemptoris* "with throte ykorven . . . / So loude that al the place gan to rynge" (611-13). The double foci here – eternal song and earthly song – emphasize the liminal quality of Mary's miracle. The child is neither dead nor alive; he is both here on earth and already one of the Brides of the Lamb. Mary, as we have seen, was traditionally associated with that moment when the soul leaves the body. For this child she extends that brief time to save him and to manifest her power. Most important, however, is the power of speech she confers on the child. He not only continues to sing the song, but he also can explain the miracle he is part of. In that sense he becomes a preacher, capable of speech and understanding apparently far beyond his seven years:

> "My throte is kut unto my nekke boon
> . . . and as by wey of kynde
> I shold have dyed, ye, longe tyme agon.
> But Jesu Crist, as ye in bookes fynde,
> Wil that his glorie laste and be in mynde,
> And for the worship of his Mooder deere
> Yet may I synge *O Alma* loude and cleere."   (649-55)

Looking at the construction of the tale one sees that this preaching culminates a strong narrative pattern: the action of the tale is focused in the little boy's power of speech, structured around moments of his speaking; the only other voice that we hear more than once is that of the Prioress. She narrates the action and, except for the little boy's speeches, minimizes direct quotations. The power of speech in the tale is hers and the child's.

The Second Nun's tale constructs similar emphases in its telling of the life of St. Cecile. In the Prologue the Second Nun says that she plans to tell the story of Mary's Mayden's death and how she won "eterneel lyf and of feend victorie." Mary's realm reappears within the next stanza and the following etymology of Cecile's name, which clearly draws on commonplace associations of light with goodness and religion. From the outset this tale stresses Cecile's possession of secret knowledge which she will share with others by means of words. On her wedding night she tells Valerian she has a "conseil." The narrative turns and moves forward on references to her speaking, as we can see in this series from the beginning of the tale: "Cecile answerde" (169), "quod shee" (172), "Telle hem that I" (176), "Telle hym the wordes whiche I to yow tolde" (180). Cecile is the one who gives words to others; she tells Valerian what to say, she explains the Trinity to Tiburce (337-42), and goes on "ful bisily to preche / Of Cristes come, and of his peynes teche" (342–43). It is she who defines and creates relationships in the tale through her language, as when she defines her marriage as a spiritual one and later takes Tiburce for her "allye": "right so as the love of Crist . . . / Made me thy brotheres wyf, right in that wise / Anon for myn allye heer take I thee" (295–97).

Of course the central action of the tale revolves around Cecile's confrontation with Almachius, the representative of earthly authority in this tale. In responding to his questions not only does she speak, but she speaks defiantly, asserting her presence, "I am a gentil womman born" (425), and replying to his questions in a series of challenges, beginning with the charge, "Ye han bigonne youre questioun folily" (428). Unable to move her by threat or persuasion, Almachius apparently is fed up with her words: "Thise wordes and swiche othere seyde she, / And he weex wroth, and bad men sholde hir lede / Hom til hir hous . . ." (512–14). He sends Cecile home, ostensibly to get this preaching female out of the public realm, to be burned. Later he treacherously sends a messenger to cut her throat. A miracle occurs as she, like the little boy, is not silenced by this assault but empowered to continue to speak, in her case to continue to preach the word of God and to instruct, as she has been doing:

> But half deed, with hir nekke ycorven there,
> He lefte hir lye, and on his wey he went.
> . . .
> Thre dayes lyved she in this torment,
> And nevere cessed hem the feith to teche
> That she hadde fostred; hem she gan to preche. . . .   (533–39)

What does this reading of the two Prologues and tales suggest about the right and the power to speak? First and most obviously, the Virgin provides this power and this right to the little boy, to the two narrators, and indirectly to Cecile whose life imitates many of the virtues associated with Mary's life. Such a pattern fits our expectations of how women claim the right to speak during this period by invoking religious forms and religious experience.[23] At the same time, however, the action of the two tales suggests a complex and somewhat contradictory message. On the one hand, aligning oneself with the Virgin and her qualities empowers the faithful to speak. On the other hand, it does not assure this speech will be welcomed or tolerated. The Prioress's tale is the story of how the child's words of praise and veneration – orthodox language of the most noble kind – offend the devil and the Jews, who combine to kill him. Those who conspire to murder the little boy are tolerated, if not supported, by the lord of the city. Authority is thus at least marginally complicit in silencing the little boy. The Virgin can and does, through Christ, grant him the power of continued speech, but it is only temporarily an earthly

---

[23] For an exploration of how two medieval women, Margery Kempe and Julian of Norwich, claim the authority both of religion and of literacy in their texts, see Lynn Staley Johnson, "The Trope of the Scribe and the Question of Literary Authority in the Works of Julian of Norwich and Margery Kempe," *Speculum* 66 (1991): 820–838.

power. In the Second Nun's tale Cecile is ultimately triumphant – her house becomes a church and her words are remembered in the story of how she used language to spread eternal truth. Nevertheless, like the little boy, she, too, is killed because of her speech. In her case, it is clear that civil authority cannot tolerate what she is saying and what her words incite others to do. In both tales speech is revealed as dangerous; to speak publicly, to tell stories, even of the highest truth, endangers one's being.

It's not surprising that we are left with this kind of paradox, for paradoxes recur throughout the *Canterbury Tales,* a work which contains the Wife of Bath's extensive Prologue and instructive tale as well as the Clerk's story of Griselda, who surrenders her will when she promises never to utter a word contradictory to her husband's wishes (IV.351–64). Within the two religious tales the pattern of affirmation traced in this paper is highly qualified. The Virgin can inspire devout women to speak, can sustain the words of those who venerate her and worship her son, but she cannot guarantee their words will be accepted or appreciated. This paradox raises tantalizing questions about whether Chaucer consciously created the pattern of tension between affirmation and restraint of speech that the Prologues and tales play out – or, indeed, if he was echoing a pattern of alignment and justification typical of religious women's public speech. Obviously, it is impossible to answer such questions. What we can say, though, is that Chaucer sets his two religious women on a different path from the one the Wife of Bath takes and from the one Griselda takes. They neither assert the authority of their own lived experience, nor do they surrender the right to speak, deferring to males to construct and utter their thoughts. Rather they follow one of the ways that women will tread for the next two hundred years as they gain the right to speak publicly and to command attention by affirming that their words are not of their own invention but inspired in them by the power of religious truth, and, in this case, by the support of the Virgin Mary. Both the Prioress and the Nun call upon the Virgin as a figure of virtuous female power and speech. Each tells a complex, fascinating, and troubling story about how in the face of human and superhuman opposition, the voices of women and children struggle to be heard.

The *Descriptio Navalis Pugnae* in Middle English Literature*

MARY HAMEL

> Actium is, of course, history, but the treatment is all Chaucer's, not
> that of any source.
>
> Robert Worth Frank, Jr.

Students of Chaucer's sea battle in the "Legend of Cleopatra," finding no
identifiable source for its rich detail and vigorous movement, have supposed
the account based on "some knowledge of contemporary sea battles."[1] The
originator of this supposition was W. H. Schofield, who argued in 1913 that
Chaucer had based the battle not merely on contemporary chronicles such as
Froissart's, which "provide us with authentic pictures of sea-conflicts in the
fourteenth century," but on eyewitness accounts of such battles: "he probably
gained most of his information from oral accounts of recent conflicts and
discussions with navy men."[2]

A few years earlier (1902), George Neilson had made much the same
argument about the equally exciting and even more detailed sea-battle of
Southampton in lines 3601–3711 of the Alliterative *Morte Arthure*: "Note how
every point of the historic battle [of Winchelsea, or Espagnols–sur–Mer,
1350] ... comes blazing into the wonderful poem ... there is more of live
chronicle of the fight of Winchelsea in the little finger of *Morte Arthure* than
there is in the entire body of Laurence Minot's song of *Les Espagnols sur Mer*."[3]
More recent studies, my own included, have argued that these correspon-
dences of detail between the *Morte Arthure* and contemporary chronicles reflect

---

* An earlier version of this article was read as a paper at the 1987 Fordham University
Medieval Studies conference, "War and Peace in Medieval Society."
[1] M. C. E. Shaner and A. S. G. Edwards, "Notes to *The Legend of Good Women*," in *The
Riverside Chaucer*, 3d ed., gen. ed. Larry D. Benson (Boston: Houghton Mifflin, 1987),
1066. All quotations from the "Legend of Cleopatra" are from this edition.
[2] W. H. Schofield, "The Sea-Battle in Chaucer's 'Legend of Good Women,'"
Anniversary Papers by Colleagues and Pupils of George Lyman Kittredge (Boston: Ginn,
1913), 142, 151.
[3] George Neilson, *Huchown of the Awle Ryale* (Glasgow: James MacLehose, 1902), 60,
62.

the contemporary practice of naval warfare more generally – and the rhetorical theme of "naval battle" – rather than specific events.[4] As John Finlayson has said,

> Neilson . . . points out that the elements of the battle – gads of iron, cutting of head-ropes, shooting of arrows, drowning of men, etc. – are all recounted in the chronicles which record the Battle of Winchelsea. None of his parallels, however, demonstrates direct borrowing, and it could be pointed out that Froissart's account of another sea-battle, Sluys, contains much the same material. . . . Mediaeval sea-battles are fairly stereo-typed, whether described by chroniclers or poets, since they talk not of strategy, but of the shooting of arrows, hand to hand fights, and drowning men. . . . the details are not those of a particular battle, but of the literary *topos* of sea-battles. (627, 634)

Comparison of the *Morte Arthure* sea-battle with that in "Cleopatra" shows an interesting number of similarities, which have been remarked before.[5] This might be taken as evidence that Chaucer and the alliterative poet were using the same battles as sources; following Finlayson, I would argue rather that the two poets were using the same literary or rhetorical topos.

Evidence for the existence of a recognized rhetorical theme of naval battle in medieval writing is scanty in the standard handbooks of rhetoric: there is a single brief reference to the *descriptio navalis pugnae* as a subcategory of *descriptio* in Priscian's *Praeexercitamina*.[6] But investigation has shown that evidence for this topos and its influence can be found in accounts of other naval battles in several kinds of texts, not only poetic but historical. In fact, the reason the two poetic sea-battles sound so much like Froissart's description of the battle of Sluys or that of Espagnols-sur-Mer or that of La Rochelle is likely that Froissart was also using the topos.[7]

[4] John Finlayson, "*Morte Arthure*: The Date and a Source for the Contemporary References," *Speculum* 42 (1967): 624–38; George Keiser, "Edward III and the Alliterative *Morte Arthure*," *Speculum* 48 (1973): 37–51; and Mary Hamel, ed., *Morte Arthure* (New York: Garland, 1984), 371–76. All quotations from *Morte Arthure* are from this edition.

[5] Both Schofield, 144n, and Frank, 43, note parallels; in their note to line 642 (p. 1066), Shaner and Edwards suggest comparing the whole scene. See also Hamel, 374 n. 3657.

[6] "Descriptio est oratio colligens et praesentans oculis quod demonstrat. Fiunt autem descriptiones tam personarum quam rerum . . . rerum vero, ut pedestris proelii vel navalis pugnae descriptio" ("*Descriptio* is speech that assembles and brings before the eyes what it is describing. Now, there are descriptions of both persons and things . . . things such as the description of combat on foot or of naval battle"). Priscian, *Praeexercitamina*, 10, quoted in Edmond Faral, *Les arts poétiques du XIIe et du XIIIe siècle* (Paris: Champion, 1924), 75. All translations are mine unless otherwise noted.

[7] One should perhaps attribute its use in the first place to Jean le Bel, the earlier prose chronicler on whose work Froissart depended for the earlier part of the war. For the relationship between the two as historians and artists, see Peter F. Ainsworth, *Jean*

Without attempting a comprehensive survey of naval battles in medieval chronicle and poetry, I have examined enough such battles in a variety of texts to draw several reasonably firm conclusions. The first is that not only was the *descriptio navalis pugnae* indeed a recognized and influential topos but it can be defined in terms of four or five clearly identified constant elements, with five more secondary elements that are frequent rather than constant; moreover, the topos has been pervasively influenced by – may even have its source in – two widely circulated premedieval Latin texts. The second major conclusion is that chronicle accounts of actual historical battles, with few exceptions that I have yet found, demonstrate the influence of the topos in their selections of detail and interpretation of events: the line between history and poetry is far from clear.[8] The third is that the Middle English version of the topos, as demonstrated in Chaucer's "Cleopatra," the *Morte Arthure*, the thirteenth-century romance of *Richard Coer de Lyon*,[9] the poems of Laurence Minot,[10] and the mid-fifteenth-century verse paraphrase of Vegetius known as *Knyghthode and Bataile*,[11] is set off from other versions in more than one way.

In addition to the Middle English texts, I have examined sea-battles in a late twelfth-century Latin prose romance, *De ortu Waluuanii* or *The Rise of Gawain*;[12] in the thirteenth-century Latin *Itinerary of Richard I*, which not only gives an apparent eyewitness account of the sea-battle described more fancifully in *Richard Coer de Lyon* but also describes another battle of special interest for this investigation;[13] two accounts of the sea-battle off Dover in 1217, one by Roger

  Froissart and the Fabric of History: Truth, Myth, and Fiction in the Chroniques (Oxford: Clarendon, 1990), 23–50.

8 Ainsworth warns against the tendency of "modern readers for whom there has always to be a watertight (but ultimately crude and surely unwarranted) distinction between 'literature' (fiction) on the one hand and 'history' (non-fiction) on the other – even in respect of medieval texts which knew no such sharp distinctions" (6).

9 Karl Brunner, ed., *Der mittelenglische Versroman über Richard Löwenherz*, Wiener Beiträge zur Englischen Philologie 42 (Wien and Leipzig: Wilhelm Braumüller, 1913), lines 2471–2650: the battle depicted is the capture of a large Saracen dromond filled with munitions.

10 *The Poems of Laurence Minot, 1333–1352*, ed. T. B. James and J. Simons (Exeter: University of Exeter Press, 1989), nos. V (pp. 37–40) and X (pp. 54–55). Both are celebrations of victories (of Sluys and Espagnols-sur-Mer respectively) rather than strictly speaking narrative accounts.

11 *Knyghthode and Bataile: A XVth Century Verse Paraphrase of Flavius Vegetius Renatus' Treatise "De Re Militari,"* ed. R. Dyboski and Z. M. Arend, EETS OS 201 (1935; reprint, New York: Kraus, 1971), lines 2840–2916. The author interpolates an account of an imagined sea-battle into his versification of Vegetius' descriptive and didactic material.

12 *The Rise of Gawain, Nephew of Arthur (De ortu Waluuanii nepotis Arturi)*, ed. Mildred Leake Day (New York: Garland, 1984), 61–79.

13 *Itinerarium Peregrinorum et Gesta Regis Ricardi*, ed. William Stubbs, Rolls Series 38, 2 vols. (London: Longman, Green, 1864), 1: 79–82 and 1: 204–209. This chronicle is a compilation of two earlier works, both based on eyewitness accounts of the events described; see Antonia Gransden, *Historical Writing in England c. 550 to c. 1307* (London: Routledge & Kegan Paul, 1974), 239–42.

of Wendover and the second by Matthew Paris;[14] the fourteenth-century Latin *Chronicon* of Geoffrey Le Baker for accounts of the battles of Sluys and Les Espagnols-sur-Mer;[15] and the French chronicle of Froissart for Sluys, Les Espagnols-sur-Mer, and La Rochelle.[16] In addition, the two earlier Latin works of importance for this project are the *Civil War* of Lucan (3.509–762),[17] with its extended and highly rhetorical account of the battle of Massilia (Marseilles) and – of course – Book 4 of Vegetius' *De re militari* (4.31–46), the most important military *and* naval manual of the Middle Ages.[18] In addition to the Latin text of Vegetius, I consulted the French translation of Jean de Meun and the adaptation of Christine de Pisan.[19]

Collation of these varied texts has led to the identification of certain constant elements in the description of naval battles, whether in poetic fiction or prose chronicle. I would designate as texts directly shaped by the topos those that have at least four of the following five elements: (1) the use of trumpets and similar instruments as a call to arms or other battle signal; (2) as one phase of battle, usually but not always the first, the ship-to-ship exchange of missiles – javelins, arrows, quarrels – sometimes compared to a shower of rain, snow, or hail; (3) as a second phase of battle, hand-to-hand fighting with spears, swords, or battle-axes on the ships' decks (a secondary element, the use of grappling-irons and chains to join ships for such fighting, is not always made explicit but usually implied if not); (4) the use of topcastles or (in earlier texts) specially built on-board towers to hurl stones and other missiles to lower decks, or the use of advantageous height in the ship itself for the same purpose (as Le Baker said of the large Spanish busses at Les Espagnols-sur-Mer, they towered over

14 Roger of Wendover, *Flores Historiarum, or The Flowers of History*, ed. Henry G. Hewlett, Rolls Series 84, 3 vols. (London, 1887), 2: 220–23, and Matthew Paris, *Chronica Majora*, ed. Henry Richards Luard, Rolls Series 57, 7 vols. (London, 1876), 3: 26–29. Matthew Paris's first account of this battle is copied from Wendover with some very minor changes; the second, briefer and less detailed, is apparently from another source. See Gransden, 359–60.

15 *Chronicon Galfridi Le Baker de Swynebroke*, ed. Edward Maunde Thompson (Oxford: Clarendon Press, 1889), 67–69 and 109–11.

16 *Oeuvres de Froissart*, ed. Kervyn de Lettenhove, 3 (Brussels: Victor Devaux, 1867), 194–206; 5 (1868), 257–71; 8 (1869), 123–40. Variations among the redactions in Book 1 do not affect this investigation.

17 Lucan, *The Civil War*, ed. and trans. J. D. Duff, Loeb Classical Library (Cambridge, Mass.: Harvard University Press, 1951), 150–71.

18 Flavius Renatus Vegetius, *Epitoma rei militaris*, ed. C. Lang (Leipzig, 1885), 150–65.

19 Jean de Meun, *L'art de chevalerie*, ed. Ulysse Robert, Société des Anciens Textes Français (Paris, 1897), 160–76; Christine de Pisan, *Le livre des faits d'armes et de chevalerie*, trans. William Caxton in *The Book of Fayttes of Armes and of Chyualrye*, ed. A. T. P. Byles, 2d ed., EETS OS 189 (1932; reprint, New York: Kraus, 1971), 180–85. I also consulted a transcription of Christine's *Livre* from Brussels, Bibliothèque Royale, MS. 10476, fols. 77–78v, generously provided by Charity Cannon Willard. See also C. T. Allmand, ed., *Society at War: The Experience of England and France during the Hundred Years War* (New York: Barnes & Noble, 1973), 126–28. I also looked at the 1408 translation made for Lord Berkeley in Pierpont Morgan MS. M 775, fols. 25–121.

the English galleys like castles over cabins);[20] (5) the defeated fighters' either leaping overboard and drowning in order to escape capture or worse deaths, or else being thrown overboard, both dead and living, by their victorious enemies – "Spanyolis spedily: sprentyde ouer burdez," as *Morte Arthure* has it (3700).

In addition to grappling (A), other secondary elements – found frequently but not so often as the "constants" I have just described – include the following: (B) an account of ships sinking or captured in the course of battle – in one case in the Battle of Massilia a ship capsizes when all its defenders and crew lean over one side;[21] (C) an exclamation or other comment on the cruelty of naval warfare in general or of this battle in particular (or both); and two elements that changed over time. First (D), Greek fire is an important element in earlier battles, from Lucan's Marseilles to Acre in 1190, but it disappeared from all but translations of Vegetius after the early thirteenth century; its place was later taken, one might say, by the projectile-casting machines and cannon that appear in Chaucer, Christine de Pisan, and *Knyghthode and Bataile*.[22] Second (E), earlier texts make much of ramming with the reinforced *rostra* or "beaks" of liburns or galleys to break up the opponents' vessels; as ship-construction changed this attack disappeared as a deliberate tactic in the thirteenth century (it was used in the battle of Dover in 1217), and the crashing-together of ships in Froissart's account of Espagnols-sur-Mer (5.261) and the *Morte Arthure* (3660–65) is as much self-destructive as tactically effective: in the former case, though the English attack is deliberate, it is the English ship that sinks.

Of the texts so far examined, then, "Cleopatra," *Morte Arthure*, *De ortu Waluuanii*, *Knyghthode and Bataile*, and Le Baker's Espagnols-sur-Mer show all five constants, each with from two to four secondary elements.[23] Let the passage from "Cleopatra" show the pattern as applied by Chaucer:

> Up goth the trompe, and for to shoute and shete,
> And peynen hem to sette on with the sunne.
> With grysely soun out goth the grete gonne,

---

[20] "Magne buscee Ispanienses, quasi castra casellis, ita nostra liburnis et navibus supereminebant" (Le Baker, 110).

[21]   Dum nimium pugnax unius turba carinae
       Incumbit prono lateri vacuamque relinquit,
       Qua caret hoste, ratem, congesto pondere puppis
       Versa cava texit pelagus nautasque carina . . . . (3.647–50)
In Duff's translation, "On one of the ships the crew, too eager for battle, leaned on the tilted gunwale and left empty the side where there was no enemy. Their combined weight upset the craft, so that she covered over both sea and sailors with her hull" (161–63).

[22] *De ortu Waluuanii* is the one battle-narrative that shows both a projectile-throwing machine and Greek fire in operation, 66–67. Vegetius, of course, mentions both sorts of weapons (4.44): "machina[e] et tormenta" and "ole[um] incendari[um]," etc. (162–63).

[23] Secondary elements: "Cleopatra," A and D; *Morte Arthure*, A, B, and E; *De ortu Waluuaniii* B, C, D, and E; *Knyghthode and Bataile*, A (implied), C, and D; Le Baker, B, C, and E.

And heterly they hurtelen al atones,
And from the top doun come the grete stones.
In goth the grapenel, so ful of crokes;
Among the ropes renne the sherynge-hokes.
In with the polax preseth he and he;
Byhynde the mast begynnyth he to fle,
And out ageyn, and dryveth hym overbord;
He styngeth hym upon his speres ord;
He rent the seyl with hokes lyke a sithe;
He bryngeth the cuppe and biddeth hem be blythe;
He poureth pesen upon the haches slidere;
With pottes ful of lyme they gon togidere;
And thus the longe day in fyght they spende,
Tyl at the laste, as every thyng hath ende,
Antony is schent and put hym to the flyghte,
And al his folk to-go that best go myghte.
　　　Fleth ek the queen, with al hire purpre sayl,
For strokes, whiche that wente as thikke as hayl;
No wonder was she myghte it nat endure.   (635–656)

The first constant, the trumpet-signal, occurs in line 635: "Up goth the
trompe, and for to shoute and shete"; the combination of trumpeting with
shouting is also found in Lucan[24] and the Acre battle in the *Itinerary*;[25]
trumpeting alone is found in nine other texts. The second constant, the
exchange of missiles, is found at the end (655) rather than the beginning of the
battle: Cleopatra flees "For strokes, whiche that wente as thikke as hayl"; such
exchanges are also compared to hail in *Richard Coer de Lyon* (2564) and
Knyghthode and Bataile (2876), to snow in Minot's Sluys (V.49), and simply to a
"shower" (Latin *imber*) in Le Baker's Sluys (68) and the second *Itinerarium* battle
(207). Chaucer adds a novel secondary element (D) to replace the missile-
exchange earlier in the battle, with "the grete gonne" mentioned in line 637.
This was probably not an anachronistic cannon, since the word "gonne" was
also used of projectile-throwing mechanisms that did not use gunpowder; the
English king in *Richard Coer de Lyon* has both "gunnes" and "mangneles" made
ready after the sea-battle, as he sails toward the siege of Acre (2651–52). These
machines were as well known as cannon for making a "grisly soun": the
onager, says *Knyghthode and Bataile*, was a bow that threw "stonys grete, / In
maner of a thonderynge" (2953–54), while the "stone-throwing ordnance" in
De ortu Waluuanii made a "din [*strepitus*] . . . which produced no less horror than

---

[24] "Innumerae vasto miscentur in aethere voces, / Remorumque sonus premitur
clamore, nec ullae / Audiri potuere tubae" (3.540–42). In Duff's translation, "then
countless cries rose together in the wide heaven, till the splash of the blades was
drowned by shouting and no trumpet could be heard" (153–55).

[25] "Congressi propius, tubis utrinque insonant; clangorem terrificum miscent" (Stubbs,
81): "As they come closer together, they sound their trumpets on both sides [and]
mix in a terrifying din."

the danger" (67). Let Chaucer himself be the final authority on the noise of non-gunpowder ordnance:

> And the noyse which that I herde,
> For al the world ryght so hyt ferde
> As dooth the rowtynge of the ston
> That from th'engyn ys leten gon.   (*House of Fame*, 1931–34)[26]

The third constant, hand-to-hand fighting, is exemplified in lines 642 ff: "In with the polax preseth he and he / . . . He styngeth hym upon his speres ord," etc. In this case the grappling (secondary element A) required to make this kind of fighting possible is made explicit in line 640: "In goth the grapenel, so ful of crokes." The fourth constant, the hurling of missiles from topcastle or tower, is shown in line 639: "And from the top doun come the grete stones." The fifth constant is only briefly represented, in line 644: "and dryveth hym overbord"; one might prefer Minot's pithy phrasing "domp in the depe" (X.24) in his poem on Les Espagnols-sur-Mer, otherwise little influenced by the topos: "Thai sail in the see gronde : fissches to fede" (X.4), a line echoing Vegetius (see below).

As for other texts, *four* constants are demonstrated in Lucan (with five secondary elements); in both battles in the *Itinerary of Richard I* (the first with five, the second with three secondaries); in *Richard Coer de Lyon* (two secondaries); in Froissart's and Le Baker's accounts of Sluys (two secondaries each); in Froissart's account of Les Espagnols-sur-Mer (three secondaries); and Minot's poem on Sluys (one secondary; note that the poem is less a concerted narrative than a series of encomia to the heroes of the battle).[27] Four constant

---

[26] The *Riverside Chaucer* editor of the *House of Fame*, John M. Fyler, glosses *rowtynge* as "roar." On the subject of the development of gunpowder weapons in the fourteenth and fifteenth centuries generally and the meaning in Middle English of "grete gunne" specifically, see Dhira B. Mahoney, "Malory's Great Guns," *Viator* 20 (1989): 291–310, especially 302–6; on the issue of the noise of trebuchets and such engines, Mahoney cites these passages from *De ortu Waluuanii* and the *House of Fame* as well as one from *Richard Coer de Lyon* (at the firing of a stone by a mangonel, "'Allas!' they cryede, and hadde wondyr. / It routes as it were a thondyr!" [4331–32]) and other texts (305–06). See also *MED*, s.v. "gonne" n., sense 1. For naval ordnance specifically, see Kelly DeVries, "A 1445 Reference to Shipboard Artillery," *Technology and Culture* 31 (1990): 818–29. It is odd that Chaucer's editors (e.g., Shaner and Edwards) are willing to ascribe so egregious an anachronism as cannon to Chaucer, whereas Lydgate's is not: on his usage of the phrase "grete gunnys" in the *Troy Book* (2.614, "gonnys grete," 6434), the editor Henry Bergen says, "Lydgate probably does not mean cannon although they were known in his time." *Lydgate's Troy Book*, Part IV, ed. Henry Bergen, EETS ES 126 (1935; reprint, Millwood, N.Y.: Kraus, 1973), Glossary, s.v. "gonnys" (348–349). See also W. W. Skeat, ed. *The Complete Works of Geoffrey Chaucer*, 2d ed., 7 vols. (Oxford: Clarendon, 1900), 3: 312.

[27] Lucan: constants 1, 2, 3, 5 and all secondaries; *Itinerarium*: first battle 1, 2, 3, 5 and all secondaries, second battle 2, 3, 4, 5 and B, D, E; *Richard Coer de Lyon*: 2, 3, 4, 5 and B, E; Froissart's Sluys: 1, 2, 3, 5 and A, C; Froissart's Espagnols-sur-Mer: 1, 2, 4, 5 and A,

and three secondary elements are also mentioned in Vegetius, though they are of course not set forth in narrative form, for this military manual describes, recommends, and catalogues rather than telling a story; yet Vegetius' discussion is far from dry or technical. For he finds naval warfare peculiarly terrible: "For what is crueller than a naval battle, where men are destroyed both by water and by fire? . . . Some men are destroyed by iron and stone; others are driven by fire into the billows; nevertheless, among so many kinds of deaths this is the bitterest thing, that the bodies, unburied, are consumed by fishes" (4.44).[28] This kind of comment is echoed so often in other texts that I have counted it as secondary element C.

Finally, two or three of our texts show three or fewer constants and two or fewer secondary elements: Roger of Wendover and Matthew Paris on Dover, Froissart on La Rochelle, Minot's second poem. How are we to interpret the relationship of these accounts to the topos? It is evident, after all, that real naval battles of the Middle Ages indeed included the elements of trumpet-signals; archery, crossbow, and arbalest exchanges; grappling and hand-to-hand fighting; the hurling of missiles from topcastles and other high places; the drowning of the defeated; and so on – that is, that the constant and secondary elements as defined earlier indeed reflect the actualities of medieval naval warfare and in the case of the historical combats may simply report observed events. Certainly the "evolving" elements of the topos – the use of Greek fire or cannon, the tactic of deliberate ramming – must reflect changing naval technology and tactics.[29] I would nevertheless argue that even in such cases as these the selection of detail and emphasis have indeed been influenced by the topos.

My conviction on this point is based partly on the pervasive influence of the two classical or pre-medieval models, Lucan and Vegetius. Though the battle of Marseilles in Lucan's *De bello civili* is a well-detailed example of the topos, with nine out of our ten elements, this poet's influence is hard to pin down, for the elements that make his description of the battle unique are frankly not those that any poet or chronicler with taste would *want* to imitate; that is, beyond the

---

B, E; Minot V: 1, 2, 3, 4 and B. Le Baker's Sluys (2, 3, 4, 5 and A, C) may be a five-constant account if the "horridus clamor" with which the battle starts (68) is interpreted as including trumpet-calls (constant 1).

[28] "Quid enim crudelius congressione nauali, ubi aquis homines perimuntur et flammis? . . . Alii ferro interimuntur et saxo, alii ardere coguntur in fluctibus; inter tanta tamen mortium genera qui acerrimus casus est, absumenda piscibus insepulta sunt corpora" (162, 163).

[29] For general surveys, see Richard W. Unger, *The Ship in the Medieval Economy 600–1600* (London: Croom Helm and Montreal: McGill-Queen's University Press, 1980); Archibald R. Lewis and Timothy J. Runyan, *European Naval and Maritime History, 300–1500* (Bloomington: Indiana University Press, 1985); and Kelly DeVries, *Medieval Military Technology* (Peterborough, Ont.: Broadview Press, 1992), 283–312. An older but still extremely valuable source is Sir Nicholas Harris Nicolas, *A History of the Royal Navy, from the Earliest Times to the Wars of the French Revolution*, 2 vols. (London: Richard Bentley, 1847). Both volumes deal with medieval warfare; the history was never completed.

conventional elements identified earlier, what Lucan contributes especially is gore and grisliness in his extended description of wounds, mutilation, and death – a remarkable catalogue of different ways to die painfully and messily. Yet it is well known that Lucan was widely read throughout the Middle Ages; Chaucer, for example, several times shows his familiarity with "the grete poete daun Lucan" (HF 1499).[30] So it is not surprising that Jean de Meun adds to his translation of Vegetius a reference to the battle of Marseilles that is clearly based on Lucan's account.[31] In another text, *De ortu Waluuanii*, one of Lucan's images, that of the missile exchange (constant 2) as darkening the air and covering the surface of the water, seems to have been imitated in different words.[32] More to the point for the question of the shaping of history by rhetoric in the chronicles, however, Le Baker's description of the aftermath of the battle of Les Espagnols-sur-Mer shows a striving for Lucanian effects: "There you might see ships painted with blood and brain-matter; arrows driven into masts, sails, beams, and castles; bowmen gathering arrows from the wounds of the dead; . . . teeth torn out, noses cut off, lips cloven and eyes plucked out. . . ."[33] For Le Baker is indeed a highly rhetorical author, one for whom the topic of naval battle was inevitably shaped by the rhetorical topos.

The case for Vegetius' influence is both stronger and more concrete than that for Lucan. An important text in this regard is the description of the sea-battle off Acre in the first book of the *Itinerary of Richard I*; it is evident that the author has filled out his account of this battle not only with the conventions of the topos but also with substantial borrowing from Vegetius. The author begins, for example, by explaining the difference between ancient and modern ships: "Ships of war were called *liburnae*. For the fleet in the battle of Actium was

---

[30] See John V. Fleming, *Classical Imitation and Interpretation in Chaucer's "Troilus"* (Lincoln: University of Nebraska Press, 1990), 56–61; Edgar Finley Shannon, *Chaucer and the Roman Poets* (New York: Russell & Russell, 1964), 333–39.

[31] *L'art de chevalerie*, 175 (4.45): "Et doit estre mis es cornes la plus grant force des liburnes et des chevaliers. Bien le moustra Brutus devant Marceille, quant Julius Cesar l'ot la laissié o toute sa navie pour combatre as cytoiens, que bien ensivi la doctrine de l'art des batailles, par coi il eust victoire" ("And the largest force of ships and men should be put in the horns [of the recommended crescent-array]. Brutus demonstrated this well before Marseilles, when Julius Caesar left him there with all his navy to battle the citizens, that he followed the doctrine of the art of battles, for which reason he had the victory"). Robert remarks that the reference to Brutus at Marseilles is an interpolation, without mentioning a possible source (175n).

[32] Lucan: "emissaque tela / Aera texerunt vacuumque cadentia pontum" (3.545–46, p. 154) – "the missiles that had been let fly covered the air and, falling, the empty sea" (my translation). *De ortu Waluuanii*: "Missilium jactu aera obfuscari, eorumque multitudine freti superficiem operiri videres" (66) – "You could see the air darkened by the hurling of javelins and the surface of the sea covered with their great numbers" (Day's translation, 67).

[33] "Ibi vidisses sanguine et cerebro naves pictas; sagittas in malis, velis, temonibus et castris infixas; de vulneribus mortuorum sagittarios sagittas colligentes . . . dentes evulsos, nasos quoque decisos, labra fissa, et oculos erutos" (Le Baker, 110, 111); my translation.

built especially at Liburnia in Dalmatia; for this reason the custom grew among the ancients of calling them *liburnae*. But all that magnificence of antiquity, diminished, has slipped away."[34] Compare Vegetius: "When Augustus fought the battle of Actium, it was . . . especially with Liburnian help that Antony was defeated. . . . Liburnia is part of Dalmatia . . . by their example warships that are now constructed are called *liburnae*."[35] A short time later, the *Itinerary* describes the battle array assumed by the Christian fleet as it approaches the Saracens: Vegetius' recommended crescent, wings toward the enemy, with the stronger ships and men in the wings. Finally, as the battle is joined the chronicler breaks off to echo Vegetius' cry – "For what is crueler than a naval battle, where men are destroyed both by water and by fire?" (see above) – with his own version: "But what can be bitterer than a fight at sea? what crueler, where such various fates entangle the combatants? Some, tortured by flames, are burned up; some, shipwrecked, are swallowed by the waves; others, wounded, perish by [the enemy's] weapons."[36]

Vegetius' commentary on the bitter choice of deaths in naval warfare is also echoed not only by *De ortu Waluuanii*[37] but also by Froissart in his report on Sluys: "This battle of which I am speaking was very cruel and very horrible; for battles and attacks on the sea are harder and stronger than on land, for one cannot flee or draw back."[38] Other echoes of Vegetius are found in Le Baker: where Vegetius identifies men who choose to engage in hand-to-hand fighting on the enemy's ships as those "who dare on account of courage," Le Baker in his account of Sluys calls such men those "who wished to and had the daring."[39] These examples show Vegetius among the chronicles; but the

---

[34] "Porro bellatrices carinas dixerunt liburnas. Est enim Liburnia pars Dalmatiae, ubi classis Actiaci belli praecipua facta fuerat: unde inolevit usus, ut apud antiquos naves bellicae dicerentur Liburnae. Caeterum omnis illa vetustatis magnificentia imminuta defluxit" (*Itinerarium*, 80).

[35] "Sed Augusto dimicante Actiaco proelio, cum Liburnorum auxiliis praecipue uictus fuisset Antonius . . . Liburnia namque Dalmatiae pars est . . . cuius exemplo nunc naues bellicae fabricantur et appellantur liburnae" (4.33, p. 151).

[36] "Quid autem navali conflictu asperius? quid saevius? ubi tam varium congressos fatum involvit; nam flammis torquentur exusti: fluctibus absorbentur naufragi: armis pereunt vulnerati" (81). See note 28 above.

[37] "Si fuge vellent consulere nec undis nec adversariis se tutum erat committere. In navi autem remanentibus mors nihilominus intentabatur. . . . socios triplici ereptos infortunio scilicet flammarum globis, undarum naufragio, hostiumque furori, illi transponit" (78) – "If they wanted to consider flight, neither to the waves nor to the enemy was it safe to commit themselves. Either way, death was imminent for those remaining on the ship. . . . He delivered his companions across to the ship, rescuing them from a threefold bane: the balls of fire, the shipwrecking waves, and the fury of the enemy" (Day's translation, 79).

[38] "Ceste bataille dont je vous parolle, fu moult felenesse et moult orible; car batailles et assaux sur mer sont plus durs et plus forts que sus terre, car on ne puet fuir, ne reculer . . ." (3.196).

[39] Vegetius, "qui de uirtute praesumunt" (4.44, p. 162); Le Baker, "qui voluerunt aut fuerunt ausi" (68). One might note also that Le Baker calls this battle "ingens et terribile" (68).

clearest evidence of the close association of Vegetius with the rhetorical *descriptio navalis pugnae* is the fictional naval battle embedded in the paraphrase of his naval chapters in *Knyghthode and Bataile* – a battle that not only turns Vegetius' descriptions of weapons and tactics into narrative but does so in the form of the rhetorical theme, with five constant and two secondary elements.

Among all these texts, the English-language poems stand out in more than one respect. The first respect is the relationship of the three later works, "Cleopatra," *Morte Arthure*, and *Knyghthode and Bataile*, to history. All other accounts so far examined except *The Rise of Gawain* purport to be historical. Chaucer's, of course, does also; but as Robert W. Frank, Jr., has said, "Actium is . . . history, but the treatment is all Chaucer's."[40] The other two late English sea-battles are purely fictional. Yet all three texts show a concern to update the traditional materials and make them more topical: most obviously, the author of *Knyghthode and Bataile* adds cannon and other firearms (2854–60); all three lay an emphasis on the cutting of rigging to collapse sails and bring down masts, a tactic recommended by Vegetius and used off Dover in 1217 and at Espagnols-sur-Mer in 1350 (according to Froissart);[41] Chaucer foreshadows Christine de Pisan's 1410 adaptation of Vegetius in speaking of the use of quicklime and slippery materials to blind and trip up the enemy;[42] *Morte Arthure* puts into practice her recommendation of broadheaded arrows for piercing and deflating sails.[43] Moreover, it is clear that both Chaucer and the *Morte Arthure*-

---

[40] Robert Worth Frank, Jr., *Chaucer and "The Legend of Good Women"* (Cambridge, Mass.: Harvard University Press, 1972), 42.

[41] "Cleopatra," 640, 646; *Morte Arthure*, 3668, 3675–78; *Knyghthode and Bataile*, 2892–94; Vegetius, 4.46, pp. 164–65; Matthew Paris, 29; Froissart, 5.264.

[42] "Cleopatra," 648–49. Christine de Pisan: "Item, grant garnison avoir est bonne de pots plains de savon mol, lesquelz gettéz et brisiéz dedens la nef des ennemis les destourne à eulx soustenir en piez tant fort y glisse, si chieent en l'eaue ceulz qui vers les bors sont, et semblablement sont bons à y lancier pots plains de chaux vive en pouldre, qui au briser tout leur en emplist yeulx et bouche, si que à paines voient" (fol. 78v). In Caxton's translation, "Item it is gode to haue grete quantyte of pottes filled with softe zande [soap?] / whiche after they be ones caste in to the shyp of the enemies they can vnuthe stande vpon theyre fete so slydrye it is so falle they thenne in to the watre that be nyghe the borders of the shypp / And semblably ben good to be cast therinne pottes full of quyk lyme made in to pouldre whiche at the brekyng of hem shal fylle al theire eyen and theire mouthes so that with peyne they can see afore them" (184–85). Quicklime was also used at Dover in 1217: "calcem quoque vivam et in pulverem redactam in altum projicientes, vento illam ferente, Francorum oculos excaecarunt" (Roger of Wendover, 2.222 – "Throwing powdered quicklime on high, with the wind carrying it, they blinded the eyes of the French"). On the problem of Chaucer's "pesen," see Shaner and Edwards, note to 648 (p. 1066).

[43] Christine: "Item, aient foison de saiectes à large fer qui soient traictes ou baille, et perce tellement le deciteront que vent ne pourra retenir; et par ce ne pourront avant aler" (fol. 78v) – In Caxton's translation, "Item they muste haue grete foyson of arowes with brode hedes that shal be shot ayenst the saille tyl that it be so pierced & so rented that it can not holde wynde noo lenger so shal they not conne goo noo ferthere" (184). Though such arrows are not shown as being used in the *Morte Arthure* battle, they are certainly prepared: "Brasen hedys full brode buskede on flones" (3619).

poet do indeed refer to specific battles of the fourteenth century: for when
Chaucer has Antony's fleet "sette on with the sunne" (636) one must be
reminded of Sluys, where both Froissart (3.195) and Le Baker (68) tell us
that the English fleet maneuvered carefully in order to attack with the sun at
their backs; in no other sea-battle I have yet seen described, actual or
fictional, does this detail occur. Similarly, when the *Morte Arthure*-poet
speaks of the Danish fleet at Southampton chained together to await
Arthur's attack – "With chefe chaynes of chare : chokkode togedyrs" (3603)
– one is reminded that (as Le Baker tells us) the French fleet was thus
encumbered at Sluys, a detail so far unparalleled in any other narrative.[44] It
appears that the *Morte Arthure*-poet indeed intended a reference to this battle;
and yet when his "Spanyolis" sprint overboard in the line cited earlier, of
course, one is meant also to remember Les Espagnols-sur-Mer – even
though, as I have argued elsewhere, Spanish vessels and sailors engaged the
English throughout the latter part of the century.[45] In this context it
becomes clear that the destructive ramming of ships at the opening of the
battle in *Morte Arthure* is likely also a reminder of Les Espagnols-sur-Mer (as
described by Froissart).[46] (These allusions do not, of course, mean that the
poem must be dated in the 1350s, any more than Chaucer's poem must be
dated 1341 because it refers to Sluys.) Only the fictional battle of *Knyghthode
and Bataile* seems divorced from actual event, yet it is less a simple fiction
than a political fantasy that envisions the defeat of the treasonous Yorkists
by the adherents of the true, Lancastrian king; the battle, in other words, is
imagined history.[47]

A second respect in which the English poems stand apart has to do with
style. For the simple fact is that three of these five texts (or four of the six,
counting Minot's as two) employ or imitate the alliterative long line. The
primary example must, of course, be *Morte Arthure*, whose verse structure in
this section at least is classical for the fourteenth century:

> Be than cogge appon cogge,   krayers and oþer,
> Castys crepers one crosse   als to þe crafte langes;
> Thane was hede-rapys hewen   þat helde vpe þe mastes.
> Thare was conteke full kene   and crachynge of chippys!
>
> (3666–69)

---

[44] Rather confusingly, Le Baker mentions the French ships' being chained together
only late in the battle; other chroniclers confirm that the French fleet began the day
in that condition but later split into three squadrons. See Robert of Avesbury, *Historia
de mirabilibus gestis Edvardi III*, ed. Thomas Hearne (Oxford, 1720), 54, and *Chronicon
Domini Walteri de Hemingburgh, vulgo Hemingford nuncupati*, ed. Hans Claude Hamilton,
2 vols. (London: Sumptibus Societatis, 1848), 2: 356.

[45] Hamel, 376, n. 3700.

[46] *Morte Arthure*, 3660–65; Froissart, 5.261.

[47] As the battle begins, the "myghtiest & booldest men of werre" say to "our foon,"
"Ye erre; / Com vndir vs, and knowe your ouer herre [liege lord] / . . . your
souuerayne; / And wil ye not? At youre perile & peyne!" (2834–39).

It has often been noted that in Chaucer's "Cleopatra," as in the tournament-mélée in Part IV of the Knight's Tale, the poet has created an impression of alliterative verse without actually following its structural rules. Some lines in the battle-passage have no alliteration at all; most have only two stressed alliterating syllables – e.g., "goth/grapenel," "ropes/renne," "polax/preseth" (640–42); only two have three terms ("grysely/grete/gonne," 637, "bryngeth/biddeth/ blythe," 647), but neither shows normal long-line structure. Yet the passage, read aloud, reminds the hearer of alliterative verse; and as Dorothy Everett has remarked, the word "heterly" (coupled with "hurtelen" in 638) "belongs to the special vocabulary of alliterative writings."[48]

Some such characterization must also apply to Minot's naval poems. Both V and X, the poems on Sluys and Espagnols-sur-Mer, are in what one has to call his "alliterative mode": the first, in six-line rhymed stanzas of essentially tetrameter verse with a good deal of anapestic movement, nevertheless includes two, three, and even four alliterating words in many of its lines. Untypically heavy are these two lines: "The gude Erle of Glowceter, God mote him glade, / Broght many bold men with bowes ful brade" (V.53–54). The Winchelsea poem is more regular: "Thai sailed furth in the Swin : in a somers tyde, / With trompes and taburns : and mekill other pride" (X.7–8). The poem does indeed have more alliteration and even a midline caesura marked, but the tetrameter habit still wins. Nevertheless both Chaucer and Minot bear witness to a sense that naval battles *ought* to be described in alliterative verse.

Even the remaining two poems show some slight evidence of this expectation. *Richard Coer de Lyon* is for the most part in very ordinary and unalliterative tetrameter verse, yet one or two brief passages stand out:

> And rappyd on hem, for the nones,
> Sterne strokes with harde stones
> Out off the topcastel on hygh.   (2551–53)

> With swerdes, speres, dartes kene;
> Flones and quarelles fleygh betwene
> Also thykke, withouten stynt,
> As hayl afftyr thondyr-ynt.   (2561–64)

> Some in the hals so hytte hee,
> That helme and hed ffleygh into the see.   (2575–76)

Knyghthode and Bataile offers more in the way of alliterative doublets such as "fleeth as foulis" (2861), "bowe" and "bent" (2864), "crosbowys yet and crankelons" (2871), an original yet natural collocation since crankelons were a kind of arrow, "armure & axe" (2889), or "helm & herneys" (2891). Two slightly more extended passages are striking:

[48] Dorothy Everett, "Chaucer's 'Good Ear,'" in *Essays on Middle English Literature*, ed. Patricia Kean (1959; reprint, Westport, Conn.: Greenwood Press, 1978), 141. For a different view, see N. F. Blake, "Chaucer and the Alliterative Romances," *Chaucer Review* 3 (1968–69): 163–69. The great preponderance of citations for "heterly" in the *MED*, however, are taken from alliterative verse.

> ... lo! clariounys crumpe
> To crye vppon, and lo! it comth adoun. ....   (2842–43)

> Summe into se go, fisshes forto fede,
> Summe vndir hacch ar falde adoun for fere.   (2896–97)

If the *descriptio navalis pugnae* is an alliterative theme as well as a rhetorical topos, that should not be surprising, considering the close relationship of fourteenth-century alliterative style to the rhetorical tradition. Nicolas Jacob's study of alliterative storms and their relationship to Latin models is obviously relevant here, though the models are different.[49] But what distinguishes the battle-topos most sharply from the storm-topos is its relationship to history: the description of naval battle, whether in chronicle or fiction, is preeminently a historical theme. For the topos is indeed based on actual practice – weaponry, tactics, signals, outcomes; thus while the topos in Middle English narrative poetry – fiction – offers scenes of lively activity grounded on concrete historical detail, it also offers the modern reader a real window on medieval naval history – and nowhere so concisely, in such a brief space packed so densely with details, with images, with movement, as Chaucer's sea-battle in "The Legend of Cleopatra."

---

[49] Nicolas Jacobs, "Alliterative Storms: A Topos in Middle English," *Speculum* 47 (1972): 695–719. One may also mention here Jean Ritzke-Rutherford, "Formulaic Macrostructure: The Theme of Battle," in *The Alliterative Morte Arthure: A Reassessment of the Poem*, ed. Karl Heinz Göller (Cambridge: D. S. Brewer, 1981), 83–95. Ritzke-Rutherford considers only English alliterative texts; it is likely that a wider purview, including prose chronicles, other types of verse, and other languages, would yield similar results for land battles: a *descriptio pedestris proelii*.

"Lad with revel to Newegate": Chaucerian Narrative and Historical Meta-Narrative*

PAUL STROHM

> If elected vice president, Yanayev said, he would campaign "against
> the political bacchanalia which the country is seeing."
>
> *San Francisco Chronicle*, 19 August 1991

Perkyn's Revelry and its Symbolic Affiliations

Whatever might be said of the Cook's Tale as a fragment, it embraces a brief
but relatively complete narrative of Perkyn Revelour's emergence, rebuke, and
social descent. The Cook's recital begins with a description of Perkyn's
"gaillard's" temperament and disposition to merriment. It progresses to a series
of interrelated examples of how he earned and enjoyed his reputation as
"revelour" par excellence, including his attendance at festive processions or
"ridyngs" (I.4377); his commitment to dancing (I.4370), hazard (I.4383–87),
and mynstralcye (I.4394); his skill at attracting adherents in the form of a loyal
"meynee" (I.4381); his comprehensive tendency to "riote" (I.4414, etc.).[1] It
ends with an emphasis upon his previous rebukes, including the fact that he
was more than once "lad with revel to Newegate" (I.4402), and a concluding
account of his worldly descent from the status of apprentice in a prosperous
guild to an underground demimonde of gambling, revelry, and prostitution.

This little narrative, unexceptional in itself, is signaled as important by the
superfluity of commentary that punctuates and surrounds it – commentary not

---

* In January 1992 I spoke at the Oxford University Early Modern History Seminar,
arranged by Robin Briggs and Miri Rubin, on "Chronicle Evidence and the Rebel
Voice" – since published as a chapter in *Hochon's Arrow*. I found a number of comments
after the talk, particularly those by my two hosts, quite stimulating, and this paper
embodies my "after the fact" reconsiderations. I wish to add thanks to Sheila
Lindenbaum for several historical suggestions and to Kimberly Keller for assistance in
research.
[1] All quotations from Chaucer's writings will be taken from *The Riverside Chaucer*, 3d
ed., gen. ed. Larry D. Benson (Boston: Houghton Mifflin, 1987).

only in excess of any immediately apparent narrative necessity but also commentary more-than-usually-heedless of the presumed perspective of its ostensible teller. For the low-life Cook, characterized by his own physical disfigurement (I.386) and churlish inability to separate his own emotional and physiological responses (I.4326) and later to be hailed out for ridicule and rejection in his own right as a debauched figure of fun (in the Manciple's Prologue), here adopts the voice of pulpit moralist and conservative satirist. The Cook's presumed purpose of telling an urban "jape" (I.4343) is pushed to the back burner, as he pauses to lecture errant apprentice, indulgent master, and everyone else who will listen.[2]

His surprising and – given his own social station – personally incongruous theme is the failings of revelers and especially those of low degree: "Revel and trouthe, as in a lowe degree, / They been ful wrothe" (I.4397–98). Then, having reported Perkyn's incarcerations, his perspective virtually merges with that of the master, as he partially ventriloquizes the master's reasoning on the advisability of releasing this unruly prentice from his service:

> But atte laste his maister hym bithoghte,
> Upon a day, whan he his papir soghte,
> Of a proverbe that seith this same word:
> "Wel bet is roten appul out of hoord
> Than that it rotie al the remenaunt." (I.4403–7)

"So fareth it," the Cook adds in amplification of this view, "by a riotous servaunt" (I.4408), and, his voice still effectively paralleling that of the master, he sends Perkyn into the world with a sarcastic "late hit": "Now lat hym riote al the nyght . . ." (I.4414).

The effect of this surplus commentary is to underscore and amplify a narrative curve running from revelry to inevitable rebuke and to imbue it with an importance in excess of any immediately apparent explanation. Chaucer's intentions for this tale and the ultimate effect to which he would have deployed this voice of urgent moralization cannot finally be known. But the short-term effect of the Cook's evocation of Perkyn's revelry and his emphatically negative pronouncements upon it is to invite the repositioning of this account of revelry-and-rebuke within a larger and highly resonant symbolic field.

The imagery of revelry as dangerous and irresponsible excess was widely prevalent within the numerous late-fourteenth-century accounts of the Rising of 1381. Needless to say, a wide gap separates Perkyn Revelour's dice games and petty cashbox pilferings from substantial transgressions like the beheading

---

[2] I agree with Lee Patterson's observations about the rejection of Perkyn's "riotous excess that threatens the social order as a whole," but I do not agree that the Cook himself is "the voice of lower-class criminality." At this point in the *Tales* the Cook's is very much the voice of middle-class moralization; only later, in the Manciple's Prologue, will the Cook be reinscribed as the representative of revelry-gone-stale and be subject to rejection in his own right. See his *Chaucer and the Subject of History* (Madison: University of Wisconsin Press, 1991), 278–79.

of Sudbury and the burning of the Savoy. If Perkyn is a rebel at all, his insurrection occurs in a register we in the last decade of the twentieth century have ample precedent for recognizing as less substantive than stylistic. Yet the Cook's brief account of Perkyn's behavior embraces an extraordinary number of historical preconditions and buzzwords and key symbols common to most accounts of the 1381 Rising. Here are just a few of the common terms that permit a resituation of Perkyn's brief bacchanal within this larger symbolic field:

Revelry itself. However innocuous we might find the attraction of this "prentys revelour" (I.4391) to holiday *ridyngs* (I.4377) and to streetlife and to other sorts of public disport, the imagery of revelry carried a heavy symbolic freight in the later fourteenth century. Accounts of the Rising of 1381 are frequently couched in terms of the outbreak of revelry and its subsequent rebuke and repression, as notably illustrated by the Westminster chronicler's claim that, during the burning of Archbishop Sudbury's Lambeth palace, the London rebels of 1381 repeatedly exclaimed, "A revelle! A revelle!³"

Perhaps the rebels actually employed ideas and occasions of revelry as staging grounds of oppositional action. (This possibility is certainly enhanced by the fact that the burning of Lambeth Palace is usually placed on 12 June, in 1381 the day of the eve of Corpus Christi.⁴) Or perhaps the imagery of revelry is simply an aspect of the chronicler's program of stigmatization, effectively burdening the rebels with all the negative associations that revelry bears for its scandalized observers, including the overprivileging of the "low" and insufficient respect for the "high," its broad erasure of the line between spectators and participants, its encouragement of temporary license. Either as incriminating description or as libelous invention, the effectiveness of revelrous imputations in discrediting the rebel program was widely recognized. Walsingham, for example, says that the rebels arranged their executions as if they were a "solemnis ludus."⁵ The Anonimalle chronicler describes the rebels in a grotesque variant of those same holiday *ridyngs* so esteemed by Perkyn and his fellow apprentices, bearing the severed head of Sudbury "en processione" through the city.⁶ The rebels in the Tower are shown lolling on the king's

---

3 *The Westminster Chronicle 1381–94*, ed. L. C. Hector and Barbara Harvey (Oxford: Clarendon Press, 1982), 2.

4 See *Westminster Chronicle*, 4. On Corpus Christi as a time of potential disorder, see Miri Rubin, *Corpus Christi: The Eucharist in Late Medieval Culture* (Cambridge: Cambridge University Press, 1991), 263–64. On the potential relation of festivity and revolt, see Yves-Marie Bercé, *Fête et Révolte* (Paris: Hachette, 1976), esp. 72–77. For explicit connection between festivity and the Rising of 1381, see Christopher Dyer, "The Rising of 1381 in Suffolk: Its Origins and Participants," *Proceedings of the Suffolk Institute of Archaeology and History* 36 (1988): 281.

5 Thomas Walsingham, *Historia Anglicana*, vols. 1 and 2, ed. H. T. Riley, Rolls Series, 28, pt. 1 (London: Longman, Green, Longman, Roberts, and Green, 1863, 1864), 1: 462.

6 *Anonimalle Chronicle*, ed. V. H. Galbraith (Manchester: Manchester University Press, 1970), 145.

mother's bed, issuing invitations as if she were a common wench, and the lowest of them reversed hierarchy by touching the beards of the "most noble" knights (Walsingham, 1: 459). Tyler himself is said to have mocked limit and ceremony by drinking ale and rudely rinsing his mouth (*Anonimalle Chronicle*, 147–48) and by playing a menacing boy's game with a dagger before the king.[7] The whole rebellion in Kent, in fact, seems to Knighton a kind of *tripudium* – a festive celebration involving frivolity and dance (131).

Apprentices as a volatile grouping. Perkyn moves mainly in a subsociety of London prentices that hovers rather ominously at the edge of many accounts of 1381. Andrew Prescott's research into the judicial records of the rebellion has shown conclusively that the majority of London rebels came not from Essex and Kent but from London itself and that, while drawing upon a wide social spectrum, their numbers were disproportionately tilted toward servants and apprentices.[8] An earlier Marxist interpretation of the London Rising sympathetically supposed it to have been an expression of solidarity with the cause of the rural peasantry.[9] In point of fact, the broad spectrum of London apprentices, servants, and journeyman-laborers (not to mention the transient and unemployed) had much to complain about in their own right, and evidence of their organizing attempts in the last decades of the fourteenth century suggests that they would have been an unstable grouping in their own right, whatever their views of labor predicaments in the countryside.

Apprentices, together with journeymen and others, may be assumed to have been on the Westminster chronicler's mind when he suggested that the London officials were paralyzed in the early stages of the revolt by the fear that the commons of the city might throw in their lot with the rebels against the remainder of the city and that the whole city should thus be lost as a result of its inner divisions: "formidabat quidem ne si invalescentibus servis resisterent, communes tanquam suorum fautores cum servis contra reliquos civium insurgerent, sicque tota civitas in seipsa divisa deperiret" (*Westminister Chronicle*, 8). We can hardly doubt the affinity of Perkyn and his peers, with their attachment to civic spectacle and propensity for uproar, to those who were in the streets in those June days and nights, nor would any fourteenth-century reader have had cause to doubt the same.

Formation of an illicit meynee. Perkyn's charisma, if not his organizational gifts, seems to have won him a devoted band of followers, somewhat derisively styled by the Cook as "a meynee of his sort" (I.4381), a band of *compeers* (I.4419) devoted to riotous conduct in the spirit of his own.[10] So, in the

---

[7] Henry Knighton, *Chronicon*, ed. Joseph R. Lumby, 2 vols., Rolls Series 92 (London: Eyre & Spottiswoode for H. M. Stationery Office, 1895), 2: 137.

[8] See Andrew Prescott, "London in the Peasants' Revolt: A Portrait Gallery," *London Journal* 7 (1981): 131–33.

[9] Perry Anderson, *Passages from Antiquity to Feudalism* (London: NLB, 1974), 205.

[10] Perkyn's associational tendencies, their rebuke by the Cook's antiassociational rhetoric, and the wider implications of this ideological field are evoked and productively analyzed in David Wallace, "Chaucer and the Absent City," in

chronicle accounts, are the rebels regularly accused of appropriating forms of sworn association normally employed by their betters. The Westminster chronicler says that the rebels on the way to Lambeth forced those they met to swear an oath of alliance to their *contubernium* or band (2), and the jurors at Scarborough claimed that the local rebels constituted themselves as a sort of retinue or sworn association by employing a livery of hoods in order to further their conspiracy.[11]

Control of written records. Perkyn's objective is to regain his *papir* (I.4404) – presumably, an indenture or contract specifying his reciprocal obligations with his master. His master, reflecting on his riotous conduct and its corrupting example to the other *servantz*, gives him his release, through ill will rather than good (I.4403–12).[12] So, by analogy, had possession of records bearing on their conditions of service been the most consistent motivation of the 1381 rebels. At Lambeth, for example, the rebels are said by the Anonimalle chronicler to have made a point of burning the registers and chancery rolls they found there: "mistrent en feu toutz les livers des registres et rolles de remembrauncez de la chauncellerie illeoqes trovez" (140). And Walsingham notes by way of explanation their determination that court rolls and muniments should be burnt so that, the memory of old customs having been rubbed out, their lords would be unable to vindicate their rights over them: "statuerunt omnes curiarum rotulos et munimenta vetera dare flammis, ut, obsoleta antiquarum rerum memoria, nullum jus omnino ipsorum domini in eos in posterum vendicare valerent" (1: 455).[13]

Perkyn's commitment to riotous misconduct, his associations with a like-minded *meynee*, and his determination to regain control of his *papir* all suggest some relationship between his temporary excesses and the more thorough-going transgressions of 1381. But what relation is here tantalizingly implied? The Cook's account of Perkyn is certainly not a "reflection" of 1381 and is not exactly an "allegory" of 1381 either. What we seem actually to encounter here is a more general relationship of mutual participation in a larger representational environment. The particular terms of this participation will be the

---

Chaucer's England: Literature in Historical Context, ed. Barbara Hanawalt (Minneapolis: University of Minnesota Press, 1992), esp. 71–81.

[11] R. B. Dobson, *The Peasants' Revolt of 1381* (London: Macmillan, 1970), 291.

[12] Reginald Call, "'Whan he his papir soghte,'" *Modern Language Quarterly* 4 (1943): 167–76. On conditions governing apprentices in the thirteenth and fourteenth centuries, see A. H. Thomas, ed., *Calendar of Plea and Memoranda Rolls, 1364–1381* (Cambridge: Cambridge University Press, 1929), xxxi–xlvii. The form of a sixteenth-century agreement, still possibly incorporating some standard features, emphasizes the responsibility of the apprentice to avoid dice and other unlawful games as well as taverns and playhouses and to be readily available for his master's service; see P. E. Jones, *The Corporation of London: Its Origin, Constitution, Powers and Duties* (London: Corporation of London, 1950), 90.

[13] A splendid discussion of the importance of writing and exclusion from writing and the sometimes-touching faith among the rebels that early charters might confirm their liberties is Susan Crane's essay "The Writing Lesson of 1381" in *Chaucer's England: Literature in Historical Context*, 201–21.

subject of the second part of this essay. I might simply observe, though, that it has several aspects, including a common reliance by Chaucer and his contemporaries on key symbols of revolt and also their frequent recourse to narrative strategies of palliation and control.

From Symbolization to Narratization

The theoretical problem of establishing a relation between the Cook's after-the-fact narrative of Perkyn Revelour and the events of the 1381 Rising has already been anticipated in certain respects by a spirited debate over the methodological procedures and implications of Robert Darnton's influential essay on "The Great Cat Massacre." In that essay, Darnton recreates an episode of the late 1730s in which a group of disgruntled printer's apprentices taunt their master by practicing various abuses, including guillotining, upon hapless cats and his wife's own favored cat.[14] The essay explores the larger field of meaning within which these events occurred, touching on witchcraft, revelry, and the practices of charivari; additionally implied, though nowhere specified, is a relation between cat-guillotining and events of the subsequent French Revolution. Roger Chartier, at odds with what he sees as Darnton's rather loose concept of symbolization and signing, argues for a more cautious mode of analysis, in which a symbol is "a sign, but a specific, particular sign, which implies a relation of representation – for example, the representation of an abstraction by a figure."[15] Interesting himself in the specificity of the cat massacre, Chartier employs his definition of symbolism to discredit Darnton's assertion that such explanatory contexts as sorcery and charivari may be "revelatory of a totality" (695) – rejecting by implication still looser symbolic affinities to the Revolution itself. In response, Darnton has advanced a more supple description of symbolization, in which the process "works as a mode of ontological participation rather than as a relation of representation."[16]

Admittedly, Darnton may not always successfully enact his view of symbolic polysemousness in practice.[17] And one may indeed question the meaning of so vague a phrase as "ontological participation" at the level of abstraction. But Darnton's concept has considerable value as a procedural tool or tool of practical inquiry. For Chartier's attempt to restrict symbolism to a "relation of representation" does insufficient justice to the status of larger representational fields that embrace many different symbolizations without necessarily specifying the particular relations between them. The cat massacre

---

[14] Robert Darnton, *The Great Cat Massacre* (New York: Vintage Books, 1985), 75–104.

[15] Roger Chartier, "Text, Symbols, and Frenchness," *Journal of Modern History* 57 (1985): 688.

[16] Robert Darnton, "History and Anthropology," in *The Kiss of Lamourette* (New York: Norton, 1990), 333.

[17] As noted by Harold Mah, "Suppressing the Text: The Metaphysics of Ethnographic History in Darnton's Great Cat Massacre," *History Workshop* 31 (1991): 1–20.

may, for example, be seen to participate in a larger textual system along with subsequent representations of the Revolution itself – a system in which the deeds and texts of the Revolution play a towering role but by no means the only role. The cat massacre and the Revolution may, that is, exist not in a relation of reference but a relation of participation within a larger system of events and signs.

In the later fourteenth century, one crucial symbolic field was constituted through and around images of revelry and revelrous behavior. Revelry was broadly available to Chaucer and his contemporaries for varied employment as what Bercé would call "un langage gestuel" (77) – a symbolic, behavioral language available for localized enactments and representations. Actual revelers in the streets might draw on this gestural language to produce a variety of actions, some festive and some insurrectionary; littérateurs like Chaucer might use it to create tales; chroniclers might use it to stigmatize rebels and rebellious acts. But all participate in a widely accessible regime for the creation and bestowal of meaning. It is within this relationship of general participation, of reliance upon a commonly held body of socially created symbols, rather than any more particularized cross reference among and between events, that their commonalty is to be found.

Now with Chartier, rather than against him, I find symbolic regimes like that of revelry to be broadly shared within a society and unlikely to be the property of any one social or cultural group.[18] The very ubiquity of a symbol like revelry nevertheless opens another interpretative problem, since all applications of the symbols are not alike. Inherent in the broad distribution of a cluster of symbols bearing on revelry and revelrous behavior is their availability for varied appropriation and use. And this very availability raises a set of coordinate issues: who is eventually to control them and for what purpose? Is, for example, a powerful symbol like revelry to be wielded as a vehicle of social transformation, as a staging ground of oppositional actions and the transgressive and possibly permanent substitution of "low" for "high," or is it to be seen as a device of social containment, a way of confirming hierarchy through temporary but closely delimited inversion?

This debate about the implications of revelry is longstanding but has remained unresolved precisely because it has been argued out in mainly essentialist terms, with the assumption that revelry must be one thing (or the other), must work one way (or the other). In fact, like other such symbols, the symbolizations of revelry can and do mean different things to different participants. Gareth Stedman Jones once put it to me this way in conversation: that all the spectators at a football match are present at the same event but experience the match differently according to whether they are sitting in the owners' box or the cheap seats and according to their different loyalties and affiliations, and other factors. So, too, with actions conceived within the symbolic language or "langage gestuel" of revelry; the same set of terms may

---

[18] Roger Chartier, *The Cultural Uses of Print in Early Modern France*, trans. Lydia G. Cochrane (Princeton: Princeton University Press, 1987), 7–11.

be wielded to produce oppositional actions or to celebrate their inevitable cessation, menacingly to articulate social hostility or reassuringly to rehearse its ultimate control.

The most conclusive way to gain control of an unruly but powerful symbol is by employing it in a narration, by assimilating it to an exemplary sequence of events that unfolds in time and that, preferably, ends with a determinate conclusion illustrating or vindicating one's claims. "Narration," in the sense in which I am using it here, can occur at the level of action in the world, when one produces a train of events that depend upon and mobilize key social symbols. Or, as in the Cook's treatment of Perkyn's revelrous heyday and ultimate rebuke, it can function textually – in this case, to control a potent and potentially socially destabilizing symbolic cluster.

The larger narrative pattern of the Cook's Tale, in which revelry is evoked within a controlling frame that guarantees its ultimate chastisement, may be viewed in convenient miniature within the narrator's derisive observation that Perkyn was "somtyme lad with revel to Newegate" (I.4402). On the face of it, the Cook's observation would seem to be a matter of derision pure and simple, supplying the conclusion that Perkyn's devious ways lead to imprisonment and that "this is the kind of revelry he deserves." But actual fourteenth-century practice supplements and complicates the line. Convicted felons and others were subject to public exposure and ridicule, frequently including a procession, either to the pillory or other public display, accompanied by emblems of the misdeed, or to a prison for confinement. In case of procession either to the pillory or to prison (or even, at intervals, procession out from Newgate for public display and then back again), minstralcy might be supplied in the form of trumpets or other instruments.[19] At the most obvious level, the purpose of the minstralcy was simply to draw notice to the punishment. But it would also seem to function as a kind of anti-ceremony, less a harnessing of mirth for purposes of transgression than a subduing of mirth to the aims of civic rectitude.

Perkyn, led with revel to Newgate, is thus accompanied with a reminder of this riotous conduct – but a reminder conveyed through an image of revelry bound over, itself now bent to purposes of chastisement. Our glimpse of Perkyn in procession is, to borrow a narratological term, synchronous, in the sense that we see him in a single moment, caught in arrest on his way to Newgate with minstrels in his party. But this synchrony includes elements of its own diachrony, in its implied sequence: Perkyn, formerly a reveler given to singing and dancing and other disport, is now arrested, and revelry is now aligned with the law and contributory to a critique of its own former devotee. Perkyn's story thus has an implied beginning (in revelry), middle (apprehension by his master and the representatives of civil authority), and end

---

[19] Representative instances of such punishments appear in *Liber Albus*, ed. H. T. Riley, 3 vols., Rolls Series 12 (London: John Russell Smith, 1862), 1: 458–59. See also Arthur Griffiths, *The Chronicles of Newgate* (London: Chapman and Hall, 1884), 34–39. I am grateful to Sheila Lindenbaum for calling my attention to these references.

(led off, with the trappings of his former revelry now redirected for purposes of mockery, to prison). The symbolic apparatus of revelry is thus loosed from its original moorings in riotous lowlife and controlled within a closed narrative system that guarantees its ultimate rejection.

The same narrative pattern, moving from revelry to its necessary rebuke, is repeated in what we have of the Cook's Tale and is repeated on a much grander scale in the later fourteenth- and early fifteenth-century chronicle narratives of the 1381 Rising. Walsingham pauses, for example, after the most ambitious of the recitals of the rise and fall of rebellion and sums up his generic and symbolic accomplishments: "Scripsimus ... historiam tragicam ... de dominatione rusticorum, et debacchatione communium, insania nativorum" ("We have now written the tragic history of the lordship of the rustics, and the wild bacchanal of the commons and the madness of the villeins" [2: 13]). Walsingham's narrative ambitions are large, and he thus claims for his work a literary form; his genre is *historia* or history, but his form is tragic – not tragedy, that is, in the Greek or classical sense but tragedy in the broad medieval sense that it recites a downfall, with a "falling" plot.[20] (The rebels might in their first heady days, in which resistance failed to materialize or melted away, have fancied themselves in a comedy. But, writing subsequent to the rebels' defeat and dispersion at London and then at St. Albans, Walsingham knows better.) Still more pertinent to the subject at hand, however, is his description of the Rising itself as a *debacchatio* – a passionate raving with Bacchic overtones. Embedded in Walsingham's final reproof, as indeed in his narration as a whole, this allusion to the rebels' brief carnival or revel makes it seem all the more futile and doomed. The fact that Walsingham has already told of the failure of the Rising and the dispersal of the rebels casts his allusion to the rebels as bacchantes in an explanatory capacity. By this descriptive stroke, such known characteristics of the carnivalesque as its inversion of the order of things, its prevailing license, and above all its temporary nature are recruited to account for the ultimate failure of rebellion.[21]

The disciplining of the rebels, as described by Walsingham, proceeded in several stages, the most consequential of which occurred when they resolved upon further sedition after their return to their homes. The king heard,

---

20 Walsingham's reliance on tragedy would seem to vindicate Hayden White's suggestion that quasi-literary "emplotment" lends meaning to a historical narrative by suggesting that it is a story "of a particular kind" (see, for instance, his *Metahistory* [Baltimore: Johns Hopkins University Press, 1973], 7–11). Readers of the remainder of this essay will, however, see that I find the organizing principles of historical narrative as no less likely to originate in the frames opportunistically or adventitiously employed to make sense of our everyday or practical experience than in the more formalized frames that have been stabilized as literary genres.

21 So, too, are the rebels bearing down on London said by the Westminster chronicler to have raved or revelrously debauched themselves (*debachabantur* [2]). The Westminster chronicler introduces the concept of bacchanal at the outset rather than the end of his narration, though it still seems intended to suggest a "brief frenzy," headed for a predictably early demise.

Walsingham tells us, that the Kentishmen were conspiring again and that they had congregated in another profane assembly to the destruction of the whole kingdom (2: 14). The king's first impulses toward wholesale slaughter being tempered by the intercession of the Kentish notables, a variety of disciplinary actions was then instituted, along mainly judicial lines. Walsingham portrays a number of the leading rebels taking an additional step toward collaboration in their own rebuke, unlike our apparently unrepentant Perkyn. Alan Treader, one of the murderers of Sudbury, is said to have been seized by the devil and to have run mad in the streets, devising his own exemplary punishment with a naked sword about his neck and an unsheathed dagger at his back: "arreptus a diabolo, insanire coepit, et, domum veniens, nudum gladium a collo suo suspendit ante pectus suum, et cultellum, [quem "daggere" dicimus] etiam evaginatum, suspendit ad tergum" (2: 15). Routinely labeled *insanus* in the chronicle accounts, the rebels are first shown transported by the crazy revelry of their bacchanal and in the end their insanity is replayed, stripped of illusion, as diabolical possession and frantic guilt.

The narrative evocation of bacchanal or revelry followed by its rebuke may serve varied purposes. The epigraph to my essay is drawn from the recent upheaval in the former Soviet Union, when, just prior to the failed conservative putsch of Autumn 1991, the old guard accused the reformers of "political bacchanalia." This representational project bore within it, of course, the seeds of a hoped-for narrative, in which the reform movement is viewed as spontaneous and involving but also as irresponsible and unrooted and – above all – ephemeral and soon to vanish with the appearance of responsible authority figures. The putsch was to be the determinate moment of closure, when the Lenten figures of old authority returned to terminate the brief sway of mardi gras. In this case, however, the insurgents in the streets, sticking flowers in gunbarrels and otherwise enacting a mythos of spring, had a different narrative in mind – a narrative in which revelry provided a staging ground for open-ended and potentially transformative actions. Unlike the apparently premature rebels of 1381, the Russian reformers were able to link their aspirations to centers of institutional authority (including their own state government with a legitimately elected and highly vocal spokesperson in power) and were able to recruit the urban officials who might loosely be characterized as the Walworths and Brembres of our day. They were thus able to continue the curve of their own narrative, in which revelrous spontaneity and improvisation were open-ended and were linked to ultimate supplantation and apparent political transformation.

Whatever their hopes, the rebels of 1381 remained subject to multiple and interlocking systems of social control. Among these elements of control were such tangible factors as the loyalty of Walworth, Brembre, Philipot, and other key leaders of the London patriciate; the presence of experienced mercenaries like Knolles and the availability of armed elements like the garrison of the Tower; and, eventually, the availability of a judicial system of rebuke and castigation. No less important as elements of control were, however, such intangibles as the rebels' own incomplete ideological program, composed of

172

ill-sorted backward- and forward-looking elements; their innate deference to the king and their inability to imagine a form of rule that did not involve reliance upon kingship; the motivation of many of their number to settle finite grudges and scores rather than to enstate new social arrangements.[22] Centrally important among these less tangible aspects of revolt is the issue of the rebels' "story" and by whom and for what purposes it is narrated and, in the course of its narration, controlled.

Narration occurs at multiple levels of action and expression. As theorists like David Carr have pointed out, our practical behavior in the world depends on our ability to narratize our own actions; as social actors we inevitably stand in "the story-teller's position with respect to our own actions" with "no elements enter[ing] our experience . . . unstoried or unnarrativized."[23] The consequence of Carr's claim is that narrative patterns (such as closure, beginning and end, departure and arrival, means and end, problem and solution [49]) are vitally involved in the production of the most mundane actions, well prior to their analytical or aesthetic uses in written texts. We may understand the rebels to have staged their oppositional actions within existing narrative frames, of which revelry was one, and the rebels do appear to have drawn upon ideas and images of revelry to produce oppositional actions. Although evidence is limited to already heavily interpreted accounts, such as the stigmatizing chronicles, the recurrence of carnivalesque images (most notably, the exclamations of the rebels at Lambeth palace) argues that the "revelle" was one of several explanatory framings by which the rebels sought to compensate for their want of a comprehensive revolutionary ideology.

Yet actions, once staged, are subject to rehearsal and reconsideration in the written record, with corresponding alteration in meaning. Carr, for example, proposes a distinction between the practical uses of narrative in producing practical actions and the various forms of written re-narration. In these terms, we may see both Walsingham *and* Chaucer as engaged in a socially active and historically important project of written re-narration, in which aspects of the Rising of 1381 are retold with a heavy emphasis on closure. Through their re-narrations, both Walsingham and Chaucer join a continuing contest over the terms of social understanding, and both join it in ways hostile to the unruly aspirations of the lower strata. Retelling the events of 1381, Walsingham and the other chroniclers draw on such characteristics of revelry as its ephemeral character to underscore the abrupt beginning, unruly middle, and definitive end of rebellion. Chaucer likewise draws upon established images of revelry-as-revolt – including its disdain for traditional relations of domination and

---

22 For particular emphasis on the diversity of rebel motives, see Andrew Prescott, "The Judicial Records of the Rising of 1381" (Ph.D. diss., University of London, 1984).

23 David Carr, *Time, Narrative, and History* (Bloomington: Indiana University Press, 1986), 61, 68. Carr's emphasis on the practical origins of narration in the production of everyday actions, as opposed to Ricoeur's assumption that experience is only retrospectively organized via narrative configuration, is conveniently set forth in his review of *Temps et Récit*, vol. 1, in *History and Theory* 23 (1984): 357-70.

subordination and its disdain for the "papers" in which such understandings are inscribed – in order to suggest the necessity for stern rebuke.

Walsingham's narrative project is a good deal more explicitly related to the events of 1381 than Chaucer's fragmentary tale. Approached as a self-sufficient system, the Cook's Tale is only about itself, and its references are meaningful only in relation to its enterprise of constructing a narration about a revelrous apprentice and his past, present, and future rebuke. But it also participates ontologically in a larger system of narratives treating revelry and rebuke in the sense that it draws upon their narrative and symbolic energy and shares a portion of their social work. So seen, Perkyn's story is not an allegory of the 1381 Rising or even necessarily a reference to it, but it participates in the narrative curve of the Rising, a sense of disturbing excitement and inevitable chastisement. It joins other post-1381 narratizations in their task of putting a quietus on rising – on the Rising – itself.

The Issue of Closure

Historical and literary narratives of revolt and repression offered a premature but highly persuasive rhetoric of closure that encouraged a view of the 1381 Rising as an event with a clear terminus and no afterlife at all. This view influenced contemporaries, constituting one of the many political and cultural forces with which those who sought decisive change had unequally to contend. The effectiveness of such closed narratives, including those founded on a movement from revel to its rebuke, may be measured in a widespread belief that the Rising was unprecedented but unique, discontinuous with other manifestations of social struggle, and was socially and politically *sans issue*. We do not wholly escape these beliefs today.[24]

[24] A tendency may be noticed among twentieth-century commentators, and especially literary people interested in "historical backgrounds," to treat the Rising (along with the Black Death and, optionally, the Hundred Years War) as an unprecedented and traumatic moment of rupture, the importance and singularity of which are enhanced by its discontinuity with events before or since. In this treatment, they reveal the influence of medieval narratives of the Rising as a sudden and overwhelming phenomenon that subsided as rapidly as it occurred. Historians have asserted their urbanity and sense of diachronic process by disallowing a sense of rupture and insisting instead that the Rising had little effect and changed little or nothing. An extreme rendition of this view is that of F. M. Powicke, with his dismissal of the Rising as "an 'incident' of no enduring importance." See his *Medieval England, 1066–1485* (London: Oxford University Press, 1931), 214. Yet this view may still be conditioned by the lingering effect of medieval narratives of flareup and subsidence, in its assumption that the Rising can be isolated or bracketed for limited analysis and an enumeration of its effects. An approach somewhat more resistant to the rhetoric of narrative closure would return the events of 1381 to the stream of history, recasting them in a narrative open, rather than closed, at the far end. This analytical effect is, for example, achieved – possibly inadvertently – by Charles Oman when, seeking to minimize the longterm significance of the Rising, he returns it to a longer-

Narratives of wished-for closure can exert a great deal of influence on the interpretation of an event. But I have perhaps gone as far as I should go in implying that a narrative can ever truly close itself or be "closed," or that the door can be shut on all its inherent possibilities for continuation or contradiction. As a fragment, Chaucer's tale stands as a particularly suggestive instance of the problems narratives have in closing themselves. Even granting the partial success of the Cook's account in underscoring Perkyn's moral and social descent, it nevertheless leaves him flourishing underground. He is welcomed by a sympathetic "compeer of his owene sort" (I.4419), a reveler who only pretends to participate in legitimate trade, and by an economically and morally emancipated wife who bleeds the brothel-owning patriarchs of the city of their profits by swiving on the side.[25] The complete story of Perkyn and his *compeers* remains untold.

The fact that Chaucer did not finish Perkyn's story – that he left his prentice *snybbed* (I.4401) or decisively rebuked but still in play – has been discussed by Chaucerians according to all sorts of critical and codicological hypotheses that I will not attempt to summarize here. Let me just conclude by adding another: the energies of 1381 inscribed within Perkyn's brief bacchanal could be thrust from view, but their work was far from done. The aspirations of 1381 were not really brought to an end by the death of Tyler or by the return of the rebels to their homes or by the multiple judicial processes of 1382. Redirected and associated with other arenas of struggle, they resurfaced as parliamentary acknowledgment of the burden of taxation on the working poor, as local impetus for manumission, as religious dissent. Associated through the shared symbolic language of bacchanalia with the most turbulent social energies of its

term account of landlord-tenant struggles: "For the next ten years the archives of England are full of instances of conflict between landlord and tenant precisely similar to those which had been so rife in the years immediately preceding the rebellion." See Charles Oman, *The Great Revolt of 1381*, new ed. with intro. and notes by E. B. Fryde (Oxford: Clarendon Press, 1969), 154. Some brief recent treatments, revealing a disposition to treat the events of 1381 as an episode in a struggle of longer duration, include V. H. Galbraith, "Thoughts about the Peasants' Revolt," in *The Reign of Richard II*, ed. F. R. H. Du Boulay and Caroline M. Barron (London: Athlone Press, 1971), 55–57 and Fryde's introduction to Oman, xxxi–ii.

25 On the civic regulation of brothels and the involvement of prominent citizens like William Walworth in their ownership and management, see Ruth Mazo Karras, "The Regulation of Brothels in Later Medieval England," *Signs* 14 (1989): 399–433. This *wyf* was operating in defiance of a number of ordinances, including the stipulation that a prostitute should be associated with a brothel and should not be attached to any one man (422, 425). Ruth Karras has commented, tellingly, that attempts at regulation were intensified by the threat posed by prostitution in creating "a group of women outside of male control" ("Common Women: Prostitution and Sexuality in Medieval Culture," a lecture delivered at Indiana University in March, 1992). On the characteristics that prostitution holds in common with other later medieval forms of women's work, including its temporary nature and lessened requirements for capital investment, see "The Regulation of Brothels," 414 and n. 60.

day – with energies, that is, that were by their nature unfinished and not subject to confident closure – Perkyn's story could hardly *be* finished in any satisfactory sense. We leave him as contemporary chroniclers left the rebels of 1381: underground, excluded from the official civil life, associated with illicit small accumulators who shadow and poach upon the sanctioned commercial activities of the day. We leave him, like the social tacticians described by Michel de Certeau, in secure control of no "proper place," still betting on a yet-to-be-narrated time in which his destinies will be revealed.[26]

[26] Michel de Certeau, *The Practice of Everyday Life* (Berkeley and Los Angeles: University of California Press, 1984), esp. 39.

"God hathe schewed ffor him many grete miracules": Political Canonization and the *Miracula* of Simon de Montfort

THOMAS J. HEFFERNAN

Depicting political opponents of the crown as the true defenders of the commonweal has a notable, albeit frequently polemical, history in medieval England. Although we expect such rhetorical polarization in the arena of political democracies, it surprises one to see it flourishing in the center of an absolutist monarchy. Yet flourish it did during the tumultuous uprising of the barons under the leadership of Simon de Montfort, Earl of Leicester, against the government of Henry III. The political commentary which surrounded the strife between Henry and his magnates is redolent with Manichean-like metaphors; the struggle was depicted as a clash between good and bad, truth versus falsehood, rebels and traitors against the sacerdotal monarch and his liege lords. Virtually every monastic chronicle which treated the affair (with the single exception of the Westminster continuation of the *Flores Historiarum*) employed a political rhetoric which was not only anti-royalist and solidly pro-baronial but depicted the two titans in the struggle, Simon de Montfort and Henry III, as saint versus sinner.[1]

In the pages that follow, I raise three related questions concerning the attempted canonization of Simon de Montfort, Earl of Leicester, and offer answers to these queries drawn from a reading of the contemporary record.[2]

---

[1] Perhaps the reason Henry received such support from the Westminster continuation of the *Flores Historiarum* is that the Westminster chroniclers were unwilling to alienate their royal patron, whose administration was close by and who chose to keep the royal treasury in the abbey. See H. R. Luard, ed., *Flores Historiarum*, Rolls Series 95, 3 vols. (London: Eyre & Spottiswoode for H. M. Stationery Office, 1890), 3: 6–137.

[2] Although Josiah C. Russell was the first to discuss at length the attempted canonizations of enemies of the monarchy, he merely touched on the case of de Montfort; see his "The Canonization of Opposition to the King in Angevin England," in *Haskins Anniversary Essays in Mediaeval History*, ed. Charles H. Taylor and John L. La Monte (Boston: Houghton Mifflin, 1929), 279–90. See also J. W. McKenna, "Popular Canonization as Political Propaganda: The Cult of Archbishop Scrope," *Speculum* 45 (1970): 608–23.

Part I seeks to answer why the particular rhetoric used by the supporters of de Montfort (his case made most strongly by the monastic chroniclers) was so indebted to the language of religion. While there are undoubtedly instances of piety in de Montfort's life, his career was singularly devoted to secular ends. Part II examines the case for de Montfort's sanctity, noting that his case uniquely abrogates all the essential topoi used and approved by the clerical hierarchy in seeking a candidate's canonization in thirteenth-century England. My analysis here is primarily indebted to a reading of the *Dictum de Kelenworthe*. I propose that the powerful charge of traitor and rebel which was leveled at de Montfort forced his defenders to the extreme measure of representing him as a saint in order to justify his actions. Part III is a description and analysis of the text of the *Miracula Symonis de Montfort* extant in British Library MS. Cotton Vespasian A.VI. The *Miracula* is a contemporary record of the cures granted those who petitioned Simon de Montfort. My discussion of the *Miracula* makes available for the first time a taxonomy of the "rank and file" who followed de Montfort and the baronial cause and who continued to proselytize his memory after the rout at the Battle of Evesham.

The case of Simon de Montfort is pivotal for the ongoing study of popular religion and literature in late-medieval England. The stories about him afford us an opportunity to view the *vox populi* coalescing around a figure of political reform, transforming that individual into a religious idol against the authority of both church and state in order to continue the struggle for social and political reform. In mid-century Simon de Montfort became for a large segment of the English population, both laity and clergy (especially the Franciscans and Dominicans who were yet instrumental in leading Innocent's Lateran reform program), a synechdotal figure behind which a disparate populist movement might continue their struggle for a greater participation in power sharing.

Simon and the Rhetoric of Religion

The *Waverley Chronicle* echoed a familiar complaint against Henry III. It characterized him as a dupe of powerful resident aliens, a man possessed of a tyrannical will who had precious little regard for the ancient customs of the realm.[3] Simon de Montfort, Duke of Leicester and leader of the barons, on the other hand, is depicted in the same chronicle as a defender of these cherished customs, seeking justice at whatever cost, even at the expense of his personal security. Of course, the irony of such invective is that de Montfort was

---

[3] For the Waverley Chronicle, see H. R. Luard, ed., *Annales Monastici*, Rolls Series 36, 5 vols. (London: Longman, Green, 1864–69), 2: 129–411; A. Gransden, *Historical Writing in England c. 550 to c. 1307*, 2 vols. (Ithaca: Cornell University Press, 1974, 1982), 1: 416, quoting J. C. Holt's translation, reads, "These laws and customs had been either excessively corrupted or wholly quashed and reduced to nothing, and it was as if instead of the law, there was [the king's] tyrannical will; and no just judgement could be easily obtained except for money."

perhaps the most powerful resident alien living in the realm. The *Melrose* chronicler, however, was not blind to this paradox and commented that Simon, the great deporter of aliens, was himself one by birth.[4]

William Rishanger, a monk of St. Alban's Abbey and the author of the pro-baronial *De Bellis Lewes et Evesham*, succinctly depicts this good versus evil dichotomy in his rendering of the prophecy concerning the de Montfort family made by Robert Grosseteste, Bishop of Lincoln. In his chronicle Rishanger alleges that Grosseteste is said to have called de Montfort's oldest son to him and, putting his hand on his head, said, "O my dearest son, both you and your father will die on the same day and in the same way succumb for the cause of justice."[5] Rishanger's incorporation of such prophecies of self-sacrifice into the record created the verisimilitude he was striving to achieve. As Rishanger well knew, the historical record corroborated the prophecy, and accordingly he recounted later in his chronicle that "Et haec sunt nomina magnatum qui in miserabili conflictu ceciderunt: Comes Leyc. [Simon de Montfort, sr.] . . . Henricus filius comitis primogenitus" at the Battle of Evesham on August 6, 1265.

While Henry III sought unsuccessfully throughout his long reign to limit the further loss of royal prerogatives surrendered by his father to the baronial movement at Magna Carta, the movement's intention was, as manifest in the *Provisio facta apud Oxoniam*, to exercise genuine control over the central administration of the realm.[6] The barons argued that, although they must consult with the sovereign, custom allowed them to choose his ministers. De Montfort emerged as the spokesman who defended this customary privilege of the English barons.[7] Henry, who was politically inept in negotiating baronial privilege, foolishly, and at times inexplicably, turned against Simon. Such slights in turn increased the barons' alienation from their king, fueled Simon's personal ambition, and led inevitably to the debacle of Lewes and Evesham. The personal animus between the king and his brother-in-law may also account for the polarizing *ad hominem* rhetoric which we find in virtually all of the chronicles that discuss the baronial movement.

---

[4] D. A. Carpenter, "Simon de Montfort: The First Leader of a Political Movement in English History," *History: The Journal of the Historical Association*, no. 246 (= vol. 76) February (1991): 3–23. Alan Orr Anderson and Marjorie Ogilvie Anderson, ed., *The Chronicle of Melrose* (London: P. Lund, Humphries & Co., 1936), 127.

[5] James O. Halliwell, ed., *The Chronicle of William de Rishanger of the Barons' Wars: The Miracles of Simon de Montfort*, Camden Society 15 (London: J. B. Nichols, 1840), 7: "O fili carissime! et tu et pater tuus ambo moriemini uno die, unoque die et morbo, pro justitia."

[6] R. F. Treharne and I. J. Sanders, eds., *Documents of the Baronial Movement of Reform and Rebellion 1258–1267* (Oxford: Clarendon Press, 1973), 9.

[7] Baronial opposition to royal privilege was active during the reign of Edward II. The barons claimed that Edward had usurped their customary rights. They appealed to the memory of Simon de Montfort as a precedent for restoration of these traditional liberties; see James Conway Davies, *The Baronial Opposition to Edward II: Its Character and Policy, A Study in Administrative History* (New York: Barnes & Noble, 1918), 344.

The rhetoric that attended the career of Simon de Montfort has a most curious chronological trajectory – from the bellicose to the sacred, from the triumphant warrior to the innocent victim. Reporting to Henry on the behalf of the kingdom of Gascony (where de Montfort was sent by Henry to bring order out of the chaos of competing rivalries), Matthew Paris referred to the widespread rumors of Simon's ruthless zeal in establishing order: "We are all unanimous in complaining of the earl of Leicester, who, charged with governing the country, brings it to ruin and expels its inhabitants with ferocity."[8] On the other hand, Adam Marsh, the great Franciscan and counsellor to Henry and friend to Simon, voices an entirely opposite view from that of Matthew of Paris, referring to Simon's moderation, long suffering, and devotion to Henry and the people of Gascony: "he ever observed towards his sovereign and his adversaries the law of mercy with the mature wisdom of a great-hearted soul."[9]

While de Montfort is referred to as an able, accomplished, judicious, and sometimes ruthless military commander in letters and chronicles of the 1250s, immediately following his death at Evesham he is celebrated almost exclusively in sacred panegyric. Such adulation continued for almost a century after his death. In a French lyric in MS. Harley 2253, the poet, while acknowledging his prowess in arms, unambiguously associates Simon with one of England's greatest saints who also died disputing the prerogatives of kingship:

> Ore est ocys la flur de pris, qe taunt savoit de guere,
> Ly quens Montfort, sa dure mort molt enplorra la terre.
> . . .
> Mes par sa mort, le cuens Mountfort conquist la victorie,
> Come ly martyr de Caunterbyr, finist sa vie. . . .[10]

The Simon mentioned in the chronicles after Evesham is now not only Simon de Montfort, Duke of Leicester, but St. Simon, popular champion of the English nation and sacred repositor of the people's trust.

How did this ambitious secular military commander – a leader who, however grievous the political situation, did indeed violate fealty and take his King captive – come to be celebrated as a saint, a champion of the church in England? Such partisanship which dressed the recently dead de Montfort in encomiastic rhetoric, in the protective robes of sanctity and divine favor, was deliberately designed to keep the struggle alive. But why was this praise couched in the language of religion as opposed, for example, to the more appropriate heroic, secular rhetoric of the *chanson de geste*? After all, there was little contemporary disagreement concerning the enormous achievements of de Montfort as a member of the knightly class.

---

[8] Charles Bémont, *Simon de Montfort, Earl of Leicester 1208–1265*, trans. E. F. Jacob (Oxford: Clarendon Press, 1930), 106–7.

[9] Bémont, 106–7.

[10] Thomas Wright, *The Political Songs of England From the Reign of John to that of Edward II*, 4 vols. [= Camden Society 6] (1839; reprint, Edinburgh: Priv. print., 1884), 2: 51.

I believe the reason for the choice of religious rhetoric is an effort to address the enormity of what de Montfort attempted to do and what he actually accomplished. The Earl of Leicester sought nothing short of the complete remaking of the way the monarchy conducted the affairs of the state. This goal was to be accomplished by force, if necessary; therefore, he took arms against his king, risked regicide, and held Henry captive. In raising the gauntlet against Henry, his king, Simon simultaneously raised it against family, for it was Henry who was chiefly responsible for arranging the hasty marriage of his younger sister Eleanor to Simon. Accordingly, Simon violated, at the very least (notwithstanding whether for noble or base principle), that deeply held medieval belief in the sacerdotal role of the monarch and loyalty to kin.

De Montfort seemed to be seeking what today might be characterized as a constitutional monarchy, with the king as *primus inter pares* in close consultation with a ruling baronial elite. Such thinking was a minority point of view and was utterly repudiated at important junctures in Simon's struggle with Henry. For example, Simon's appeal to King Louis IX of France to determine whether Henry's oath to uphold the *Provisions of Oxford* ought to have made him legally bound to support the application of the *Provisions* resulted in Louis' famous *Mise de Amiens* (see especially clauses 14 and 17). The *Mise* reaffirmed the power of the monarchy and abrogated the *Provisions of Oxford* as being unwarranted usurpations of traditional kingly prerogative.[11]

The panegyrists who wished to defend de Montfort had to seek a sufficiently serious rationale to counter the enormity of what he had done. It was a well established tradition that to attack the king was to attack God's vicar. Thinkers like John of Salisbury and Giles of Rome saw the very character of the state as determined by the ruler. To rule was a call to the highest ethical actions. The king therefore sought to become in Dunbabin's apt expression "virtue personified."[12] Such attitudes, although there were obvious dissenters, were widely held in thirteenth-century England and France.[13] Indeed, it is doubtless the case that Simon de Montfort himself clung tenaciously to such traditional thinking concerning the ideal of kingship. If he did not share this belief, I think it unlikely that he would have sought an adjudication from King Louis IX concerning Henry's obligation to uphold the *Provisions of Oxford*. Therefore, the only possible rationale with sufficient gravity to counter the claims of the royalists was for Simon's defenders to fashion one whose rhetorical authority was rooted in religion. Simon de Montfort, Earl of Leicester, was, in his war against the rightful king, implementing God's plan to rid England of a tyrant.

---

[11] Treharne, 288, c. 17: "Item, dicimus et ordinamus, quod dictus rex plenam potestatem et liberium regimen habeat in regno suo, et eius pertinentiis; et sit in eo statu, et in ea plenaria potestate, in omnibus et per omnia, sicut erat ante tempus predictum."

[12] Jean Dunbabin, "Government," in *The Cambridge History of Medieval Political Thought c.350–c.1450*, ed. J. H. Burns (Cambridge: Cambridge University Press, 1987), 483.

[13] In the famous "Song of Lewes," composed shortly after Simon's victory, we read the following: "therefore let him who reads know that he cannot reign who does not keep the law" (Wright, 2:27–28).

The post mortem rhetorical panegyric added a powerful weapon to the arsenal of the anti-royalists, investing their conflict with a theological legitimacy.[14] Through this strategy, the strife which erupted throughout the realm after the rout at Evesham could be represented as an engagement between the annealing forces of God and a monarchy grown corrupted by the world. An entry in the *Melrose Chronicle* written shortly after the debacle of the battle of Evesham illustrates the depth of feeling in the houses of the regular clergy and may reflect a populist view: "it should be made clear that anyone possessed of sense ought not to censor nor call Simon de Montfort by the name of traitor. He was no traitor; but he was the most faithful protector and follower of the church of God in England, a shield and defender of the kingdom of England. . . ."[15]

The People Raise up a Saint

The *Chronicle of Battle Abbey* was not only sympathetic to de Montfort and his cause and opposed to that of Henry but believed de Montfort died a martyr's death and was indeed a saint.[16] While it was not without precedent in twelfth- and thirteenth-century England to seek canonization for individuals who publicly trumpeted anti-royal sympathies, such efforts – with the single exception of Simon de Montfort – seem to have been chiefly directed at celebrating the memory of a member of the clergy who stood up for God and principle.

All post-Conquest English political canonization attempts which involved opponents of the royal prerogative from Becket's administration at Canterbury through Henry III's reign were members of the clerical hierarchy: Thomas à Becket, Archbishop of Canterbury (d. 1170, canonized 1173); Hugh, Bishop of Lincoln (d. 1200, canonized 1220); Stephen Langton, Archbishop of Canterbury (proposed but failed canonization); Edmund of Abington (d. 1240, canonized 1246); Robert Grosseteste (d. 1253, proposed but failed repeated attempts at canonization); and Thomas Cantilupe, Bishop of Hereford (d. 1282, canonized 1320). All of these individuals, with the exception of Edmund of Abington, were reformers whose zeal spared neither crown nor church.

The attempt to canonize de Montfort and the miracles attributed to him are of great interest because de Montfort is the singular exception to this clerical

---

[14] Although I am using the terms royalist and anti-royalist throughout this paper, such terms are not meant to convey, for example, that de Montfort did not believe in the sacerdotal role of the monarchy. The Earl of Leicester, like his baronial confrères united in their struggle with Henry, was opposed to Henry's particular abuses of his royal prerogatives and not to the idea of kingship. De Montfort was no proto-democrat.

[15] Rishanger, xxvii: "et sciendum quod nemo sani capitis debet censere neque apellare Simonem nomine proditoris. Non enim fuit proditor, sed Dei ecclesiae in Anglia devotissimus cultor et fidelissimus protector, regni Anglorum scutum et defensor. . . ."

[16] Gransden, 422, n. 178.

dominance of candidates for canonization who opposed their king. Moreover, de Montfort fell outside what characterized the normative backgrounds for saints in mid-thirteenth century England. Simon de Montfort was married with children; his major accomplishments were in feats of arms; and, although pious, he was enormously ambitious, at odds with the papacy, and broke fealty with his sovereign. Thus, virtually all the traditional medieval English topoi (celibacy, asceticism, humility, learning, and loyalty) used to fashion a case for canonization were missing in the exceptional case of the sanctity of Simon de Montfort.

What reasons were given to support de Montfort as a candidate for canonization and on what grounds did his supporters legitimate their rationale? A fruitful area of study which may answer these questions is the chronicles which report on the battles of Lewes and Evesham, the *Dictum de Kelenworthe*, and the important but little studied *Miracula Simonis de Montfort*. Our earliest historical record that a movement was underway to canonize the recently dead de Montfort comes from the royalist camp. These efforts are referred to in a brief remark made in clause 8 of the *Dictum de Kelenworthe*, promulgated in late October 1266. The *Dictum de Kelenworthe* is a royalist document expressly designed to bring reconciliation to the realm. As Sanders noted, the *Dictum* was an effort to redress the "rash words" attributed to Henry III on the battlefield of Evesham, where he is reputed to have said that the rebels had forfeited all lands and goods and his supporters that day might keep whatever they had seized from their opponents. This draconian disinheritance of his opponents was in turn sanctioned by the Parliament, which met in Westminster in September 1265.

The upshot of the parliamentary legislation was to inflame the sense of grievance of those already alienated from the crown and to galvanize sporadic pockets of resistance to Henry and his supporters throughout the realm. Clause 12 of the *Dictum* specifically attempted to remedy this situation by allowing those who were disinherited (referred to as the *exheredatorum*) by the Winchester Parliament of September 1265 to ransom through payment the lands confiscated after Evesham. But while Henry and his counsellors in the *Dictum* attempted to create a spirit of reconciliation for most of their former opponents, they remained obdurately opposed to de Montfort and certain other leaders of the rebellion.

Accordingly, the royalists would have been especially sensitive to any efforts to legitimate the name of de Montfort. Clause 8 of the *Dictum* underscores the depth of the concern on the part of the royalists that a populist movement to canonize de Montfort was gathering momentum. Moreover, if such a movement were successful, it would diminish Edward's victory and give the moral high ground to the opposition. The language of clause 8, therefore, is carefully designed to thwart any such populist movement and, as such, is constructed so as to place sanctions on both the clergy and the laity:

Rogantes humiliter tam dominum legatum quam dominum regem ut ipse dominus legatus sub districtione ecclesiastica prossus inhibeat, ne S.

comes Leycestrie a quocumque pro sancto uel iusto reputetur, cum in
excommunicacione sit defunctus, sicut sancta tenet ecclesia; et mirabilia
de eo uana et fatua ab aliquibus relata nullis unquam labiis proferantur; et
dominus rex hec eadem sub pena corporali uelit districte inhibere.

[Humbly beseeching both the lord legate and the lord king that the lord
legate shall forbid absolutely under the jurisdiction of the church, that
Simon the earl of Leicester be considered a saint or just man, since he died
an excommunicate, and thus the holy church holds. And the vain and the
silly miracles attributed to him by others shall not at any time pass
anyone's lips. And the lord king rigorously agrees to forbid this
[discussion of miracles] under the pain of bodily injury.][17]

While clause 8 is a general condemnation of the memory of Simon de
Montfort, it singles out two particular issues which were believed especially
injurious to the commonweal, namely that Simon de Montfort must not be
revered as a saint and all discussion of miracles attributed to him must cease.
The legitimacy of these prohibitions was founded in the joint authority of
papacy and crown. Notice that the first part of clause 8 concerns an issue of
religious belief and thus is rightly proscribed by the church. The second point
concerns the behavior of these believers which presumably, if unchecked,
might lead to sedition and was forbidden by the civil authority under "pain of
bodily injury."

The bifurcation of jurisdictional authority of clause 8 represents the *modus
vivendi* which church and state in England had achieved under the authority of
the crown. In particular, on this sensitive issue of excommunication – from the
beginning of the thirteenth century (traditionally referred to as the caption of
excommunicates) – the English monarchy had positioned itself as the
disciplinary arm serving the episcopacy in their capacity as ecclesiastical
judges. Clause 8 is thus a classic rendering of this alliance and illustrates the
mutuality of cooperation between the church hierarchy and the civil authority
when their common interests were threatened.[18]

The first interdiction is both juridical and ecclesiastical: it stipulates that
Simon can be considered neither a saint nor even just since he died an
excommunicate outside the bosom of the church. This interdiction is then
legitimated by the authority of the lord legate. While clause 8 also served as a
general prohibition for any of the populace to reverence de Montfort, it would
appear, given what we know of the relationship between civil and ecclesiastical
authority at that time, that it was chiefly directed at the clergy. This
denunciation of de Montfort as saint and the reminder of his excommunicate

---

[17] R. E. Treharne and I. J. Sanders, 322.

[18] J. A. Watt, "Spiritual and Temporal Powers," in *The Cambridge History of Medieval
Political Thought c.350–c.1450*, 394–95. The complex *via media* achieved by the two
jurisdictional authorities of church and state in England, when it concerned issues of
excommunication, Watt suggests were implementing "a truism known to all
canonists from the rubric to a text of Isidore: 'What priests are powerless to
accomplish by exhortation, the force of discipline may exact by fear.'"

status were a cue to the episcopacy of their obligation as judges against such individuals and to the lesser clergy of their obedience to their bishops.[19] The framers of clause 8 may have believed that such an interdiction would have the immediate effect of limiting the freedom of the clergy to proselytize in the name of de Montfort.

Within the very varied ranks of the English clergy, de Montfort's most ardent supporters appear to have been the Franciscans and Dominicans. By mid-century, these two groups were well established throughout England and were in the vanguard for promoting the reformist program of the Fourth Lateran Council. Preaching was their chief tool in this evangelistic ministry. Thus, such a sanction like that mentioned in clause 8 would have the effect of limiting the mention of de Montfort's name in liturgical settings such as the sermon and the divine office. There is indeed a fragment of an office written in memory of Simon de Montfort extant in British Library MS. Cotton Vespasian A.VI and in Cambridge University Library MS Kk.4.20. In the British Library manuscript, the fragmentary *Matins* hymn ends the collection of miracles we shall be discussing below.[20] If his supporters persisted in their public show of support, they would be subject by virtue of clause 8 of the *Dictum* to papal censure through the legate and/or their clerical superior. The mendicants were under the direct jurisdiction of Rome, so the fact that the papal legate is the authority for the interdiction in clause 8 would cause their efforts at promulgating de Montfort's memory to be in public violation of a widely publicized ecclesiastical sanction.

An obvious route around this interdiction was to challenge the legitimacy of the excommunication. Amaury de Montfort did this very thing. In a

---

[19] It is difficult to know how seriously one should consider the excommunication. For example, a colleague sympathetic to Simon's ideas, Thomas Cantilupe, Bishop of Hereford, was formally canonized while still under the ban of excommunication pronounced earlier by his metropolitan, John Pecham, Archbishop of Canterbury.

[20] There is a fragmentary office composed in Simon de Montfort's memory, printed in George W. Prothero, *The Life of Simon de Montfort, Earl of Leicester with Special Reference to the Parliamentary History of his Time* (London: Longmans, Green, 1877), 379–80, 388–91 and in Wright, 2:50. It reads: "Anno Domini M.cc.lx.v octavo Symonis Montisfortis sociorumque ejus, pridie nonas Augusti.

> Salve, Symon Montis-Fortis,
> > Totius flos militiae,
> Duras poenas passus mortis,
> > Protector gentis Angliae.
> Sunt de sanctis inaudita,
> Cunctis passis in hac vita,
> > Quemquam passum talia;
> Manus, pedes amputari,
> Caput, corpus vulnerari,
> > Abscidi virilia.
> Sis pro nobis intercessor
> Apud Deum, qui defensor
> > In terris extiteras."

communication to Pope Clement IV sometime before April 1267, he stated that his father had asked for and obtained absolution and made clear signs before his death of his repentance.[21] A number of the chroniclers who discuss the events immediately prior to the battle of Evesham report behavior which also suggests that Simon may have repented. That section of the *Lanercost Chronicle* (1201–1297), written by the Franciscan Richard of Durham, an ardent supporter of de Montfort and his cause, goes so far as to state that immediately before the Battle of Evesham de Montfort heard mass and received communion "auditio officio et accepto viatico." Such claims were undoubtedly the basis of Amaury's petition to Pope Clement IV. Given the degree of political bias which exists in the chronicles, however, there is little hope of determining with certainty whether de Montfort repented before entering the fray against Edward. Furthermore, this very claim, made in a number of the chronicles, has the aura of hagiology about it.

The second admonition contained in clause 8 is both dismissive and exacting. Its arch tone and the particular nature of its subject suggest a largely lay population as its intended audience: these *mirabilia de eo [sunt] uana et fatua* and those who persist in telling them will be severely punished. While the rapid appearance of miracles on the death of a saint in English medieval cultic practice is not without precedent, seldom, if ever, do we have such a rapid collusion of the secular and clerical hierarchy united against such occurrences. For the royal authorities, within a year after Evesham, to single out putative miracles for interdiction suggests that the cult of Simon de Montfort must have been gaining adherents at a very rapid rate, and these faithful adherents must have been discussing these miracles throughout the realm. And since, as we will see, the majority of those who were advantaged by the miracles of Simon were lay people of low status, it would appear that this threat of bodily punishment was directed principally at the peasantry and those who corroborated these stories.

Vox populi: The Miracula of Simon de Montfort

We are fortunate in being able to probe the historicity of the concerns voiced in clause 8, since we have a near contemporary record detailing the miracles which were reported. British Library MS. Cotton Vespasian A.VI contains an acephalous account of the miracles attributed to Simon de Montfort. In

---

21 W. H. Bliss, ed., *Calendar of Entries in the Papal Registers Relating to Great Britain and Ireland: Papal Letters A.D. 1198–1304,* .13 vols. (London and Dublin: Eyre & Spottiswoode for H. M. Stationery Office and Stationery Office for the Irish Manuscript Commission, 1893–1978), 1:434. It is in the same letter of Pope Clement IV to his legate, Ottobono, that mention is made that Amaury petitioned for church burial for his father's body. This is most interesting, since it appears to contradict some of the chronicles, which presume his body was disposed of in an open sewer. The date of the Pope's memorandum to Ottobono is April 1267, twenty months after the Battle of Evesham.

addition to mentioning the nature of the miracle rendered, the narrative also supplies the names of the petitioners, the names of witnesses to the miracle, the place of origin of the petitioner, and, lastly, the status and gender of the petitioner. The acephalous state of Cotton Vespasian A.VI may reflect mutilation by those opposed to de Montfort's cause. James O. Halliwell speculated that "De miracula" may have become separated from a no longer extant chronicle of Evesham Abbey.

Although anonymous, there are certain internal suggestions that the *Miracula* may have been written by a monk(s) of the Abbey of Evesham. The author had detailed knowledge of events which transpired in the abbey as a result of the miracles. He notes even small bequests to the abbey from those petitioners who were cured through the intercession of de Montfort: "De hoc perhibet testimonium Johannes de Hyke, qui candelam suam apud Evesham detulit."[22] While its Evesham provenance, uncritical biases in favor of the baronial movement, and its importance in the emerging cult of de Montfort do limit its reliability, these very prejudices illustrate precisely the sort of climate that clause 8 of the *Dictum de Kelenworthe* was trying to stifle. Therefore, the *Miracula* is a very apt document for our analysis of the populist attempt to canonize Simon and thus continue the struggle for civic reform.

The *Miracula* is a narrative account of the miracles which occurred to approximately 205 individuals. The records vary in length from an average of about 75 words to approximately 350. The prologue to the *Miracula* contains no date. We have, therefore, to date the text from the records themselves, some of which are dated. There is no systematic dating in the records. Typically, the date, when given, is of the form year plus its proximity to an important liturgical celebration. The earliest dated record which I have found is given as the vigil of the Holy Cross 1265 (usually celebrated September 13/14): "in vigilia sanctae Crucis, anno gratiae M cc lxv." This date is a mere month after the death of Simon at Evesham and is indicative of the speed with which his cult was being taken up and, perhaps, suggestive of the zeal of those who continued to resist Henry's victory. The latest date cited in a record is the Nativity of the Blessed Virgin 1277 (celebrated in England on September 8): "qui die Lunae proximo ante nativitatem beatae Mariae, anno Domini M°.cc°. septuagesimo vii." Such a late date (fully twelve years after the Battle of Evesham, the fifth year of King Edward's reign and the beginning of his campaign against the Welsh leader Llywelyn, who was betrothed to Simon de Montfort's daughter Eleanor) underscores the continuing widespread affection for de Montfort and his cause. Further, it suggests that the political grievances, which grew principally from Henry III's difficult relationships with his barons, may still have had supporters.[23]

All three estates representing the medieval populace are depicted in the *Miracula*. The records are, however, not consistent in that some contain more

---

[22] Rishanger, 83.
[23] Michael Prestwich, *Edward I* (London: Methuen, 1988), 106–7.

usable historical detail than others. A typical record will inform us as to the name of the petitioner, sometimes giving either a surname or identifying a male parent and sometimes a location: "Quidam puer Johannes nomine, filius Philippy de Sancta Maria in Creiden, Kent." Women are sometimes fully identified through marriage: "Margareta uxor Willelmi Mauncelle, de comitatu Gloverniae." However, in other records, their name and/or place of residence is simply given "Quaedam mulier nomine Matilda de Blythe." Even such small variation from a formulaic entry as this would suggest that the entries were originally made by different hands.

The *Miracula* identifies petitioners from at least sixteen different English counties, some as distant as Northumberland, Kent, and Devonshire. The greatest number of pilgrims, however, are identified as coming from the Midlands. No shire is represented by more than four petitioners (e.g., Lincolnshire, Northamptonshire). The reasons for this concentration from the Midlands is probably twofold: de Montfort's supporters were concentrated there and the location of the shrine in Evesham would have made this an easier pilgrimage for those in the Midlands. Petitioners are also identified as coming from Ireland, Scotland, France, and possibly from Germany.[24]

Although the records sometimes give the most indeterminate entries (e.g., "a certain man came and asked for . . ."), they occasionally have sufficient information so as to allow us to identify different socio-economic classes. For example, I have identified at least nine women and three men who were themselves from the highest class of society. One prominent woman from Gloucester is intriguingly identified as "Domina comitissa Gloverniae." It is difficult to know precisely what degree of position the scribe was describing when he penned *comitissa*. Certainly, the petitioner is of high status. But should we understand this expression to point unambiguously to a countess (*comitissa* is attested as "countess" as early as 1085) or as part of a generally accepted formula for identifying someone of high birth?[25] The strained political climate of the time complicates a ready assumption that this is a reference to the Countess of Gloucester. Although Edward I and the Earl of Gloucester were at odds from most of the late 1260s, it is difficult to believe that this is a reference to the Earl of Gloucester's wife or to a high-born woman of that house, since the Earl of Gloucester was himself frequently an antagonist of de Montfort and his sons. One might have expected that, if this had been someone from that household, the identifying entry in the *Miracula* would have been more opaque, but it is not. Therefore, I believe that we should read this as a reference to a woman from Gloucester of high birth, wealth, and independence, very possibly the Countess herself, since the narrative also states that out of thanksgiving for the miracle, "iterum misit armigerum suum Evesham."

[24] I have been unable to locate the place name "parochia de Inteberg."
[25] R. E. Latham, *Revised Medieval Latin Word-List from British and Irish Sources* (London: Oxford University Press, 1965), 98. If this is a formulaic expression for describing a woman of high station, I have been unable to find it elsewhere.

There is a single example of this anonymous sort of entry, reporting a man of high birth from Derbyshire (three records cite Derbyshire as a petitioner's place of residence): "Quidam nobilis de Derebeschire." Seven individuals are identified as being knights. A typical entry for this group reads, "Galfridus de Say, miles, de Essex." The bulk of the lay petitioners, in so far as I am able to make certain identifications of class (153 in number), are from the lowest estate. The clergy are represented with thirty three petitioners. The narrative records members of both regular and secular clergy as petitioners at the shrine. The regular clergy are identified as members of the Cistercians, Benedictines, Praemonstratensians, both male and female, and from the abbatial rank to that of the choir monk. From the ranks of the mendicants are four Franciscans and one Dominican friar. Two petitioners are simply identified as belonging to an order of canons.

In estimating the number of individuals involved in a miracle, I have restricted myself to counting only the major petitioner, since most of the records also list witnesses who testify to the truth of said miracle. However, in certain instances, it is misleading to count only the primary recipient of the benefaction. For example, of these 205 petitioners recorded in the text, 127 were adult males, fifty were adult females and twenty six of the petitioners were children (nineteen males and seven females) and two individuals whose sex is not identified. In some instances, the children were brought to the shrine at Evesham by one or more parents and thus, while the miracle was performed for the child, the parent is mentioned as a crucial member in the narrative record. In some of the miracles which involved children, the child had already died and the parent is the main suppliant. In instances where the parent is an integral part of the narrative record, I have counted both parent and child in my sum of 205 individuals.

For example, in the following record, one William Child, identified as a member of the constabulary and an enemy of de Montfort, has just lost his son to an illness. He was directed to seek help from de Montfort by a mendicant, possibly a Dominican:

> Willelmus cognomento Child, constabularius de Kynggis, habens puerum fere mortuum, dictus Willelmus tantem dolorem concepit in mente, quod nullum gaudium vel laetitiam potuit habere. Casu superveniente venit quidam praedicator, socius ab antiquo, vidit nimiam anxietatem et dolorem, voluit ab illo declinare; ultimo dictus praedicator quaesivit, si contrarius fuit aliquando comiti Symoni. At ille, "Sic, quia privavit me multis bonis." Cui ille, "Pete veniam a martire, et recuperabis filium tuum." Interim infans expiravit. Et ecce dolor super dolorem! et jacuit se super lectum, et parum obdormuit. Et vidit in sompnis Christum descendere de coelis, et tetigit eum, dicens, "Quicquid petieritis in honore Comitis mei, dabitur tibi"; et surgens cum festinatione, mensuravit puerum, et denario plicato super eum, statim aperuit oculos. Et sic, per merita Comitis, sanus et in columis redditur patri suo. De hoc perhibet testimonium constabularius de Flopesbury, Clemens Londoniarum, una cum patre praedicti mortui.

[William surnamed Child, constable of Kings, had a son who was dying and this brought the father great sorrow which no joy or pleasure could alleviate. It happened that an old friend, a friar preacher [*praedicator*], saw his grief and anxiety and wished that he should tell him about it. The preacher asked him if he was ever at odds with the Count Simon. That man said: "Yes, because he deprived me of many goods." To which the other responded: "Seek grace from the martyr and your son will recover." In the meanwhile the child died. And behold there was sorrow on sorrow! And the father [grieving] threw himself on his bed and slept. And he saw in his dream Christ descend from heaven, and he touched him saying "Whatever you ask in the name of my Earl, it will be given to you." And rising in great haste, he measured the boy, [and folded it ten times about him]. Immediately he opened his eyes. And thus, because of the virtue of the Earl, [the child] was returned to his father whole and sound. Concerning this event, the constable of Flopesbury, Clement of London, and the father of the aforesaid dead child, are witnesses.][26]

Despite this record's hagiology, it contains much solid historical material. First, there is the petitioner, an individual identified by first and last name, one William Child. His exact occupation, that of constable, and place of residence, in the village of Kings, is given. As a constable of either a parish or a manor, Mr. William Child would have been from a higher class than the peasantry and may have been a lesser vassal of the local seigneur. In addition, Child is described not only as a contemporary of Simon de Montfort, but we learn he must have been a public supporter of Henry sometime during the period between 1258 and 1265, since he lodges a complaint against de Montfort. Notice that William, at the friar's prodding, acknowledges that his enmity for de Montfort was due to de Montfort's having taken his property against his will. This line of questioning by the preacher is a non sequitur, since nothing before it prepares us for it. But even here we may have the glimmer of a historical shard. William Child's remarks about Simon de Montfort's having been the cause of his goods' being lost may well be a reference to the effect of the *Provisions of Oxford* which stipulated the appointments of new sheriffs throughout the shires and the investigation into the practices of all local officials, sheriffs, bailiffs, coroners, escheators, and so on, with an eye toward dismissing those who had acted unfairly. William may have been one of those

---

[26] Rishanger, 82–83. The word *mensuravit* in the phrase "mensuravit puerum" refers to the placement of a length of cord or twine on the child. This same twine had been placed against the corpse of the saint. Having been pressed against the hallowed corpse, it was believed that the cord was invested with a numinal, healing power. The cord was then placed against that physical part of the petitioner which was being prayed for. The word *mensuravit* is derived from the past participle of *metior, -iri* and designates a custom which appears brand new in England at this time. It is first recorded with this application in mind in England as late as 1257 (see Latham, 296), a scant eight years before our earliest record. The word is used in virtually every record which cites a cure of an illness in the *Miracula*.

who were dismissed in the administrative reshuffling, which resulted under the *Provisions* until Henry abrogated the *Provisions* in the spring of 1261.

Additionally, if we view the record from its situation as an example of the didactic rhetoric of hagiography – that is, as a narrative intent on demonstrating the power of this new Christian saint – the figure of William Child then represents the stock topos of the unbeliever who is converted. But the hagiography is inseparable from the politics, for this record of the recovery of the dead son of William Child, Sheriff of Kings, suggests that it is only through an acceptance of the wisdom of de Montfort and the principles of his party that the cancerous strife eating away at the bowels of the commonweal can be healed.

In sum, within eleven years of the battle of Evesham, we have every facet of medieval society making pilgrimages in direct violation of clause 8 of the *Dictum de Kelenworthe* to pay homage to and seek favor from the memory of this political hero whom they had now invested with the halo of sanctity. The policies of the baronial party, although vanquished by the combined administrative might of Henry and Edward, sought to regain that lost ground through the medium of popular religion and the unsuccessful canonization of their dead leader, Simon de Montfort, Earl of Leicester. The very existence of such cultic movements may have served as a reminder to Edward that his father's politics frequently led to disastrous ends and, additionally, that the peace of the realm dictated a monarch more inclined to listen to his barons and the parliament.

Thrift

PEGGY A. KNAPP

> The boy did not know he was hearing Ovid, and it would not have
> mattered if he had known. Grandfather's stories proposed to him that the
> forms of life were volatile and that everything in the world could as easily
> be something else. The old man's narrative would often drift from English
> to Latin without his being aware of it ... so that it appeared nothing was
> immune to the principle of volatility, not even language.
>
> E. L. Doctorow, *Ragtime*

A bit later the boy in Doctorow's novel reflects that it "was evident to him that
the world composed and recomposed itself constantly in an endless process of
dissatisfaction." What he comes to see is the continual flux of both the world
we refer to and the signifying systems through which we try to seize it and
render it coherent. That continual flux presents a multi-faceted problem for
those of us who attempt to study the past, for the linguistic records we rely on
may either reveal cultural change quite directly or coyly occlude it. Our belief
that the narrative art of the past allows us in some measure to understand how
people lived and thought about their lives – to speak to the dead, as Stephen
Greenblatt has put it – depends at bottom on our finding a strategy for
capturing meaning from the volatile welter of potential implication which
language is.

Traditional philology approaches linguistic change by charting the first
occurrences of words and syntactic structures, their geographical range,
transmission from one language group to another, and the like. Deconstructive
analysis, on the other hand, attempts to show the slippage between signifier
and signified, the unexpectedly lurking traces of "hostile" within the friendly
invitation of the "host," to cite the example of an influential essay by J. Hillis
Miller.[1] I intend here a direct contribution to neither of these projects, although
the insights and strategies of both are called upon. I want to read verbal
histories as indications of the struggle among social groups to "detach one
meaning of [a] concept from ... public consciousness and supplant it within
the logic of another political discourse," as Stuart Hall puts it.[2]

[1] J. Hillis Miller, "The Critic as Host," *Critical Inquiry* 3 (1977): 439–47.
[2] Stuart Hall, "The Problem of Ideology – Marxism without Guarantees," *Journal of
Communication Inquiry* 10.2 (1986): 40–41.

Narrative fictions are especially empowered participants in this struggle because of their hold on imagination, both public and private. But while social groups are jockeying for position, the infrastructure is also changing – which is to say, the social world as well as language is composed and recomposed, as Doctorow's character intuited. In this essay I mean to "put you a case," in Thomas More's lawyerly phrasing, by citing occurrences of a particular word – *thrift* – through a couple of centuries of wear and tear. I also hope to demonstrate that many texts now thought of as canonized "works of art," rather than merely naturalizing and thus reinforcing structures of power, have subtly demystified social inequalities and the language which legitimizes them. I want to follow *thrift* from the late fourteenth to the early seventeenth century in order to see how certain complex works – in this case primarily works by Chaucer and Shakespeare – perform the social function of enhancing or unsettling dominant discursive positions through their management of the verbal nuance.

Thriving in the Middle Ages

Thrift is first found in its connection with the verb "to thrive." As early as *Hali Meidenhede* (1230) and as late as the late nineteenth century, it is found meaning "thriving," either physical or spiritual. Both Langland and Chaucer use it in this sense, and New England farm communities still refer to especially abundant crop growth as "thrift." John Trevisa, in translating Bartholomaeus Anglicus (1398), rendered *virorem* as "þrift" and *non proficiunt* as "faileþ of perfect þrifte." In Early Modern English, *thrift* occasionally took on the meaning of "the means to make something thrive," as in George Ripley's "also I wrorȝte jn sulphour & in vitriall . . . and thus I blewe my thryfte at ye cole. . . . My clothys were bawdy my stomake was never holle" (1500) or Lodge's "your giddy brain made you leaue your thrift" (1580).[3] Sometimes this thriving is imagined rather directly as monetary or military profit ("pore mennys thrift"), sometimes as a more general or even a distinctly spiritual increase. The "ill thrift" that two of the shepherds in Towneley *Secunda Pastorum* wish on the third when he asks for food is a simple curse (150), until the birth of Christ appears in the play to complicate the meaning of food itself.

What constitutes "thriving" is clearly dependent on social, religious, and economic conditions. Between the late fourteenth and the late sixteenth centuries, shifting social values stretch the word between two quite distinct meanings: nobility in condition or manner and economy with resources – in other words, propriety and frugality. How the two potentialities within the term are deployed allows us to glimpse the shift in wealth from lands, titles,

---

[3] Passages from Trevisa's translation (226/17) and Ripley's *The Compend of Alchemye*, MS Bodleian (1883) are quoted from the collection of the *Middle English Dictionary*; Thomas Lodge, "Reply to Gosson," *The Complete Works of Thomas Lodge, 1580–1623?*, 4 vols. (New York: Russell & Russell, 1963), 1: 3.

and inheritances to moveable, monetary earnings and in the ideological force of *thrift*, which works to naturalize first the former and then the latter situation. We need not suppose that all members of their earliest audiences understood these instances in the same way but rather that differing class, theological, and gender affiliations may have allowed different accents to be heard.

In Middle English generally, "propriety" is much more likely to appear as the first meaning of *thrift* than "frugality"; I found about five times as many passages among those dated before 1500 which clearly meant "propriety" (not counting Chaucer).[4] Armies consist of thirty thousand knights "thryfty in armes" in the Alliterative *Morte Arthure* and many other narratives, ladies bear "thrifty" children, readers are warned against "unthrifty" language, and many events take place "in thrifty wise." A medical treatise from 1425 suggests getting a "thriftye phisicien" to superintend a patient's purge (104) and describes how "thriftilye" to sew up an incision (107), bind up a wound (126), and cauterize the root of a canker (150).[5] These medical uses seem especially persuasive cases of "appropriate," "proper to the situation," since we might assume that the writer is striving to be especially exact.

The Proceedings of the Privy Council seem to regard "thriftimen" as a kind of estate, along with prelates, knights, squires, and "other cominaltees within the countree of Lincoln aforesaide" (1443); and in Fortescue the term seems to indicate an echelon of the citizenry without rank but with some property, unlikely to join an uprising "ffor dred off lesynge off their gode" (1475).[6]

The Paston letters deplore a riotous neighborhood with "so many vnthriftys that it was gret parell to thrifty men to duelle there" (2.581). This usage of *thrifty* seems to contain the element "frugal" along with its implication of "proper," "decent." Frugality does not enter into the instance in Caxton's *Book of the Knight of the Tower* (1484) in which "unthrifty women" are defined as "euelle women of her body." A rather late example – and a very striking one – of thriving non-materially is Miles Coverdale's "The entrie vnto immortall thrifte is throughe losse of transitorie thynges" (1549), but it does seem to depend for its effect on an understanding that thrift usually involved keeping a tight hold on "transitorie thynges." A naive rather than conscious irony is achieved when John Lydgate describes the elaborate banquet King Cethus prepares for Hercules and Jason. The narrator lacks the descriptive power, he says, to present the diversity of courses served up: "þer-with-alle þe noble officeris / Ful þriftely serued han þe halle . . . / With alle deintes þat may rekned

---

[4] I am grateful to the people at the *Middle English Dictionary* library in Ann Arbor, Michigan for allowing me to use the unpublished slips with which they are preparing the T volume of the Dictionary and especially to Karen Mura, now of Susquehanna College, for scholarly advice.

[5] *Paston Letters and Papers of the Fifteenth Century*, ed. Norman Davis, 2 vols. (Oxford: Clarendon Press, 1976); the medical handbook is Glasgow, Hunterian Museum MS. 95, a photocopy of which is in the MED library.

[6] *Proceedings and Ordinances of the Privy Council of England*, ed. H. Nicolas, 7 vols. (London: Eyre & Spottiswoode, 1834–37), 5.414; Sir John Fortescue, *The Governance of England*, ed. Charles Plummer (Oxford: Clarendon Press, 1885), 148; see *OED*.

be" (*Troy Book* 1.1538–41).[7] Here the sense of propriety as abundance and display is directly at war with the other potentialities of *thrift*.

In Middle English, frugality defined in terms of protecting money is not often represented without some hint of more general impropriety,[8] but even when its major emphasis fell on prudent saving – that is, at its least spiritualized – *thrift* retained its very positive aura. Its history is an instance of the successful appropriation into the early modern period of the cultural privilege a term had accrued in Middle English. In his *Meditations* (1608–11) Bishop Hall comments that "So devotion is counterfaited by superstition, good thrift by niggardliness" (*OED*).

Some writers manage to call up both propriety and frugality as strong constituent meanings of *thrift,* as in the Ashmolean *Secretum*:

Yf any kyng have eyther of these 2 vices, that is to sey, avarice or prodigalite, he oweth thurgh thryfty counseill and full grete diligence, to purveye to gete vnder hym a discrete, trewe, chosen man, vnto whom he shall commytte the disposicion of the comone wele.[9]

The "thryfty counseill" is certainly appropriate, proper, but because of the particular vices the king is worried about, it must also be parsimonious counsel not wastefully sought. Similarly, when the poem "On the Corruption of Public Manners" accuses the rich as "Ye prowd galonttes ... With youre schort gownys thriftlesse, / Have brought this londe in gret hevynesse" (Wright, 2: 251), it imputes both immodesty and extravagance to this mode of dress.

Here is Lydgate's *Fall of Princes* on *thrift*:

To swich fals lustis duryng al thi lyff,
List nat forberen in thi latter age,
Thou vsist many riche restoratiff
In suiche vnthrifft tencrece thi corage,
Of ribaudi thou fill in such dotage, –
How maist thou thanne rebuke me? For shame!
Which in such caas art blottid with diffame.   (7.474–80)[10]

---

[7] Coverdale's *Paraphrase of Erasmus upon the New Testament* (Phil. 5), see *OED*; *Lydgate's Troy Book*, ed. Henry Bergen, EETS ES 97 (London: Trübner, 1906).

[8] A few instances of solely monetary *thrift* do occur, as in Lydgate's *The Hors, the Shep, and the Ghoos* (1470): "In thyn expences make no waste / Grete excesse causeth unthrift in haste"(*Münchener Beiträge zur romanischen und englischen Philologie* 19 [Erlangen: Deichert, 1900], 28); and "Also they bere the golde owte of thys londe, / And souketh the thryfte awey oute of oure honde" ("English Policy" in *Political Poems and Songs relating to English history, composed during the period from the accession of Edw. III to that of Ric. III*, ed. Thomas Wright, 2 vols., Rolls Series 14 [London: Longman, Green, Longman, and Roberts, 1859–61] 2: 174 [*MED*]).

[9] *Secretum* (33.14), EETS OS 276 (London: Oxford University Press, 1977).

[10] "Corruption of Manners," in Wright, *Political Poems and Songs* 2: 251 (*MED*); *Lydgate's Fall of Princes*, ed. Henry Bergen, EETS ES 123 (London: Oxford University Press, 1924).

The passage addresses certain moral improprieties of the aging. They are the more blameworthy because the appetite to perform them must be supplemented through the use of "restoratiffs" – that these are "riche" suggests that "vnthrifft" is wasteful of resources, that they increase "corage" (here, clearly, sexual appetite, although sometimes in Middle English, bravery) suggests turpitude. The balance falls on lack of thrift as a moral failing but interestingly implies economic imprudence as well.

A different balance is struck by the preacher's metaphor in one of the Worcester Sermons: "& tey se a man þat is but a wretche, þat is but vnþrifti, haþ noyþer fruit nor leues vp-on hym, is nat able to come to non estat, no degre of wrschepe her-afterward."[11] The force of the figure is that the unthrifty man becomes a barren tree, as in traditional indictments of general unworthiness indicating an unproductive life, both spiritually and temporally. But the monetary implications of *thrift*, emphasized by *estat*, which is also a bifurcated word heading toward meanings connected with property, gives the metaphor itself a thrifty doubleness in which both meanings function, either together or separately, for differently situated hearers or readers.

Such complex effects, made possible by certain fluidities in the social formation, are the stock in trade of poets like Chaucer. As instances of the "playfully creative ambiguity" Dominick LaCapra defended from the flatness of the ideal speech situation, Chaucer's range of effects in managing the implications of *thrift* is astonishing. The nonironic feudal sense "propriety" is sometimes unchallenged, sometimes undercut by faint traces of playfulness, and sometimes marked by strong suggestions of the emergent sense of the mercantile, the calculating.

In the courtly *Troilus and Criseyde*, for example, *thrift* usually either means simply "thriving," "fortunate," or it clearly refers to aristocratic proprieties. Both hero and heroine are referred to as the "thriftiest" – for Troilus the attribution is linked with friendliness, gentility, and freedom (grace); for Criseyde with attractiveness (1.1081, 2.737).[12] At a crucial moment in Book 1, when the arrow of love enters Troilus's heart as he glimpses Criseyde in the temple, he "gan hir bet biholde in thrifty wise" (1.275). Here Troilus's looking is thrifty, proper, because it almost immediately becomes prudent and secretive as he keeps his sigh unheard and composes his face into its "pleyinge chere" to hide his loss of composure. These are the actions of a prince who cannot put his emotional state on public display, a leader among youths whose male camaraderie depends on uncommitted gazing on women, and a lover who (it would seem instinctively) observes the secrecy proper to "courtly love."

Pandarus tells Criseyde of Troilus's love through a torturously deferred chain of "confidences": news of a great secret, praise of Troilus, urgings that

---

11 *Three Middle English Sermons from the Worcester Chapter MS F. 1011*, ed. D. M. Grisdale (Leeds: University of Leeds School of English Language Texts and Monographs, 1929), 36.

12 I have used *The Riverside Chaucer*, 3d ed., gen. ed. Larry D. Benson (Boston: Houghton Mifflin, 1987) for all quotations from Chaucer.

his niece be less widow-like, assurances of his own loyalty to her, and finally direct disclosure. Pandarus *is* calculating, but he uses the word *thrift* to characterize Criseyde's success in winning a prince's affection: "And right good thrift, I prey to God, have ye, / That han swich oon ykaught withouten net!" (2.582–83). In the plainest sense, "thriving," "lucky," this is an appropriate ploy in convincing Criseyde that her fears of a love entanglement are groundless, that she is the one with freedom and control. Book 2's sorrowful opening with Proigne's "sorowful lay" waking Pandarus (2.64) and Pandarus's acknowledgment of his own wiliness (2.267–73), however, produce a sense of foreboding which counteracts that reading of *thrift* for the reader and makes Criseyde the one with snares and nets. Since Criseyde fears responsibility as much as danger, the tactic proves successful for Pandarus's suit.

So far Criseyde has not been a plotter; her beauty is a power of nature like that of the "faire gemme" (2.344). But to help her decide how to respond to Troilus's interest, she sets herself a "caas" to debate, in the course of which she reflects that Troilus might have "the thriftieste" woman in the town for his love (2.737). While the trend of the stanza suggests that this means "most desirable" or "worthiest," the details of her fabricated "caas" concern the risk and secrecy surrounding such a love. Her reflection that Troilus's dependence on her ("And yet his lif al lith now in my cure. / But swich is love, and ek myn aventure" [2.741–42]) constitutes an entrepreneurial advantage is nicely captured by the ambiguities of "aventure" as either "chance" or "exploit." With these reflections she does begin to consider shaping events through calculated actions, even while she fears that the lives of lovers necessitate them (2.799–805).

In such an intricate web of words, even the formulaic uses of *thrift*, like wishing someone "good thrift" or swearing "by one's thrift," can register a slight irony. Helen's "Good thrift have ye!" later in Book 2 (1687) probably retains its neutral sense of "Have a good day," but Pandarus's "by my thrift" (3.871) may be taken literally in its emergent sense as well, for Pandarus is claiming (to readers, not to Criseyde) that she will reveal her love to Troilus "by his thrift," meaning "through his cunning." Still more pointedly, "by my thrift" is Criseyde's oath promising her to return to Troy (4.1630). At stake in this avowal are her belief that she can outmaneuver her calculating father for all his "queynte pley" (here swearing to her self possession and cunning) and her claim to be trustworthy (to risk everything to fulfill her plighted *trouthe*). The trouble is that the two claims require two different senses of *thrift*, the first the emergent "cunning," the second the courtly "noble."

As part of the little drama Pandarus stages in Book 3, Criseyde takes leave of Helen and Deiphebus "ful thriftily" (3.11), by this time suggesting both "properly" and "without waste [of time]." Pandarus responds to Criseyde's willingness to see Troilus in bed by her "good thrift on that wise gentil herte!" (3.947), and now they are deeply joined in a plot which uses the language of courtly propriety but manipulates appearances from behind the scenes. Later in that book, a tinge of the comedic is signalled by a description of Troilus caressing his beloved as "good thrift bad ful ofte" (3.1249). Exuberant, freely-willed propriety certainly dicates such caresses when a lover has won his lady's heart, but there is a shadowy suggestion here that Troilus had better get his loving while he can – frugally – since the permanent happiness and security both he and Criseyde long for is not likely in the Troy they inhabit.

In *Troilus and Criseyde*, the social proprieties are not just referred to but defined, and that definition contains a hint of the calculation which seems necessary to courtly propriety. Calculation, in turn, retains the taint of its connection with Criseyde's trecherous father, who left his city when "this Calkas knew by calkulynge ... that Troie moste ben fordo" (1.71–74; cf. 4.1398). And throughout the poem, Pandarus is shown to be manufacturing proprieties, disguising the lovers' motives and actions from each other and perhaps even from themselves. In this overtly feudal, courtly fiction, it would seem that the modulations of the word *thrift* constitute a small gesture toward subverting the naturalness of the aristocratic code, a hint that it is a construction for protection rather than an inherent sign of nobility.

On the road to Canterbury, some distance from the courtly scene of the *Troilus*, of course, a wider range of "proprieties" is called for, most of them suited to more pragmatic, sometimes market-oriented, sensibilities. Skill and practicality are shown in the way the Yeoman's peacock arrows are "thriftily" arranged under his belt (I.105), and the oath the miller in the Reeve's Tale swears – by his thrift – is to outwit the students and save his best grain. The "thrifty tale" the Man of Law at first says he cannot conjure up (II.46) is a memorable one suitable for his heterogeneous audience and useful for him as a contestant in the storytelling competition. Within his tale the merchants of Syria are sought after for their "thrifty" merchandise (II.138), in a fully economic usage for *thrift*, which then may be read back into the Man of Law's earlier desire for a thrifty story and forward into her father's mercenary motives for marrying Custance to the Sultan. The bourgeois Harry Bailly admires Custance's story as a "thrifty tale" (II.1165), an "improving" one, but by his lights: proper, unoffending to status quo morality, just the thrifty work he had interrupted the Miller to effect. The "thrifty clooth" the Wife of Bath denies having at home (III.238) is of a kind befitting (i.e., proper to) her artisan dreams of grandeur, but she may be imagined as glancingly complaining that even the humbler cloth of a more frugal style is denied her by the imputed niggardliness of her husbands. In the Merchant's Tale, January's description of Damyan as "a thrifty man right able" (IV.1912) suggests a delightfully unself-conscious irony. Damyan is "proper" as blind January sees him but able and cunning, to January's disgrace, as the tale presents him. Still further down the social scale, the husband in the Shipman's Tale admonishes his wife to govern in his absence as befits a "thrifty houshold" (VII.246), a clear double entendre involving proprieties and frugalities which are poles apart.

In the Franklin's Tale, Aurelius and his brother meet a young clerk on the road to Orléans, who greets them *thriftily* in Latin, a proper address, it would seem, to identify both his social class and educated graces (V.1174). But his *thrift*, as craft, is quickly linked to his uncanny knowledge of why they have come and therefore reminds the reader of the denunciation of magical practices the Franklin-narrator has just finished delivering:

> and swich folye
> As in oure dayes is nat worth a flye –
> For hooly chirches feith in oure bileve
> Ne suffreth noon illusioun us to greve.   (V.1131–34)

It connects forward as well to the vexed question of whether the rocks were really "removed" sufficiently for Aurelius's side of the agreement to be regarded as fulfilled. The emergent meanings which suggest at their worst calculation also flit glancingly through this thrifty greeting: the nameless clerk's test of freedom (another term which undergoes the social strains under discussion) is about money.

Chaucer's usage readily includes instances of *thrift* simply as frugality and good luck with money, as in the Canon's Yeoman's Prologue and Tale, where both *thrift* and *thrive* occur very often.[13] In line 603 of the Yeoman's Prologue, *thriftily* is a variant of *craftily*. The Tale begins and ends with warnings that anyone who comes into the alchemical trade will lose his thrift: whoever "casteth hym therto, / If he continue, I holde his thrift ydo" (VIII.738–39) and "Medleth namoore with that art, I mene, / For if ye doon, youre thrift is goon ful clene" (VIII.1424–25). What will be lost is both moral and social thriving. In a complicated plot full of markedly Chaucerian ironies, the desire for wealth improperly indulged ends in the loss of both inner and material wealth.

Harry Bailly warns the raucous Miller not to insist on speaking immediately after the seemly Knight by begging him to "werken thriftily" (I.3131). I like this instance especially, since it makes use of a term from courtly proprieties to chide one of the lower-class pilgrims, holding him, as it were, to a standard set by his "betters." Yet by the end of the Miller's ingenious and bawdy tale, almost everyone is laughing together (except Oswald the Reeve, a special case because he thinks himself the butt of the Miller's joke). In other words, the Miller's insistence on his improper intrusion into the order and decorum of the tales has produced a re-ordering, a parsimonious (because brief) and worthy (because conducive to festive harmony) contribution to the pilgrimage. This moment fuses the sense of *thrift* as propriety with that of frugality without losing the edge of either and yet with the social import of humorously turning the usual order of protocol on its head.

Chaucer's verbal effects are made possible by a general pattern of usage in which "propriety," linked with feudal social ideals, predominates over "frugality," with its hint of emergent market economies, monetary and intellectual. Frugality with resources is not scorned in the Middle Ages, but neither is it the overarching metaphor for value. The sixteenth century's economic shift from the traditional village to a much more prominent urban

---

[13] There are five instances of *thrift* and *thrive*, in the Canon's Yeoman's Tale, more than in any other tale.

and mercantile mode of production and exchange is matched by a new sense of personal responsibility concerning doctrinal matters made possible by the Reformation. Between Chaucer's era and Shakespeare's we see the gradual distributional shift to an economic inflection for *thrift*, often related to currency. This shift may be attributed in part to attempts by Protestants to foreground economic trusteeship as a moral matter. Lutheran and Calvinist arguments that all callings are equally holy opened a field for moral speculation, at a time when new modes of trade and investment, greater social mobility, and wider circles of literacy required new ethical speculation. As these newer social and ethical discourses increasingly succeeded in including the still very positive term *thrift* within their domain, it waned in usefulness as a mark of aristocratic propriety, becoming increasingly associated with a range of virtues we would now call "middle class."[14] Between Chaucer's work and Shakespeare's there occurs a clear case of appropriating the high positive valence of a term, in which a romance hero and heroine can be described as "thriftiest," for use "within the logic of another political discourse" (in Hall's phrase), the newer discourse of calculated earning, deciding, and saving.

Early Modern Thriftiness

The range of meanings for *thrift* in the sixteenth century is indicated by George Whetstone, who entitled one section of his *Rock of Regard* (1576) "The Garden of Unthriftiness" because it has in it "a number of vain, wanton, and worthless sonnets" which "make the rest of the book more profitable by exposing 'hot desires'" (313); by Thomas Tusser, who named a section of *Five Hundred Points of Good Husbandry* (1573/1580) "The Ladder to Thrift" and advised both parsimony and moral propriety; and by Robert Greene, who tells the fable of the ant and grasshopper in *Groatsworth of Wit*, in which the thrifty ant wins, the grasshopper repents, admonishes the young, and dies comfortless.

Thrift is a favorite term for Thomas More, and he uses the word in both light and weighty English works and with its full range of senses. In "A Merry Jest," *thrift* means thriving, the means to thrive (especially as a specific craft), saving, and, less directly, propriety; the theme of the poem is about staying within one's proper craft. (This usage is a good reminder that there can be a Catholic as well as a Protestant moral argument for craft.) In the course of the debate over sanctuary in his *History of King Richard III* (1513), Buckingham argues that few, if any, ever sought sanctuary from "favorable necessity." "Unthriftiness" has brought the thieves and manquellers who hide in churches to nought. The charge implies simultaneously the leaving of a craft (by which one might have thrived), the impropriety of the seeking of sanctuary, and the monetary prodigality which accounts for their need to steal or to hide their doings.

---

[14] Much has been written on the appropriateness of referring to class in discussing the fifteenth and sixteenth centuries. I mean here only to indicate some features of social life – its increasing urbanity, literateness, Protestantism, and social mobility.

More replies to the attack on the doctrine of purgatory made by Simon Fish. In *The Supplication of Souls* (c. 1529), More contests Fish's claim that the poor should be given the alms currently used to support a self-indulgent clergy. More's ingenious answer (which nonetheless risks making a devasting concession) is that still worse social ills would result from the sudden turning loose of so many clerics "vnthryfty / lewde / and nought . . . as he wolde haue them all seme" (156.25–26). A bit later, speculating on the effects of replacing Catholic preaching with Luther's or Tyndale's, he alleges, "Then shall folk waxe ydle and fall to vnthryftynesse. . . . Then shall vnthryftys flok togyder and swarme abowte and eche bere hym bolde of other" (168.13–16).[15] The two passages castigate both social impropriety and economic waste. More is perfectly capable of meeting Protestant reformers on their own pragmatic ground rather than moving to more traditional theological arguments in assessing the social role of the clergy. In the first passage, he provides a *reductio* of Fish's assertion that overnumerous clergy impede egalitarian social progress by arguing that if they are really as wicked as they are made out, defrocked they would merely add to the population of outlaws. The word "vnthryfty" makes this point in both the system of production and consumption and that of moral "works." The second passage is a vision (which looks back to Gower's in *Vox Clamantis* and forward to Ulysses's "untuned string" speech in *Troilus and Cressida*) of a world without the restraining power of hierarchy. Idleness is easily elided into crime, gang violence, disregard of law, and finally treason against master and state. The role "vnthryftynesse" plays here is crucial: thrift is respect for the "natural order," which bolsters its claims through both the coercive power of masters and rulers and the ideological power of God's anointed. More claims to see the social transformations which might follow from Protestant readings of the gospel, and his reply stresses power in accents not unlike Machiavelli's.[16]

Shakespeare uses "thriftless" in *Twelfth Night* to describe Olivia's bootless sighs for Viola/Cesario in its most basic sense: unlikely to thrive. And yet one might easily see an implication of the impropriety of romantic attachment between females in Viola's choice of this word and even, in view of the stress

---

[15] I have used the Yale Edition of *The Complete Works of St. Thomas More*, 15 vols. (New Haven: Yale University Press, 1961-), vols. 2 and 7.

[16] The sixteenth-century translator of More's *Utopia*, Ralph Robinson, has Hythloday report that the Utopians are allowed to "bestow the time well and thriftily upon some other Science, as shall please them" when their regular work does not occupy them (56). This appropriation of both strands of meaning for *thrift* is in keeping with the dense and complex weaving together of moral and economic issues in the fable of *Utopia*. See *Utopia, written by Sir Thomas More and translated by Ralph Robinson* (Hammersmith: Kelmscott Press, 1893). Sir Philip Sidney's *New Arcadia* delivers a neat sermon on the economic *via media* in his account of a moated castle which was "the work of a noble gentleman, of whose unthrifty son" Dido's father had bought it (244.34). The present miserly owner maintained it so badly that Pyrocles opines: "if that were thrift, I wished none of my friends or subjects ever to thrive" (246.26–27); see *The Countess of Pembroke's Arcadia: The New Arcadia*, ed. Victor Skretkowicz (Oxford: Clarendon Press, 1987).

on monetary images in the wooing scene ("leave the world no copy" [I.v.243], "schedules of my beauty" [I.v.245], "will" [I.v.247] as inheritance, and "recompens'd" [I.v.253]), an implication of the prodigality of Olivia's "spending" her beauty in an improper infatuation.[17]

In *Richard II*, the "thriftless sons" who waste their "scraping fathers' gold" clearly use monetary frugality as the vehicle of the metaphor, although the tenor is York's aristocratic "honor" being senselessly wasted by Aumerle (V.iii.69). York returns to the word, as he curses Bolingbroke for the pardon he is about to grant Aumerle: "Ill mayst thou thrive if thou grant any grace!" (V.iii.99). The scene in which this occurs begins with Bolingbroke, now Henry IV, inquiring "Can no man tell me of my unthrifty son?" (V.iii.1), which is itself, in all the meanings of thrift, the over-arching theme of the Henriad. Hal has abandoned, as Henry sees it, the craft of chivalric military prowess and political acumen ("thy place in council thou hast rudely lost") in the service of his dynasty; he has literally and figuratively spent the royal family's credit; and he has behaved without aristocratic propriety. (John Harington, translator of Ariosto's *Orlando Furioso*, describes the Prodigal Son of the Scripture in the same terms as King Henry: "given over to all unthriftiness, all looseness of life and conversation" [38-39]; this description matches the Common Council's language restricting plays: "unthrifty waste of the money of the poor and fond persons."[18] In Hal's failure to protect the family's interests, Henry sees a recurrence of the very reason he had returned to England from banishment: "my rights and royalties / Plucked from my arms perforce – and given away / To upstart unthrifts" (II.iii.122).

In the 1590s, when Puritan insistence on thriftiness was an everyday concern to Londoners, especially those who defended the stage from the "unthrifty waste" that the theater was accused of entailing, *The Merchant of Venice* plays out the entire range of socially available meanings. Bassanio attempts to present his "quest" for Portia's hand as a courtly romance in which *he himself* risks all to win the lady – that is the point of his elaborate classical imagery in asking Antonio to lend him the money in I.i. His use of *thrift*, then, is an attempt to call up associations like those of Chaucer's *Troilus*. But since the passage is an unrelenting plea for a monetary loan, it is difficult to read Bassanio's "I have a mind presages me such thrift" as anything less than a prediction of not just general success but monetary success. Irony is produced by the clash between Bassanio's intended sense of the word and the force of the context the scene provides.

Later in Act I, Shylock certainly means money by "my well-won thrift, / Which he [Antonio] calls interest" (I.iii.50–51), but he is evoking the newer range of meanings of *thrift* most closely associated with Puritan thinking. Like Bassanio, he intends to call up positive associations for *thrift* but from a

---

[17] I quote Shakespeare's plays from *The Riverside Shakespeare*, ed. G. Blakemore Evans et al. (Boston: Houghton Mifflin, 1974).

[18] Joseph Quincy Adams, *A Life of William Shakespeare* (Boston: Houghton Mifflin, 1923), 109.

different – more self-conscious and shrewder – vantage point: Jacob's sheep are "a way to thrive . . . / And thrift is blessing" (I.iii.89–90). Later he tells Jessica that "Fast bind, fast find" is a "proverb never stale in thrifty mind" (II.v.54–55), in a phrasing which will haunt him during the trial scene, when in his thrift he binds himself to an unalterable (as he thinks it) legal code. Modern comment on this play has often discussed it as a direct, although complex, analysis of Elizabethan anxieties over the power of the cash nexus and the growing legal establishment which regulated but also legitimized it.[19] The seemingly nostalgic denouement of the play, its return to idealized feudal values, does not altogether dispel the thrill of horror the courtroom crisis has evoked. When Lorenzo makes his list of lovers' trysts on beautiful evenings, he ends with "In such a night / Did Jessica steal from the wealthy Jew, / And with an unthrift love did run from Venice" (V.i.14–16). It was an unfrugal love, surely, a love which did not count the cost, and that implication is surely the one Lorenzo himself intends. But perhaps it was also an improper love in more than just its lack of parental authorization – sentimental and overly optimistic about the bottomless plenitude of the old feudal, Christian mode of life. This small doubt registers alongside the larger obstacles to a festive comedic closure in the final act of the play.

In sum, then, Bassanio attempts to suggest that his premonition of *thrift* results from his uncalculating aristocratic propriety, but because the term itself is bifurcated and the occasion concerns money, we are not led to take him at his own valuation. Shylock's appeals are also to *thrift* as a virtue, but it is the virtue of a very different social formation, one in which the control of money is openly acknowledged. His appeal to thrift of this kind neither convinces Antonio nor appeals to the young Venetians, but the play as a whole discredits extravagence as well as this species of calculating self-discipline, including the emotional extravagance to which Lorenzo refers.

Hamlet's "where thrift may follow fawning" (III.ii.62) surely trades on the single meaning of gain, and so does the Player Queen's avowal that second marriages are made with "base respects of thrift, but none of love" (III.ii.183). In fact, in both of these cases monetary thrift seems the enemy of aristocratic propriety. But the really interesting instance of thrift is Hamlet's explanation of Gertrude's o'erhasty marriage: "Thrift, thrift, Horatio, the funeral bak'd meats / Did coldly furnish forth the marriage tables" (I.ii.180–81). The wit involved bears Hamlet's distinctive stamp – it suggests the displacement of deep and bitter emotion and the pesky wakefulness of penetrating intellect. It discloses Hamlet's grievance within his only frank friendship yet pretends to blunt or play with that disclosure. It imputes impropriety of a serious sort by using a word which (in 1600) still can mean "propriety," but which in this passage displaces the direct

---

[19] A very full analysis of this issue is given by Walter Cohen in "*The Merchant of Venice* and the Possibilities of Historical Criticism," *ELH* 49 (1982): 765–89; and from somewhat different points of view by Lars Engle in "'Thrift Is A Blessing': Exchange and Exploration in *The Merchant of Venice*," *Shakespeare Quarterly* 37 (1986): 20–37; Karen Newman in "Portia's Ring: Unruly Women and the Structures of Exchange in *The Merchant of Venice*," *Shakespeare Quarterly* 38 (1987): 19–33; and John S. Coolidge in "Law and Love in *The Merchant of Venice*," *Shakespeare Quarterly* 27 (1976): 243–63.

sarcasm toward the second meaning of "middle-class parsimony." It almost seems to refer to Claudius's claim (earlier in the scene) that discretion fought with nature to explain the quickness of the marriage. Like Hamlet's "a little more than kin and less than kind," it comes close to accusation but commits him to no treason – just the tactic he will accuse himself of continually during the rest of the play. He not only unpacks his heart with words but with ambiguous, teasing words. In his taunts, he is accusing Claudius and Gertrude of inaugurating a new, diminished order, in which base respects of thrift replace the epic virtues of Hamlet's father's reign.

These retrospective uses of *thrift* might be taken to indicate a nostalgia for the feudal past, except that they invoke that past in a way that nibbles away at its status as an ideal. Hamlet's enthusiasm for the former age might be described as a desire for return to a "prelapsarian" state in which his Oedipal energies were kept in check by the authority of an unassailable father. Henry's political ambitions rest on his ability to reestablish the authority of a regime in which no one can kill a king with impunity, even though it was he himself who had discredited it by his successful usurpation, a pattern played out as tragic irony in *Macbeth*. Both instances signal a robust skepticism about a past in which to thrive is to be proper, and that signal is writ large in *The Merchant of Venice*, where the connection between economic realities and social proprieties is directly scrutinized. The ambiguities of *thrift* in the Shakespeare plays are not easy to decode, but that very difficulty suggests a painful attempt to investigate the social order rather than a glib coverup for oppression.

"Thrift" provides us a path through certain social struggles in late medieval and early modern England. Early in this history, its implication of propriety may be seen in most instances to naturalize a social scheme built on carefully delineated feudal hierarchies. It bestows value rather unproblematically when conventional standards are met. Even when tinged with "frugality," the Middle English examples include that dimension in an overall estimate of appropriateness. Until Chaucer. With Chaucer's unsettling playfulness, even a serenely aristocratic tale like *Troilus and Criseyde* seems to innoculate the exemplary thrift of both hero and heroine with a touch of worldly expense-minding. A free-for-all like the Miller's Tale, of course, opens the question of narrative thriftiness for the whole Canterbury anthology. By the late sixteenth century the weight of the term had shifted toward its economic implications under the pressure of mercantile and Reformation cultural influences, its strong positive valences captured for new social ideals.

The examples before us – the "thrifty" beauty and modesty of Criseyde, Harry Bailly's sharp command that the Miller behave "thriftily" by deferring to his superiors, More's Buckingham imputing both impropriety and financial prodigality to seekers of sanctuary, and Shylock's thrift, well won by charging interest – seem to trace an intelligible linguistic history. Much as is revealed, this excursion also reminds us how much has been lost, just as Doctorow's boy, watching his neighbors skate on the frozen ponds of New Rochelle, "saw only the tracks made by the skaters, traces quickly erased of moments past, journeys taken."